Andy Murray of Britain is overcome with emotion after defeating Novak Djokovic at the All England Club in 2013. Murray's victory marked the first time a British man had won Wimbledon in 77 years.

TENNIS' GREATEST STARS

Mike Ryan

FIREFLY BOOKS

For my niece Maisie, who's 15, with love.

A FIREFLY BOOK

Published by Firefly Books Ltd. 2014

First printing

Cover and interior design: Peter Ross / Counterpunch Inc.

Printed in China

The publisher gratefully acknowledges the financial support for our publishing program by the Government of Canada through the Canada Book Fund as administered by the Department of Canadian Heritage.

PUBLISHER CATALOGING-IN-PUBLICATION DATA (U.S.)
A CIP record for *Tennis' Greatest Stars*/978-1-77085-293-8 is available from the Library of Congress

LIBRARY AND ARCHIVES CANADA CATALOGUING IN PUBLICATION
A CIP record for *Tennis' Greatest Stars*/978-1-77085-293-8 is available from Library and Archives Canada

Published in the United States by
Firefly Books (U.S.) Inc.
P.O. Box 1338, Ellicott Station
Buffalo, New York   14205

Published in Canada by
Firefly Books Ltd.
50 Staples Avenue, Unit 1
Richmond Hill, Ontario   L4B 0A7

CONTENTS

INTRODUCTION

When I was 12 my parents brought me to Wimbledon. It was a typically finicky English summer day, and after taking in the hallowed grounds and some strawberries and cream, we wandered among the many satellite courts, far removed from the exclusive seating and bright lights of Centre Court.

Two things struck me that day: the grandiosity and tradition of the event, and the sublime skill of the players. You can't truly appreciate either until you experience them in real life. The British, as they do, have perfected the ritual, and the players were true specimens. The speed with which they delivered the ball and the relentless drive they gave to chasing it down — the impossible shots they made and managed to return — all seemed to defy physics, geometry and gravity. To witness players so well-honed is to realize the massive gulf that separates you from elite athletes, leaving you astonished by the ability of the human body while accepting the limitations of your own.

Impressive as they were, these players weren't even highly ranked. What would it take for them to reach the big courts and big time? What is that little something that separates the many stars who've ever played tennis from the transcendent few who make it look so easy, 50 of whom are profiled here?

All the featured players in this book won the genetic jackpot, yes, but their minds and lives away from the game are what fascinate us and paint a portrait of success. And not one story is the same. Strip away the tennis parents and the coaches and the entourages of today, and who are they? What does it take, psychologically, to be a champion? Do you need to internalize it all, like Ivan Lendl, or do you need to rage against your inner demons for all the world to see, à la Jimmy Connors and John McEnroe?

Not surprisingly, the players with the most supportive parents are the ones who were able to separate themselves from the game and be content off the court, people like Lindsay

Jimmy Connors celebrates a victory over Paul Haarhuis at the 1991 U.S. Open. Connors would make a stunning run to the semifinals in his last appearance at the American championship.

Court 18 of the All England Lawn Tennis and Croquet Club is manicured during the 2011 edition of Wimbledon.

Rafael Nadal hugs the championship trophy after defeating Novak Djokovic to win the 2013 U.S. Open.

Davenport, Jim Courier and Rafael Nadal. Some, like Steffi Graf and Andre Agassi, suffered domineering parents but found peace and tranquility in the latter parts of their careers (and in each other's arms). Others, such as Jennifer Capriati, Martina Hingis and Arantxa Sanchez Vicario, were driven to the top by family but ultimately torn away from them. Would any of these players have been more or less successful with a different upbringing?

There are also the eccentric characters from tennis' early days, people who may have withered in today's media world or thrived on reality TV. What would smartphones have captured Suzanne Lenglen doing? What would Bill Tilden tweet? Would Helen Wills Moody withdraw completely instead of being hounded by TMZ?

My personal favorites are players like Martina Navratilova — those who faced down governments and inequality and who ultimately made a deeper impact on society than on their sport. Many players have philanthropic pursuits, but the bar was set, and set high, by Billie Jean King and Arthur Ashe. It's no coincidence that their names adorn the USTA Tennis Center, home of the U.S. Open.

Each player profiled in the following pages pushed the very limits of mind and body to reach the pinnacle of the sport. On the court, tennis is a game of two people trying to crush each other's wills. There's nowhere to hide and there's no one to lean on. Thousands of people in the stands and millions watching on TV see two athletes at the peak of human physiology battling each other while also dueling with their own doubts and demons. It's a marathon played at a sprinter's pace, and one shot can break a player's spirit. That's what makes the game so raw and visceral.

As *Sports Illustrated* tennis writer S.L. Price says: "It used to seem odd that the first question asked when people found out I cover tennis was about a player's sex life, but it makes sense. Stare at someone long enough, and you can't help but wonder about it all: Parents, religion, fashion sense, politics, tipping. Out of that calculus springs interest, then fandom, and then — for the very rare player — an investment verging on the religious."

There's very little about sex lives in the following pages, but hopefully there is enough information and insight to feed your fanaticism — maybe even tip it over into religious fervor.

Enjoy.

Mike Ryan

The statue of Arthur Ashe by sculptor Paul DiPasquale is unveiled on Monument Avenue in Richmond, Virginia, on Wednesday July 10, 1996. The statue pays homage to Ashe's efforts as both a groundbreaking tennis star and humanitarian.

ARTHUR ASHE

A BRIEF HISTORY OF TENNIS

According to the book *Tennis: A Cultural History* by Heiner Gillmeister, tennis may owe its genesis to a dark children's tale from the 12th century, in which minions took the soul of a French cleric named Pierre and knocked it back and forth across the fiery pits of hell. Seems as good a theory as any about the origin of people hitting something at each other for fun.

But in truth, that story and the actual birth of tennis are hard to verify. What is known is that monks in Europe used their hands to bat balls against the monastery walls and back and forth to each other. Rackets were introduced in the 16th century for a game in Italy called *gioco di racchette*.

Long tennis, or *longue paume*, an outdoor game with rackets and nets, was played in the time of Queen Elizabeth I, but no codified rules were developed and the game didn't catch on.

The aristocracy also played indoors; Shakespeare wrote about it in *Henry V*, and Henry VIII had a court in Hampton Court Palace, which is still in use. Played exclusively by the wealthy, it was called court tennis, real tennis or royal tennis.

The root of the word *tennis* is unknown but one possibility is that it is from the French word *tendere*, which means "to hold" and which players apparently called out as a warning to opponents just before they served. There's no definitive record of this, however, so another hypothesis is that it comes from the French word *tenez*, or "take it."

Ten is a common French prefix and gives rise to many logical theories, and there are towns in France and Egypt named Tennis, which some believe may have been the birthplace of the game. Others think the back-and-forth motion of the *tens* — a weaver's shuttle — could be the inspiration.

There's also debate about the origin of "love" in the scoring system. It could come from *l'oeuf*, the French word for egg (an egg representing the numeral 0), or from *lof*, a Dutch/Flemish word for honor, taken from the phrase *omme lof spellen*, which means "to play for honor." The 15, 30 and 40 scoring increments are thought to represent the quarters of a clock face, with 40 being shorter and easier to say than 45. Deuce is a rare instance of consensus, coming from the French *deux*.

Modern lawn tennis, the game we know today, was first written about in March of 1874 in the British papers *Court Journal* and the *Army & Navy Gazette*, a month after retired British army officer Major Walter Clopton Wingfield filed patents for "A Portable Court of Playing Tennis." He developed his game while serving in India, but skeptics said he simply moved the indoor game outside and that it was much like a game called "pelota," which J.B. Perera had introduced 15 years earlier.

Wingfield's patented set included four tennis bats, balls, poles, netting, a brush for painting the lines and an instruction manual called *The Book of the Game*. He dedicated the book to "the party assembled at Nantclwyd [Wales] in December 1873." It's thought this may be where this particular game was first played, although no proof of that exists; it may have also been at Earnshill in Somerset, a Wingfield family estate.

The sport spread quickly around the British Isles. Sets were purchased by royalty, members of parliament and the military and also taken to Canada, India, China and Russia. It became popular because it was more active than croquet, which was a fashionable pastime, and could easily be played on the ubiquitous croquet courts.

The All England Croquet Club, founded by Dr. Henry Jones in 1868 in Wimbledon, was one of the first to introduce tennis, changing its name to the All England Lawn Tennis and Croquet Club in 1877.

Another early adopter of the new sport was the Marylebone Cricket Club, home of Lord's Cricket Ground. With Wingfield and Jones at odds over the rules of tennis, a meeting was called

Early tennis, as seen at the first modern Olympic Games in Athens, Greece, in 1896.

at MCC, where 25 official rules were drawn up and released in May of 1875.

The inaugural Lawn Tennis Championships was held in 1877 at the All England Club, months after Wingfield failed to pay the £50 to renew his patent. Wingfield wasn't involved and soon faded from the game.

Spencer Gore beat William Marshall in straight sets for the first title of the first recognized tournament of lawn tennis, making Wimbledon the birthplace and spiritual home of modern tennis — and giving it bragging rights it enjoys to this day.

One of the changes made for that first tournament was designing a rectangular court, instead of the hourglass shape Wingfield had envisioned. In the coming years Jones made further changes to Wingfield's game, adjusting the height of the net to three and a half feet at the net post and three feet at the center of the net. These measurements remain the standard for today.

Two other improvements installed in the early years of the Lawn Tennis Championships were using byes in the first round to even out the number of players (the first Wimbledon had three semifinalists) and introducing the seeding system, which was proposed by mathematician Charles L. Dodgson, who was better known by his nom de plume — Lewis Carroll.

The first tennis superstars were the Renshaw twins, who dominated in the 1880s. Willie won Wimbledon every year from 1881 through 1886, failing to defend in 1887 because of an early case of tennis elbow. He recovered and added one last championship in 1889. His seven titles weren't equaled for 111 years, when Pete Sampras won his seventh in 2000.

Brother Ernest won in 1888, and together they won seven of the first 10 doubles titles after doubles were introduced in 1879. Women's doubles and mixed doubles didn't arrive until 1913.

The Scottish Championships started in 1878, followed a year later by the Irish Championships, which included the first women's tournament. The women played in the privacy of Dublin's Fitzwilliam Club, open to members and guests only, while the men played publicly in Fitzwilliam Square. The first female champion was 14-year-old May Langrishe.

In 1884 Wimbledon held its inaugural women's tournament, won by 19-year-old Maud Watson, who beat her older sister Lillian in the final. A semifinalist was Blanche Bingley (later Bingley Hillyard), who won the singles title six times and competed for the last time in 1913 at the age of 49.

Major Rowan Hamilton brought a Wingfield tennis set to Canada in 1874, and the country's original tournament was played in 1878 at the Montreal Cricket Club. The first national

championship for men was played in 1890 after the Canadian Lawn Tennis Association was founded in Toronto that year, with the women's championship following two years later.

Lawn tennis had already spread quickly around the world: clubs were founded in Brazil, India and Scotland in 1875; in Germany and the U.S. in 1876; in France and Ireland in 1877; in Australia, Hungary, Italy, Peru and Sweden in 1878; in Denmark and Switzerland in 1880; in Argentina in 1881; in the Netherlands in 1882; in Jamaica in 1883; in Greece and Turkey in 1885; in Lebanon in 1889; in Egypt in 1890; and in Finland and South Africa in 1891.

Author Leo Tolstoy was an early adopter of tennis, with a court at his estate and a tennis scene in the 1877 novel *Anna Karenina*.

Some believe Mary Outerbridge, of a prominent Staten Island family, brought the first tennis equipment to the United States from Bermuda in 1874 and should be credited with introducing it, while others claim Dr. James Dwight played the first games outside Boston sometime that same year.

The first recorded tennis played in the United States was in October of 1874 at Camp Apache in the Arizona Territory, between Ella Wilkins Bailey, the wife of an army officer, and her sister Caroline.

Founded in 1876, the New Orleans Lawn Tennis Club was the first tennis club in the United States. In 1880 the initial U.S. Nationals were played, but they weren't made official until the U.S. National Lawn Tennis Association was formed on May 21, 1881, at the Fifth Avenue Hotel in New York City. The USNLTA represented 33 clubs, with R.S. Oliver of the Albany Lawn Tennis Club its first president.

It was the world's first national tennis association, and the U.S. Championships were first held in 1881 at the Newport Casino in Rhode Island, a center of American wealth and style in those days and now the home of the International Tennis Hall of Fame.

Dr. James Dwight's cousin Dick Sears won the first seven U.S. titles, and as a team they won the doubles event in five of the first seven years.

In 1887 the initial U.S. Women's Championship was held at the Philadelphia Cricket Club, where it stayed until moving to Forest Hills, New York, in 1921. Ellen Hansell earned the first title.

Dwight is considered the father of American tennis. In 1884 he became the first foreigner to triumph in England when he took the Northern England Championships; he was the president of the USNLTA, later renamed the USTA, for 21 years; he wrote two seminal instruction books and he helped start the Davis Cup in 1900.

Boston's Longwood Cricket Club, near where Fenway Park now stands, introduced tennis to the city in 1878. The land was rented from David Sears, the uncle of national champion Dick, and played host to the first Davis Cup, between the United States and Great Britain.

By 1889 British players were playing in American tournaments, stirring up a transatlantic rivalry that gave Dwight the idea for an international challenge. Fellow Harvard man Dwight Davis had been on a tour of the United States and Canada with a group of players in 1899 and felt the goodwill generated by tennis could be spread. Together, Dwight and Davis introduced the International Lawn Tennis Challenge Trophy in 1900, which became known as the Davis Cup.

Davis was the captain of the first U.S. team, which consisted of two other Harvard students, and the first tournament was played on the school's home courts of Longwood. They challenged the British Isles team, which was selected as much for their spare time and money to travel as for their playing prowess.

The singles were played simultaneously on adjacent courts, and with the home crowd and familiar turf the Americans won handily, 3-0.

The Americans defended their title at the second Davis Cup in 1902, but with Reggie and Laurie Doherty, the best British players of the time, added to the team, Britain won its first Davis Cup in 1903. It remained in British hands for four years.

In 1905 the tournament included Australasia for the first time, and the team from Australia and New Zealand captured the Cup in 1907, beating the United States in the semifinal and Britain in the final. They held the Cup until 1912, when the British Isles won it back.

After that the Australasians and Americans had a stranglehold on the trophy until 1927, when France's "Four Musketeers" — Jean Borotra, Jacques Brugnon, Henri Cochet and Rene Lacoste — beat the United States for their first of six Davis Cup victories in a row.

After the French earned the title in 1927, the decision was made to designate the national championships of the four countries that had won the Davis Cup as the homes of the major tennis tournaments. Collectively known as the majors, these four tournaments later became the Grand Slam tournaments. And so the Australian, French and U.S. Championships joined Wimbledon as the highlights of the tennis calendar and have remained that way ever since.

The majors were anointed by the International Lawn Tennis Federation, which was later shortened to the International Tennis Federation. American Duane Williams proposed the

Don Budge with the Davis Cup in 1937. He defeated Gottfried von Cramm to give the United States the 3-2 victory over Germany to capture the title.

idea for a worldwide association but perished on the *Titanic* before it came to fruition on March 1, 1913. His son Dick, a future U.S. champion, was also on board but swam to safety.

The 15 original members of the ILTF were Australasia, Austria, Belgium, Denmark, France, Germany, Great Britain, Hungary, Italy, Netherlands, Russia, South Africa, Spain, Sweden and Switzerland.

The official international rules of tennis were drafted on January 1, 1924, when the ILTF was recognized as having the authority to control lawn tennis throughout the world. The United States, which had originally turned down membership, joined at this time. Any rule changes continue to be decided at the ITF's annual general meeting.

The sport was becoming more popular in the 1920s thanks to the dominant play and eccentric personalities of Bill Tilden and Suzanne Lenglen, both of whom brought tennis into the tabloids. A 13,000-seat stadium was built at Forest Hills as a result of the success of Tilden and the U.S. Davis Cup team that decade, and Wimbledon was moved down the road in 1922 to accommodate a new stadium with a capacity of 14,000 for the fans who wanted to see Frenchwoman Lenglen. The defense of France's first Davis Cup in 1927 necessitated the building of Roland Garros in Paris.

Lenglen and Tilden were also two of the first players to expose the folly of amateurism in the sport. Tournament organizers and sponsors were getting rich, and together with the ILTF they insisted that the players retain their amateur status to play in the majors and most other important tournaments. Lenglen turned pro in 1926 and toured the United States and Canada, earning hefty paychecks and leaving a trail of lovers and headlines in her wake. Tilden joined the professional ranks in 1931 after he had spent much of his family fortune on friends and vanity projects.

Most professionals, even the successful ones, barnstormed around America, playing in a variety of ill-equipped venues in big cities and small towns. Under the control of the promoters, the players scrambled for cash and lived out of suitcases. Meanwhile, the amateurs chased the majors while trying to survive on under-the-table payments and part-time jobs.

Both brands of tennis were popular in the 1920s and '30s, but after World War II professional team sports were on the rise, and tennis ceded the spotlight. It was also dropped from the Olympics after the 1924 Games in Paris and didn't return until the Seoul Olympics in 1988.

The 1950s and 1960s brought a wave of powerful and personable Australians who dominated the Davis Cup and the majors. Roy Emerson had a then-record 12 singles and 28 total

major victories, Rod Laver won two Grand Slams and Margaret Court won 62 major titles, including 24 in singles, a record (male or female) that still stands. Ken Rosewall and Evonne Goolagong were also popular players and champions of the era.

Their success raised the profile of tennis once again and, with it, the debate of amateurism versus professionalism. "Shamateurism," the act of tournament organizers finding increasingly unique and creative ways to funnel money to amateur players to ensure their participation, had consumed the sport. With professional circuits poaching the best players from the amateur ranks with hefty pay and bonuses, professional tennis became the only way forward if the national tennis associations and the major tournaments wanted to keep the top talent performing at their events.

Wimbledon held a separate professional tournament in August 1967 as a test; when the sky above the All England Club didn't fall, the Lawn Tennis Association announced that Wimbledon would be an open tournament in 1968.

USTA president Bob Kelleher was next up, changing the U.S. Championships to the U.S. Open for the 1968 tournament. The ITF didn't support the changes, but with two majors proceeding against their wishes there was no turning back; momentum had swung and the other two majors followed suit and became open tournaments soon after.

The very first open tournament was in Bournemouth, England, in 1968, won by Rosewall and Virginia Wade. Englishman Mark Cox made history as the first amateur to beat a professional, downing Pancho Gonzalez and Emerson.

The inaugural open major was the 1968 French Open, coming before Wimbledon and the U.S. Open on the calendar. The Australian Championships was the last to change, becoming the Australian Open a year later.

In 1970 the different tournaments around the world came together to form the Grand Prix circuit, which included a points system that was the brainchild of Hall of Famer Jack Kramer. That system was in place until the birth of the Association of Tennis Professionals and the advent of computer rankings, which began on August 23, 1973.

In 1971, Laver became the first player to win $1 million in career prize money, and by the end of the decade 15 other men and three women had joined him. But even with some players earning big money, the majority of the players felt the tennis associations weren't acting in good faith and were unhappy with working conditions and remuneration.

Spearheaded by Arthur Ashe, who, as an amateur, won the first U.S. Open in 1968, the top male players got together at the 1972 U.S. Open and formed a players' union — the Association

Australian stars Roy Emerson (left) and Rod Laver on September 10, 1962. Laver defeated Emerson in the final of the U.S. Championships to claim his first Grand Slam.

of Tennis Professionals — with executive director Kramer and president Cliff Drysdale.

Left out by the men, Billie Jean King and *World Tennis* magazine publisher Gladys Heldman formed the Women's Tennis Association in 1973. Later that year, the U.S. Open became the first tournament to award equal prize money to men and women.

It was also the year of "the Battle of the Sexes" between King, who won $117,000 in 1971 to become the first woman to earn six figures, and Bobby Riggs. The retired player and avowed chauvinist challenged the top female player in an attempt to show that male players were superior. The match created widespread attention and record TV ratings, and King struck a blow for women and the equal rights movement by winning handily.

From 1974 to 1989 the men's tour was overseen by the Men's Tennis Council, which consisted of members of the ATP, members of the ITF and individual tournament directors. At the 1988 U.S. Open, ATP CEO Hamilton Jordan, the former chief of staff for U.S. president Jimmy Carter, held a press conference announcing the formation of the ATP Tour.

The ATP Tour debuted in 1990 and the women's equivalent, the WTA Tour, was formed in 1995, when the players' association merged with the Women's Tennis Council.

The ITF oversees the Davis Cup, the Fed Cup and the four majors while also hosting entry-level tournaments so that future stars of the game can earn qualification for the professional tours. The ATP and WTA operate independently but in conjunction with, and under the auspices of, the ITF. Each tour hosts its own series of events in varying tiers, and the three associations come together at the four Grand Slam tournaments.

The ATP Tour holds 61 tournaments in 30 countries across three platforms: the ATP World Tour, the ATP Challenger Tour and the ATP Champions Tour. The World Tour encompasses the Masters 1000 events, which consist of nine main non-majors — five in Europe, three in the United States and one in Canada — and the season-ending Masters, which is now called the Barclays ATP World Tour Finals. The eight players who earn the most points on the World Tour throughout the year are invited to participate in the Finals.

The WTA Tour, which became the Sony Ericsson WTA Tour in 2005, now holds 54 events in 33 countries, including the year-end WTA Tour Championships for the season's top players.

Representing more than 2,500 players from 92 nations, the WTA marked its 40th anniversary in 2013 with the "40 Love"

campaign celebrating the women who blazed a trail for today's stars. Before the WTA was born, the total annual prize money for female tennis players was shy of $2 million; it's currently over $118 million.

In 1992, 18-year-old Monica Seles set a record for women by winning more than $2.6 million in a season, which was surpassed by Arantxa Sanchez Vicario two years later. In 2007 Justine Henin was the first to earn more than $5 million in a season, and in 2013 Serena Williams won $8.5 million, with some $12 million more in endorsements. Maria Sharapova collected $6 million in prize money in 2013 and $29 million overall, second only to Roger Federer in total earnings among all tennis players.

Ivan Lendl retired in 1994 with a record of more than $21 million in career prize money, which Pete Sampras had more than doubled by the time he retired in 2002. When Federer, Rafael Nadal and Novak Djokovic call it a day they will far exceed that, and when endorsements are factored in they're among the highest-earning athletes in any sport in the world.

Tennis is one of the few sports with global reach, and with new tournaments being introduced in new markets, an already brief off-season continues to be shortened. More than half of all tournaments are played on hard court, and combined with travel demands, playing the majority of a season's events in modern tennis is extremely taxing on the players' physical and mental health.

But the thirst for elite-level tennis is not abating, and when there's money to be made for tournaments, sponsors, local economies and players, the schedule will continue to expand.

With the growth comes a new generation of players, many from nontraditional tennis countries. It's no longer just a game for the nobility, and several of today's stars have proven that you don't need to go to an elite tennis academy or belong to a country club to embark on a Hall of Fame career.

You don't even need Major Wingfield's kit — just a paddle, a ball and a wall.

Spain's Rafael Nadal returns the ball to Serbia's Novak Djokovic during their semifinal match at the 2013 French Open. Nadal would go on to win the match and the tournament to claim his record-setting eighth French title.

PIONEERS AND PERSONALITIES

Sensational stars from the 1920s to the 1970s

Australian stars John Newcombe (left) and Rod Laver (right) — flanking team captain Neale Fraser — celebrate defeating Stan Smith and Erik van Dillen of the United States to secure the 1973 Davis Cup for Australia.

Don Budge

FATHER OF THE
GRAND SLAM

Don Budge returns a shot to Frantisek Cejnar of Czechoslovakia during their fourth-round match at Wimbledon in 1938. Budge defeated Cejnar on his way to winning the championship — the third major of his eventual Grand Slam.

To varying degrees, Don Budge can attribute both his most legendary victory and the end of his career to Adolf Hitler.

Budge's father played for storied soccer club the Glasgow Rangers but moved to Oakland, California, before World War I, where his son was born in 1915.

Young Donald looked more Glaswegian than Californian with his pale skin and red hair, but he grew up playing American sports like football, baseball and basketball. It was only after he was convinced to play in the boys' state tennis tournament in 1930 and won easily that he took up the sport seriously.

By the time he was 19, Budge was good enough to be a reserve on the 1934 Davis Cup team. He'd also started emulating legendary player and fellow Californian Helen Wills Moody. As a champion, her dominant play and calm demeanor — on and off court — were an inspiration to the budding tennis star.

Budge played with a heavy racket and developed one of the best backhand shots the game has known. His 6-foot-1 frame lent itself to heavy serves, and he learned to hit the ball early on the bounce, almost always with power. He didn't smoke or drink while he was training or over the course of tournaments, and when asked what made him successful he said: "Discipline. You have to have discipline to go to bed early."

Budge also played a gentleman's game, always composed and rarely showing any flashes of anger, either at himself or his opponent — even when that opponent was instructed to win the Davis Cup and bring it back to Germany by Hitler himself.

In 1937, Budge had ascended to the number one ranking in tennis as he won a clean sweep of Wimbledon that year; he beat German Baron Gottfried von Cramm in straight sets in the men's final, won the men's doubles with Gene Mako and captured the mixed doubles with Alice Marble.

The Davis Cup featured a rematch between von Cramm and Budge, and before the match the baron got a call from the Führer. Hitler wanted the Davis Cup. "Gottfried came out pale and serious and played as if his life depended on every point," said Budge.

The German won the first two sets 8–6, 7–5 and was up 4–1 in the third before Budge took a more aggressive approach and stormed back to take the set 8–6. He'd win the next two sets 6–4, 6–2 to win the match, which has been called the greatest match in the history of tennis.

"The brilliance of the tennis was almost unbelievable," wrote tennis journalist Allison Danzig. "In game after game they sustained their amazing virtuosity without the slightest deviation or faltering on either side."

Budge beat von Cramm again in 1937, this time in a tight five-set final match at the U.S. Championships. It was Budge's first U.S. title, and it came in the same year he won the Sullivan Award as the top amateur athlete in the United States, presented at the World's Fair by Babe Ruth. He was also named the Associated Press Male Athlete of the Year for 1937.

Remarkably, Budge was even better in 1938, winning the Australian title, the French Championships, Wimbledon (where he became the first man to win without losing a single set), and the U.S. Championships. He was the first person to win the Grand Slam, a term, some argue, that was coined for his achievement that year. It took more than 25 years for Australian Rod Laver to become the next Grand Slam winner, and they remain the only two men who have won all four major tournaments in one season.

Budge didn't get a chance to play von Cramm again in the 1938 Davis Cup, a tournament fraught with political implications on the eve of World War II. By this time Budge and von Cramm had become friends, and Budge organized a petition signed by the tennis stars of the day to send

Don Budge smashes the ball for a point against Bobby Riggs in the final of the 1942 U.S. Pro Tennis Championships. Budge took the match in three sets, 6–2, 6–2, 6–2.

to Hitler to protest the imprisonment of von Cramm, who had been jailed for his anti-Nazi stance, friendship with Jews and rumored homosexuality. It fell on deaf ears.

Having reached the pinnacle of the amateur game and with little money, Budge became a professional. He made his debut in 1939 in front of a crowd of nearly 17,000 people at Madison Square Garden, a straight-sets victory over Ellsworth Vines. On the pro tour Budge had a winning record against Vines, Fred Perry and an aging Bill Tilden.

When the United States entered the war, Budge signed up for the Air Force. A shoulder injury suffered in training effec-

tively ended his tennis career. He didn't give up playing completely, however; in 1973 he won the Wimbledon Veterans Doubles title at the age of 58 with partner Frank Sedgman.

Twice married with two sons from his first marriage, Budge spent his post-tennis career on the board of advisors for Prince rackets and on the committee that chose the world champion each season. He remained an affable and popular man throughout his life and spent his golden years indulging in his passion for jazz and literature.

Budge died in 2000 at the age of 84 of a heart attack.

CAREER HIGHLIGHTS

Australian Championships
Singles champion 1938

French Championships
Singles champion 1938

Wimbledon
Singles champion 1937–38
Doubles champion 1937–38
Mixed doubles champion 1937–38

Davis Cup Team Member
1935–38

U.S. Championships
Singles champion 1937–38
Doubles champion 1936, 1938
Mixed doubles champion 1937–38

Associated Press Male Athlete of the Year
1937–38

International Tennis Hall of Fame
1964

Roy Emerson

HE JUST WINS

Australian Roy Emerson, wearing his
Fred Perry whites, makes a backhand return
in this circa-1960s photo.

Whether there was something in the water or it's just a statistical anomaly, the Australian countryside churned out two of the biggest stars in tennis history in the 1960s, including the only double Grand Slam winner in the game—Rod Laver.

Like Laver, Roy Emerson grew up in rural Queensland and built up his arm strength by working on the family farm.

Born in 1936 in Blackbutt, Emerson milked countless cows before his family moved to Brisbane to further his tennis ambitions with better coaching and competition. He was sent to an elite private school but dropped out a year before graduation to join the Australian Davis Cup team at age 17.

An athletic 6 feet tall with jet-black hair and a golden smile, "Emmo" was a popular player on tour who didn't let a good time get in the way of his match preparation.

He was a smooth and efficient serve-and-volley player, and despite enjoying the spoils of his Philip Morris cigarette sponsorship, he was one of the era's fittest players.

Emerson also lived by the Australian code of toughness the players of his time shared: "You should never complain about an injury. We believe that if you play, then you aren't injured, and that's that."

Emerson won his first Australian title in 1961 and lost in the final the following year as Laver embarked on his first Grand Slam run. Over the 1961 and 1962 seasons, Emmo played in the final of 19 straight tournaments.

After Laver joined the professional ranks in 1963, Emerson won the first of his five straight Australian titles en route to his individual record of six Australian championships.

That's just one of Emerson's all-time records, which include eight Davis Cup victories and 28 major titles in singles and doubles play. Of the 28, 12 were singles—six Australian and two each at the French, Wimbledon and U.S. Championships.

The 12 singles majors were a record that stood for 33 years, until Pete Sampras tied it at Wimbledon in 1999 and broke it there one year later. Emerson wasn't aware he held such an esteemed mark until tennis writers pointed it out as Sampras approached it. "Nobody paid attention to that sort of thing then, or kept track," said Emerson. "We just played."

In 1964 Emerson had a winning streak of 55 matches, second only to Don Budge's 92 in 1937–38. He won three of the four majors that year, just falling short of the Grand Slam when he lost in the quarter-finals in Paris.

The golden generation of Australian tennis also included Fred Stolle, whom Emerson beat in the 1965 Australian final after coming back from two sets down. He also faced Stolle in the final of his two Wimbledon victories, in 1964 and 1965, and in the U.S. final in 1964.

With Australia on top of the tennis world and Emerson a proud part of it, the Australian Lawn Tennis Association barred him from the Davis Cup team when he left the organization over their refusal to pay expenses outside the country. Eventually they relented, persuaded by Emerson's number one world ranking.

Emerson won the decisive match in six of the eight Davis Cup titles he was part of, going 21-2 in singles and 13-2 in doubles.

Immaculately dressed and groomed at all times, Emerson also made others look good. He's the only man to have won all four majors in both singles and doubles, winning the doubles crown at each at least three times and taking it six times with five different partners at the French Championships.

Emerson's final major championship was in 1971, early in the open era, when he partnered with old friend Laver to win the men's doubles at Wimbledon, and in 1978 he and son Anthony won the U.S. Hard Court Father-and-Son title.

Roy Emerson plays against Mike Sangster of Britain in a second-round singles match at Wimbledon in 1965. Emerson defeated Fred Stolle in the final for his second consecutive title at the All England Club.

"Emerson was the best doubles player of all the moderns," according to rival Jack Kramer, "very possibly the best forehand court player of all time. He was so quick he could cover everything. He had the perfect doubles shot, a backhand that dipped over the net and came in at the server's feet as he moved to the net."

A consummate teammate and leader, as Emerson eased into retirement he was player/coach with the Boston Lobsters of World Team Tennis in the 1970s, with a young Martina Navratilova as their star.

But in a sport that saves its biggest accolades for individual accomplishments, Emerson stood alone.

"There is this about Emerson first," said Mexico's Davis Cup captain Pancho Contreras in 1964. "He is always a winner. He has won them all—Wimbledon, Forest Hills, the Davis Cup. But he wins in the Caribbean, too—Trinidad, Barranquilla. He wins in Europe. He wins the little ones. He just wins."

CAREER HIGHLIGHTS

Australian Championships
    Singles champion 1961, 1963–67
    Doubles champion 1962, 1966

Australian Open
    Doubles champion 1969

French Championships
    Singles champion 1963, 1967
    Doubles champion 1960–65

International Tennis Hall of Fame
    1982

Wimbledon
    Singles champion 1964–65
    Doubles champion 1959, 1961, 1971

U.S. Championships
    Singles champion 1961, 1964
    Doubles champion 1959–60, 1965–66

Davis Cup Team Member
    1959–67

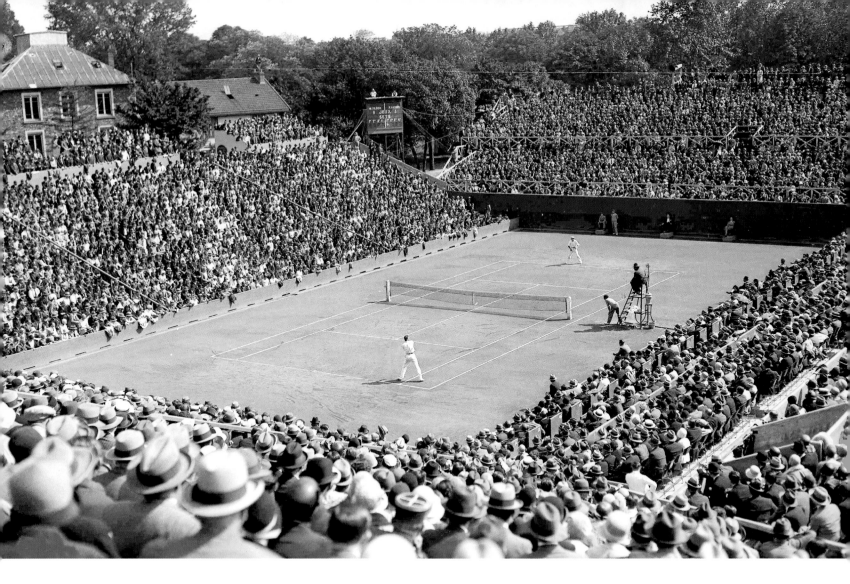

Rene Lacoste

GAME CHANGER

Rene Lacoste, in the far court, awaits the offering of Bill Tilden in the semifinal of the 1929 French Championships. Lacoste won the championship over his fellow countryman Jean Borotra in a five-set scorcher, 6–3, 2–6, 6–0, 2–6, 8–6.

Rene Lacoste was a revolutionary. Whether introducing the knit polo shirt that he remains famous for or inventing a new style of racket to replace wooden ones, he was always pushing the limits and boundaries of tennis.

Lacoste, who was born in Paris in 1904, was also his own tennis creation. He announced to his father at age 15 that he wanted to be a tennis player. An affluent automobile executive, his father gave him five years to become world champion or follow in his business footsteps.

Lacoste became a meticulous student of the game under the tutelage of French star Suzanne Lenglen. He won his first tournament in 1921, and within the five years his father allotted he had reached the upper echelons of the game, earning the nickname "the Crocodile" along the way.

Legend has it that in 1923 Lacoste bet a crocodile-skin suitcase he'd seen in a store in Boston that he'd win his match that day. He lost, but a *Boston Post* writer covering the match heard about the wager and gave him the nickname.

Lacoste liked it. He asked his friend and fashion designer Robert George to sew a crocodile on his blazer pocket, and a fashion movement was born.

Five years after promising his dad he'd be world champion, Lacoste lost to compatriot Jean Borotra in the 1924 Wimbledon final, a title he'd take a year later in a four-set rematch. He also beat Borotra for the French crown in 1925 and again in 1926, the same year he became the first Frenchman to win the U.S. Championships, which he defended in 1927.

Lacoste's opponent in the 1927 U.S. Championships final was Bill Tilden, an

American who had dominated the first half of the 1920s and would later be voted the best tennis player of the first half of the 20th century. Lacoste's first win of consequence against Tilden had come a year earlier at the 1926 Davis Cup. The loss was Tilden's first in Davis Cup action after 16 straight victories. It was an upset and a changing of the guard in world tennis.

Alongside Borotra, Henri Cochet and Jacques Brugnon, Lacoste was part of France's "Four Musketeers," who in 1927 broke the seven-year American stranglehold on the Davis Cup, with Lacoste beating Tilden for the second year in a row.

Lacoste also bested Tilden at the 1927 French Championships. Then 22, Lacoste took the 34-year-old Tilden the distance in a record-setting French final, a five-set, 61-game marathon in which Lacoste overcame two match points to win the final set 11–9.

And that became a familiar score. In the 1927 U.S. final at Forest Hills, Lacoste sat in the backcourt and wore Tilden out, winning an 11–9, 6–3, 11–9 thriller.

"I never played better," said Tilden after the match. "That Frenchman is a machine."

It was "the Year of the Crocodile" beyond the tennis court as well. In 1927 Lacoste introduced the revolutionary breathable short-sleeve knit tennis shirt to cope with the heat of American summer; he met the love of his life, Simone Thion de la Chaume; and he wrote his first book, simply titled *Tennis*.

In 1928 Tilden got a measure of revenge by beating Lacoste in the Davis Cup, but the French held their title. It was the last time Lacoste played internationally, and after winning the French Championships in 1929, again over Borotra, he retired from tennis at just 24.

Lacoste had more than held up his end of the bargain with his father. He was the best tennis player in the world for a brief but glorious time, and despite poor health that hastened his retirement, he was far from finished leaving his mark.

In 1967 the forked-shaft steel racket Lacoste invented was released as the T2000 and popularized by Jimmy Connors, the same year his daughter, Catherine Marie, won the U.S. Open golf title. She

Rene Lacoste, wearing a button-up shirt (with rolled sleeves) and his signature hat, watches a backhand return. Lacoste revolutionized tennis with the invention of the short-sleeve knit polo shirt that eliminated cumbersome buttons and long sleeves.

was the first foreigner, first amateur and youngest player ever to win the Open.

Aside from the now-familiar racket shape Lacoste created, he also wrapped the handle in surgical tape, pioneering a new grip; he designed and built the ball machine and filed more than 20 patents between the mid-1960s and 1980s, including a watershed 1982 design that changed the golf driver.

And then there's the signature crocodile logo that's still worn over the heart by millions around the world. But the modest Lacoste wouldn't even take credit for that.

"I cannot explain it but it just caught on. People wanted to wear that little alligator. Isn't it strange how life works—the elements of pure luck that are involved?…I was very, very lucky."

CAREER HIGHLIGHTS

French Championships
Singles champion 1925, 1927, 1929
Doubles champion 1925, 1929

Wimbledon
Singles champion 1925, 1928
Doubles champion 1925

U.S. Championships
Singles champion 1926–27

Davis Cup Team Member
1923–28

International Tennis Hall of Fame
1976

Rod Laver

AUSTRALIAN TREASURE

Rod Laver smashes a return shot to compatriot Neale Fraser at the 1960 U.S. Championships. Laver was known for his powerful stroke.

Rodney George Laver earned his nickname "the Rocket" the ironic way.

"He was anything but a Rocket," said Harry Hopman, the captain of Australia's Davis Cup team, "but Rod was willing to work harder than the rest, and it was soon apparent to me that he had more talent than any other of our fine Australian players."

The third of four children and the only left-hander in the family, Laver was born in Rockhampton, in rural Queensland, Australia, on August 9, 1938, a month before Don Budge became the first man to win the tennis Grand Slam.

Known for his grit and determination, as well as for his red hair and Popeye-like forearms, Laver toiled on his parents' cattle farm and practiced with his siblings on their homemade court. Bowlegged and just 5 foot 8, the power and spin gener-

ated by a flick of his mighty wrist more than compensated for his physical shortcomings.

Laver's first international victory was the U.S. Junior Championships when he was 17, and at 21 he claimed his first major title — the 1960 Australian Championships. He won the title over Neale Fraser, coming back from two sets down to win in five, the final two each 8–6.

Laver lost the 1961 Australian final to compatriot Roy Emerson, but he reclaimed the title in a rematch in 1962, the start of a remarkable year.

At that year's French Championships, Laver saved a match point in a five-set quarterfinal victory, and he went the distance again in the semifinal to set up another duel with Emerson. By then Laver had built a reputation as a player who was at his best when his back was against the wall and a comeback seemed impossible.

And again, Laver defeated Emerson for a major title—his second of the season.

Wimbledon was a smoother ride; Laver was the defending champion and emerged from a final four that was all-Australian, beating Fraser in the semifinal and Marty Mulligan in the final, both in straight sets.

At the U.S. Championships Laver lost only one set on his way to the final, where, for the third time in major competition, he got the best of Emerson. With his four-set win, Laver became the second man and third person to win the Grand Slam, following Budge and Maureen Connolly, who won in 1953.

With the Slam and fellow Australian Margaret Court's three majors in 1962, interest in amateur tennis was at an all-time high. The professional game was suffering as a result, and for the second time since World War II there was no pro tour in the United States. The professional players decided to pool their resources and lure Laver with an offer of $125,000. It worked.

After five years playing in subpar facilities in the professional wilderness, Laver was back playing against the best in the world after the International Lawn Tennis Federation approved 12 open tournaments, with amateurs and professionals competing against each other.

Immediately Laver took back his crown at the first open Wimbledon in 1968 and defended it in 1969, winning in four straight appearances with a 31-match undefeated streak, a record that stood until Bjorn Borg broke it in 1980.

In 1969—in what was now the Australian Open—Laver won a five-set endurance test in the semifinal that included a 22–20 second set in 105-degree heat, keeping cool with the help of a wet cabbage leaf in his hat. The final was a little easier—a straight-sets victory over Andres Gimeno.

The French Open final was also a straight-sets victory for Laver, and after he successfully defended his Wimbledon title, he was one tournament away from becoming the first person to win the Grand Slam twice.

The U.S. Open at Forest Hills in 1969 was nearly washed out, with heavy rain making the grass courts almost unplayable. The final was delayed two days, but Laver

Rod Laver makes a backhand stab at the 1960 U.S. Championships in Forest Hills, New York. Laver was runner-up at the tournament.

donned spiked shoes on the soggy turf and dispatched Australian Tony Roche in four sets.

Laver is still the only player to win the Grand Slam twice, and with an even 200 tournament victories in his career, he holds two records that appear unassailable.

In retirement Laver became a fixture on the tennis circuit, making a point of traveling from his southern California home to the Australian Open, where the main stadium was named Rod Laver Arena in 2001. Laver's native country named him an Australian Living Treasure, and he remains one after suffering a serious stroke in 1998. He was nursed back to health by the love of his life and wife of 46 years, Mary Shelby Laver, who passed away in 2012.

Since then the Rocket has slowed down a little, but he's still one of the game's great ambassadors, a universally respected elder and arguably the best player who ever lived.

CAREER HIGHLIGHTS

Australian Championships
Singles champion 1960, 1962
Doubles champion 1959–61

Australian Open
Singles champion 1969
Doubles champion 1969

French Championships
Singles champion 1962
Doubles champion 1961
Mixed doubles champion 1961

French Open
Singles champion 1969

Wimbledon
Singles champion 1961–62, 1968–69
Doubles champion 1971
Mixed doubles champion 1959–1960

U.S. Championships
Singles champion 1962

U.S. Open
Singles champion 1969

Davis Cup Team Member
1959–62, 1973

International Tennis Hall of Fame
1981

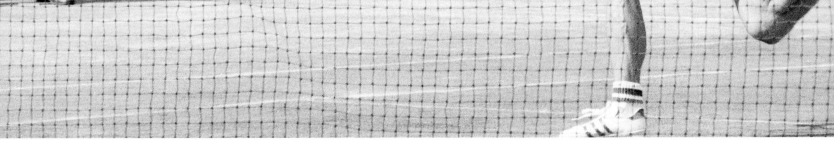

John Newcombe

GOOD TIMES, GREAT TENNIS

John Newcombe returns the ball to Ken Rosewall during their semifinal match at the 1973 U.S. Open. Newcombe won 6–4, 7–6, 6–3 to advance to the final, where he beat Jan Kodes 6–4, 1–6, 4–6, 6–2, 6–3 for his second U.S. title.

In 2000 John Newcombe was enjoying a comfortable retirement in his hometown of Sydney. With the exception of his presence during the annual awarding of the Newcombe Medal (given to Australia's player of the year) and some tennis commentary, he remained largely out of the spotlight. That is, until a future American president reminisced about a night of excess nearly a quarter-century earlier.

Asked about a 1976 drunk-driving conviction at a press conference two days before the U.S. presidential election, George W. Bush simply said, "I was out drinking beer with John Newcombe."

At the time Newcombe was 32 and a winner of 25 major titles. Bush was 30 and his father was the director of the CIA.

Upon learning of Bush's comments, Newcombe and his wife—former German player Angelika Pfannenburg, whom he

married in 1966—planned to go to their farm in Australia's Hunter Valley to avoid the media. But it was too late. Before they could leave, Newcombe's office in Sydney was surrounded by American journalists.

In 2000 news traveled instantaneously; in 1976 it could be swept under the rug, which was probably a good thing for fun-loving "Newk." Arthur Ashe liked to tell a story about Newcombe filling a bathtub full of beer following a win at Wimbledon, and another where he wrenched his back while drunk.

The odd injury aside, however, Newcombe's off-court activities didn't hurt his game. He's one of only two players to win the Wimbledon and U.S. titles as both an amateur and a professional—the other being fellow Australian Rod Laver. He won a total of 66 singles titles, 34 as an amateur and 32 as a professional.

Born in 1944, Newcombe was more interested in other sports growing up and didn't focus on tennis until he was 17. Only two years later, in 1963, he was on Australia's Davis Cup team, which won four straight titles from 1964 to 1967.

He was the last amateur to win Wimbledon in 1967 before the open era began and professionals were allowed to play. He also won consecutive crowns in 1970 and 1971—the latter final a classic five-set victory over Stan Smith—before missing the tournament in 1972 and 1973.

Newcombe's game was best suited to grass, and he would have been favored to continue his dominance at the All England Club, but the politics of the day ended his streak. In 1972 he was part of World Championship Tennis, an organization that was feuding with the International Tennis Federation because the ITF refused to recognize the competing tour and its players. In 1973, Newcombe led a boycott of Wimbledon because the Association of Tennis Professionals, the fledgling players' union, was in a dispute with the ITF over player rights. After the ITF banned ATP member and Yugoslavian player Niki Pilic because he wasn't "in good standing" with his national tennis association (a result of playing in a professional tournament instead of the Davis Cup), the players decided to test the powers of their new union against the ITF establishment and boycotted Wimbledon in solidarity with Pilic.

The 6-foot, 170-pound Newcombe was a natural leader, and he cut a dashing figure with his signature mustache and tousled hair. He was as warm and friendly off the court as he was strong and fit between the lines. His attacking serve-and-volley game earned him seven major singles titles—a French championship short of a career Grand Slam. However, he did win at least two of each of the other majors.

With good friend and countryman Tony Roche, Newcombe was also a formidable doubles player. Together they won Wimbledon five times, setting a modern record. They're one of five teams, all Australian, to win each of the four majors, and they lead all teams with 12 total major victories.

Fan favorite John Newcombe makes a backhand stab in this undated photo.

Newcombe's combined total of 25 major titles stands second all-time behind the 28 won by compatriot Roy Emerson.

Fortunately for him, Newcombe's rabblerousing in the 1960s and 1970s—on behalf of the players and while enjoying the tour's nightlife—came before electronic media and constant scrutiny. He believes today's game is in good hands despite instant, international news.

"We've got two unbelievable examples of exemplary character at the top in Nadal and Federer," he says. "It feeds down."

Still running a tennis camp in Texas that he opened in 1968, Newcombe was asked about the events of that now famous 1976 night.

"George wanted to show how a Texan could out-drink an Aussie. It didn't quite work out the way he planned it."

CAREER HIGHLIGHTS

Australian Championships
Doubles champion 1965, 1967
Australian Open
Singles champion 1973, 1975
Doubles champion 1971, 1973, 1976
French Championships
Doubles champion 1967
French Open
Doubles champion 1969, 1973
Wimbledon
Singles champion 1967, 1970–71
Doubles champion 1965–66, 1968–70, 1974

U.S. Championships
Singles champion 1967
Doubles champion 1967
Mixed doubles champion 1964
U.S. Open
Singles champion 1973
Doubles champion 1971, 1973
Davis Cup Team Member
1963–67, 1973, 1975–76
Davis Cup Team Captain
1995–1999
International Tennis Hall of Fame
1986

Fred Perry

OUTSIDER TO ICON

Fred Perry lunges for a ball delivered by Gottfried von Cramm in the 1936 Wimbledon final. Perry took the championship 6–1, 6–1, 6–0. It was his final Wimbledon victory and the last for British men until Andy Murray prevailed in 2013.

Frederick John Perry retired from amateur tennis almost 80 years ago, yet his name remains synonymous with British sport and fashion. Outside the United Kingdom, however, Fred Perry's tennis career is often largely forgotten. Instead he is known for his eponymous clothing line, the quintessentially British street fashion with the iconic laurel wreath logo.

Perry's name also represented a failure for Britain; he was the last native son to win Wimbledon until Andy Murray finally prevailed in 2013 — a span of 77 years.

Although Perry is beloved in his native country now, he wasn't embraced in his time. The upper crust didn't care for his working-class roots in Stockport, south of Manchester, and the tennis establishment felt his intensity on the court was an affront to proper etiquette.

Perry didn't let that get in his way; "bloody-mindedness was one of my specialties," he said, "and revenge was never against my principles either."

Born in 1909, Perry first focused his bloody-mindedness on table tennis while attending school in the London borough of Ealing. In 1929 he became world champion. He promptly retired and picked up a bigger racket, hoping success on the tennis court would move him a few rungs up the social ladder.

In the wake of Perry's mother's death in January of 1930, his father agreed to fund his tennis ambitions for one year. In the third round of the 1930 edition of Wimbledon, Perry showed promise in dispatching Umberto De Morpurgo, an Italian baron. In fact, some members of the Lawn Tennis Association were so impressed by Perry's play that they added him to a summer tour of the Americas.

The tour was a success on the court and off, as Perry won the Argentine national championship and reached the final of the Davis Cup the following summer, while also squiring around Hollywood starlet Jean Harlow.

While rightly perceived as a bit of a playboy, Perry didn't let it affect his game. Early in his career he vowed to be the fittest player on tour, and he trained with the Arsenal football club to get there. As a result his stamina enabled him to retrieve difficult balls late into matches, and he lost only two five-setters in his career.

Perry also played psychological games with his opponents, like changing into crisp white pants and a new shirt for the fourth set to give the impression he was fresh. He also leaped over the net to congratulate his opponents after matches.

In 1933 Perry led England to its first Davis Cup victory in 21 years. A year later he won the Australian Championships before taking his first Wimbledon title, a moment tainted by a Wimbledon committee member who told Perry's vanquished opponent, Australian Jack Crawford, that the better man did not win.

A line was drawn in the sand, and Perry was driven. He won Wimbledon the next two years, and with a French Championships win in 1935 he earned a career Grand Slam with victories in all four majors, the first man and only British player to accomplish the feat.

After he broke a rib and bruised a kidney late in the 1935 season, it looked like Perry's Wimbledon reign was in jeopardy at the 1936 tournament. But he was determined to retain the crown, if for no other reason than to spite the Lawn Tennis Association. His victory was resounding, beating Gottfried von Cramm in a rematch of their 1935 final, 6–1, 6–1, 6–0. In his three-year reign as Wimbledon champion, Perry didn't lose a set in the final.

After defending the Davis Cup and regaining his U.S. title, Perry retired as an amateur at age 27. He promptly went back to the United States and used the proceeds from his first professional tour to buy a stake in the Beverly Hills Tennis Club, which was soon crawling with celebrities and beauty queens. He gave lessons

Fred Perry holds a collection of his trophies.

to Charlie Chaplin, Errol Flynn and the Marx Brothers, and he married four times.

However, Perry's real postcareer legacy was in fashion. Fred Perry the brand was born in the 1940s, when former Austrian soccer player Tibby Wegner came to Perry with the concept that became the first sweatband. In 1952 they came up with the signature slim-fit cotton shirt with the laurel wreath—a classic symbol of sporting success that Perry had worn on his touring blazer and Davis Cup uniform—which they cleverly marketed in the early years of televised tennis by giving them to players, commentators and cameramen at Wimbledon.

The shirts soon became international fashion and were adopted by various musical subcultures, one of which was known as "the Perry Boys." From the Mod movement to Rude Boys to Britpop, they became a symbol of Britain and a flag on the chest.

Perry eventually sold the company and spent his life raising a family with Bobby, his fourth wife, and traveling the world. He made peace with the powers that be at Wimbledon, and they named the entrance gate after him and erected a statue in his honor. He died in Melbourne after watching the 1995 Australian Open, still waiting for a British heir to his Wimbledon throne.

CAREER HIGHLIGHTS

Australian Championships
  Singles champion 1934
  Doubles champion 1934

French Championships
  Singles champion 1935
  Doubles champion 1933
  Mixed doubles champion 1932

Davis Cup Team Member
  1931–36

Wimbledon
  Singles champion 1934–36
  Mixed doubles champion 1935–36

U.S. Championships
  Singles champion 1933–34, 1936
  Mixed doubles champion 1932

International Tennis Hall of Fame
  1975

Ken Rosewall

AGELESS WONDER

Ken Rosewall makes a forehand return at Wimbledon. Despite winning every other singles major, Rosewall was never able to triumph at Wimbledon. He did, however, twice win the doubles crown at the All England Club.

Throughout the 1960s, Australians Rod Laver and Roy Emerson stood astride the tennis world, winning 23 major singles titles between them. So it's not surprising that a third, more reserved Australian was a little overshadowed.

Laver may be the only man to win the Grand Slam twice, and Emerson may hold the record for most Australian championships, but Ken Rosewall showed them a thing or two about longevity.

In 1972, at the age of 37, Rosewall won his fourth Australian title, and more than forty years later he's still the oldest man to win a major championship in the open era.

But that wasn't a swansong or a victory by a wily veteran taking one last kick at the can in his native country; it was the start of a remarkable Rosewall run.

Although he couldn't compete in the French Open or Wimbledon in 1972 because the International Tennis Federation was in a dispute over player eligibility with World Championship Tennis (the tour he belonged to), Rosewall did face Laver in the WCT finals. The Aussies gave the crowd in Dallas and millions more on television a five-set epic. Rosewall, down 5–4 in the fifth-set tiebreaker, stormed back to take the decisive fifth set 7–5 in a match considered among the best of all time.

In 1974 Rosewall made it as far as the U.S. Open final and was still ranked second in the world at the age of 40. He's one of the few successful players who spanned the three different eras of tennis: elite amateur, professional, and open-era tennis, which began in 1968. He won 50 tournaments in the open era—32 in singles and 18 in doubles—all of which came after he turned 33. He won the very first open tournament, the British Hard Court Championships, and the first open major, the French. His last victory was in 1977, just two weeks shy of his 43rd birthday, and he finished that season ranked 12th in the world.

Barred from entering the Grand Slam tournaments during his prime after turning professional, Rosewall would have had far more than his 18 Grand Slam titles in singles, doubles and mixed doubles. His two French titles came 15 years apart, and his U.S. championships were separated by 14 years. He didn't win Wimbledon as a singles player, but he made it to four finals over 20 years, and the first and last of his four Australian victories were 19 years apart; his final appearance was a semifinal loss in 1977—24 years after his first title.

Rosewall also competed in the Davis Cup 20 years after his first appearance, helping Australia beat Czechoslovakia in 1973 to recapture the crown.

"I was lucky, because the game didn't change a great deal from the start of my career to the end," said the humble son of a grocer from Sydney. "I was only average in school, and I didn't know anything about business. Tennis was my game and my livelihood, so I just kept playing."

Born in 1934, Rosewall was 18 when he won his first Australian title in 1953, after his father, Robert, the only coach he ever had, taught the natural lefty to play right-handed. He practiced incessantly on the clay courts of his blue-collar neighborhood, so much that it cost him his accounting degree.

Rosewall developed a deadly backhand and was blessed with great balance and anticipation as well as a body that stood up to the rigors of decades of tennis. His serve was extremely accurate, compensating for a lack of power, and there were few weaknesses in his overall game.

Said Australian pro Dick Crealy: "With Rosewall, you think you're playing well but he seems to anticipate everything you do. And he never misses. He doesn't maul you the way Laver does. He just breaks your heart."

At 5 foot 7, though generously listed by some as 5 foot 9, and playing for most of

Ken Rosewall (right) and Rod Laver share a moment after the conclusion of the 1968 French Open. Rosewall took the contest 6–3, 6–1, 2–6, 6–2.

his career at around 142 pounds, Rosewall was jokingly called "Muscles" as a young player and was very seriously dubbed "the Doomsday Stroking Machine" by tennis writer and historian Bud Collins as he marched through the years.

The second man with over a million dollars in career earnings after Laver, the failed accountant did concede that one thing changed as he got older: "I'm just a little heavier in the wallet."

But that money didn't change Rosewall. He remained notoriously thrifty and down to earth. "Ken's just a very decent little bloke," summed up Arthur Huxley, a close friend for many years.

Now living on an olive farm in Queensland and still playing occasionally despite a minor stroke in 2011, Rosewall says the Australian greats of those three bygone eras still remain friendly and in touch.

Asked if any current players could break his record for oldest major winner, Rosewall suggested Roger Federer might have the conditioning and love of the game.

"I'd like to say Roger reminds me of myself, but I'm not sure if I belong there with him."

CAREER HIGHLIGHTS

Australian Championships
Singles champion 1953, 1955
Doubles champion 1953, 1956

Australian Open
Singles champion 1971–72
Doubles champion 1972

French Championships
Singles champion 1953
Doubles champion 1953

French Open
Singles champion 1968
Doubles champion 1968

Wimbledon
Doubles champion 1953, 1956

U.S. Championships
Singles champion 1956
Doubles champion 1956
Mixed doubles champion 1956

U.S. Open
Singles champion 1970
Doubles champion 1969

Davis Cup Team Member
1953–56, 1973, 1975

International Tennis Hall of Fame
1980

Bill Tilden

THE CHAMPION SHOWMAN

Bill Tilden is decked out in a trilby and thick sweater for a post-Wimbledon match against Frenchman Martin Plaa at the Ibrox Stadium in Glasgow, Scotland, on July 6, 1938.

Considering that Selina Hey Tilden lost three children to diphtheria within three weeks of each other in 1884, it's not surprising that she would coddle her youngest child, William Tatem Jr.

Born in 1893 in the affluent Philadelphia neighborhood of Germantown, Bill Tilden wasn't allowed to go to city parks and was homeschooled by his doting mother. His father, a prominent Republican who entertained two presidents, remained aloof and distant.

When Selina became ill, her son was sent to study at Germantown Academy in 1908. He also went to live with his maiden aunt and cousin, in a home Tilden would retreat to for much of his adult life.

His mother died of a stroke in 1911 while he was attending the University of Pennsylvania. Four years later Tilden lost his father to kidney failure and his only surviving sibling, older brother Herbert, to pneumonia. Already a nervous young man who had difficulty making friends, Tilden was adrift without his family. He became a recluse until cousin Selena suggested he'd be trapped in his aunt's house forever if he didn't make something of his life.

A decent tennis player as a boy, Tilden took up the sport in earnest, but in his first U.S. Championships in 1916 he lost in straight sets in the first round. Tilden, however, had the time, inheritance money and connections to focus on tennis, and he went about building his game, brick by brick, shot by shot.

In 1919, at the relatively advanced tennis age of 26, Tilden made his first U.S. Championships final, losing 6–4, 6–4, 6–3 to Bill Johnston. He was humiliated and vowed to improve his backhand shot, which Johnston had exploited. To improve,

Tilden made a deal with a wealthy insurance executive in Rhode Island who owned one of the few indoor courts in the country; he agreed to teach the man's son in exchange for his own use of the court. He became so obsessive about the game that he would literally write the book on tennis—*Match Play and the Spin of the Ball* was a bible to many of the world's top players for years to come.

The practice paid off handsomely, and "Big Bill" Tilden avenged his defeat by beating "Little Bill" Johnston at the U.S. Championships in 1920. His game transformed, he won Wimbledon the same year, the first American to do so. Until a bad knee derailed him six years later, he didn't lose a match of any consequence, going undefeated at Wimbledon and in the Davis Cup in the years he entered and winning six straight U.S. titles, five of them over Johnston.

Tilden didn't lose a single match in 1924 and was ranked number one in the world for six straight years (1920–25) and in the United States 10 consecutive times (1920–29). His amateur record was 907-62, and he won a total of 138 tournaments and 10 majors.

Despite his success, Tilden fancied himself more than a tennis player. He sunk much of his fortune into vanity projects in the hope of becoming an actor, but his chops treading the boards didn't match his footwork on the court, and the shows invariably failed.

The real theater for Tilden was on the court. He was a consummate showman who arrived at matches in a camel-hair coat and bowed to the crowd after shots. Tall and rail thin despite a diet heavy of steak and ice cream, he was an elegant player with a complete game who could easily slip between styles, and he often did to confound opponents and please the galleries.

Tilden's homosexuality was an open secret in a less tolerant time, but by all accounts he led an asexual life, and the young men he took under his wing were simply protégés. It was only as his tennis powers and celebrity declined years after his retirement in 1930 that he began to act on his sexual urges. While visiting cousin

Bill Tilden shown during an exhibition match. The star turned professional in 1931 and participated in professional matches to help fund his other interests, primarily theater production.

Selena in the late 1930s, she gently suggested his sexuality was becoming more apparent and he should be careful. Tilden never spoke to her again.

In 1946 Tilden was arrested for contributing to the delinquency of a minor after being caught with a teenager in a car on Hollywood's Sunset Boulevard. He spent a little under a year in prison and did a second stint in 1949 when he was caught with another young man, a violation of his probation.

Days after being released the second time, Tilden was voted the best player in his sport in an Associated Press half-century poll by the largest margin of any athlete. But by then, most of his friends had turned their backs on him, and he was a pariah in the tennis world.

Tilden died alone and almost penniless in his Los Angeles apartment at the age of 60. A modest headstone that simply read "William T. Tilden 2nd 1893–1953" was placed on his grave in the family plot in Philadelphia at the foot of his mother's. It remains the only monument to the greatest tennis player of the first half of the 20th century.

CAREER HIGHLIGHTS

French Championships
Mixed doubles champion 1930

Wimbledon
Singles champion 1920–21, 1930
Doubles champion 1927

Davis Cup team member
1920–30

U.S. Championships
Singles champion 1920–25, 1929
Doubles champion 1918, 1921–23, 1927
Mixed doubles champion 1913–14, 1922–23

International Tennis Hall of Fame
1959

Maureen Connolly

WHAT COULD HAVE BEEN

Maureen Connolly makes a backhand return against Angela Mortimer in their third-round matchup at Wimbledon in 1952. Connolly won the tournament, her first of four straight.

The history of tennis is littered with child prodigies who didn't fulfill enormous promise. Maureen Connolly is one of those players. However, her talent wasn't squandered because of overbearing parents, a Svengali coach or a substance abuse problem—as has been the case with many others. For Connolly, it was simply cruel fate.

Born in San Diego in 1934, Connolly was raised by her mother, Jessamine, and a stepfather she loathed. Though Jessamine wanted her to be a dancer, Maureen

couldn't help but be drawn to the local tennis courts.

She was equally passionate in her love of the game and her animosity toward opponents. Fomenting this anger was encouraged by her coach, Eleanor "Teach" Tennant, a professional at the Beverly Hills club who gave lessons to Hollywood stars like Clark Gable, Errol Flynn and Marlene Dietrich and who coached both Alice Marble and Bobby Riggs to Wimbledon titles in 1939.

"Eleanor Tennant contributed to my hate complex," Connolly later wrote, "but there was fertile soil for the seed. She believed one should not make friends with opponents, one should remain aloof. I translated this into hating my foes. Miss Tennant, I am positive, had no idea a seed of hatred would flower in my breast with such a dark bloom."

It was a dichotomy in Connolly. In her obituary, the *New York Times* said: "Off the court, Maureen was a bubbling young girl, full of gaiety and friendliness for everyone, fond of hamburgers, baseball games, dancing and music of every kind."

But her nickname "Little Mo" reflected her on-court persona. Bestowed upon her endearingly by San Diego sportswriter Nelson Fisher, it was an allusion to the World War II American battleship *Missouri*, also known as "Big Mo," because of her cannonading shots from the baseline and the fire she carried inside when she set foot on the court.

The partnership with Tennant worked early on. After losing her first two matches at the U.S. Championships when she was only 14 and 15, Connolly won her first title at 16 in 1951, the youngest winner in tournament history.

Connolly then went on an incredible run of 50 straight wins in the majors, going undefeated at Wimbledon and the French and Australian championships, and taking 19 straight at Forest Hills after those early U.S. championship losses.

It wasn't just the streak, it was the way Connolly won—with ease. After ascending to the number one ranking at age 17 in 1952—the year she won Wimbledon and the U.S. Championships and parted ways with Tennant—she dominated in 1953. In her 22 matches at the Grand Slam tournaments, she ceded an average of only three games a match. She won the Australian Championships over her doubles partner, Julie Sampson, and lost just one set in taking the French Championships. Her toughest test in the majors was the 1953 Wimbledon final, which she won 8–6, 7–5 over Doris Hart and called the most satisfying of her career.

Entering the U.S. Championships that year with the first three major titles under her belt, Connolly strolled through the tournament, winning the quarterfinal 6–2, 6–3, the semifinal 6–1, 6–1, and the final 6–2, 6–4. With the victory she became the first woman to win the Grand Slam—capturing the Australian, French, Wimbledon and U.S. singles titles in a calendar year—a feat replicated just twice since, by Margaret Court in 1970 and Steffi Graf in 1988.

Connolly skipped the Australian Championships in 1954 but defended her French and Wimbledon titles, not losing a single set in the latter. But she wouldn't get the chance to go back to New York.

After Connolly won her second national title in 1952, the people of San Diego held a parade in her honor and gave her a horse named Colonel Merryboy as a gift. She was riding outside San Diego before the 1954 U.S. Championships when a cement truck drove past and startled the horse, causing a collision that crushed Connolly's right leg, breaking the fibula and severing the calf muscles—and ending her career when she was only 19.

Over a remarkable three and a half years she was the undisputed number one ranked player, won nine straight majors that she entered and was named the Female Athlete of the Year three times by the Associated Press.

"Tennis is a wonderful game and I leave it with no regrets," said Connolly. "I've had a full life with lots of travel and I've met lots of wonderful people. Now I'm going to be a little housewife. It's a new career and I'm awfully happy with it."

A year after her accident Connolly married Norman Brinker, a Navy officer and U.S. Olympic equestrian, with whom she had two daughters, Cindy and Brenda. In retirement she worked as a ten-

Maureen Connolly is seen here in a mixed doubles match at Wimbledon. Her best finish as a mixed pair was in the semifinal in 1954.

nis correspondent and was on the board of Wilson sporting goods. She also founded the Maureen Connolly Brinker Tennis Foundation in 1968 to fund clinics and help junior players who couldn't afford to play nationally.

The foundation remains active today, but Connolly never got to see it grow or American tennis thrive. On June 21, 1969, she succumbed to cancer at just 34 years old, leaving behind a legacy as one of tennis' most dominant performers.

CAREER HIGHLIGHTS

Australian Championships
Singles champion 1953
Doubles champion 1953

French Championships
Singles champion 1953–54
Doubles champion 1954
Mixed doubles champion 1954

Wimbledon
Singles champion 1952–54

U.S. Championships
Singles champion 1951–53

Wightman Cup Team Member
1951–54

Associated Press Female Athlete of the Year
1951–53

International Tennis Hall of Fame
1968

Margaret Smith Court

QUEEN OF THE COURT

Australia's Margaret Court is shown in action while winning the Pacific Coast International Open in Berkeley, California, on October 5, 1969.

The woman with the most appropriate last name in tennis history is also its most dominant.

Margaret Court married into her apropos surname, but, as either Margaret Smith or Margaret Court, the Australian owned the sport in the 1960s and '70s the way no one had before, and no one has approached her since.

However, Court's reputation, especially in Australia, has taken a beating—the kind of which she never endured on court. After converting from Catholicism in the 1970s, Court went on to become a Pentecostal minister and founded the Margaret Court Ministries in the '90s. She's now the senior pastor at a church in Perth and appears regularly on the Australian Christian Channel.

When the Australian government was debating legalizing same-sex marriage, Court spoke out against it, saying that God intended marriage to be between a man and a woman only. These views drew protests at her namesake tennis court in Melbourne at the Australian Open, as well as admonishment from openly gay former opponents Martina Navratilova and Billie Jean King.

Court has maintained her stance on gay marriage, and while it remains a lightning rod for controversy, her on-court career cannot be questioned.

"She was such a queen for so many years," King said. "I needed all I could get against her. It was very difficult."

The rivals faced off in five major finals, with Court beating King in arguably the best Wimbledon women's final ever played. The final score was 14–12, 11–9 in a match that took two hours and 27 minutes. The win earned Court the third title of her Grand Slam in 1970.

And it was King who bestowed the nickname "the Arm" on Court.

Rosie Casals, the woman Court beat in the U.S. Open final to seal that Slam, agrees. "It was about the arms that always seemed to stretch up, out, sideways. She could always reach everything. And those long legs that would take her up to the drop shots. Arms and legs, I always remember that's what she was."

Court was always all limbs. As a tall, gangly 15-year-old in 1958, she left her home in Albury, New South Wales, to train in Melbourne. She moved in with former star player Frank Sedgman and his family, and he put her on a rigorous training regimen. Her work ethic became legendary; long before it was common practice, she was lifting weights and increasing her endurance with distance runs. It led to a powerful, relentless style of tennis.

With this marriage of innate ability and high-level training, Court started to dominate the sport, winning the first of seven straight and 11 total Australian titles in 1960 at age 17.

Having also won twice each at the French Championships, Wimbledon and the U.S. Championships and tired of living out of a suitcase, she retired in 1966 and married Barrymore Court, the son of the premier of Western Australia, in 1967. It was his desire to see the world that convinced her to rejoin the tour.

The brief respite did nothing to dull Court's game; in 1969 and 1970 she won seven of eight majors, her one loss coming in the 1969 Wimbledon semifinals to eventual champion Ann Jones. In 1970 she became just the second woman to win the Grand Slam—all four majors in a calendar year—after Maureen Connolly did it in 1953. Only one other woman has accomplished this feat since—Steffi Graf in 1988.

Having already won the doubles Grand Slam with compatriot Kenneth Fletcher in 1963, Court became the first and still the only person to accomplish this feat in both singles and doubles.

Court retired for good in 1977 when she found out she was pregnant with her fourth child, and today her records are seemingly unassailable. Court ended her career with 197 singles titles, 158 in doubles and 59 in

Margaret Court lunges for a backhand return against Billie Jean King in the 1970 Wimbledon final. Court prevailed in the hotly contested match 14–12, 11–9. She would later win the U.S. Open to become the second woman ever to win a Grand Slam.

mixed doubles for a grand total of 414 tournament victories, winning all three titles (singles, doubles and mixed doubles) at the same tournament 27 times. She won 24 Grand Slam singles titles, a record for men and women that still stands, as well as 38 women's and mixed doubles crowns, and she was ranked number one in the world for seven years in the 1960s and '70s.

Asked how she'd fare in today's game against the likes of the Williams sisters, Court replied: "If we had been brought up at this time with the rackets they are using now, I think most of us would have fitted in. Navratilova would have fit in and Billie Jean would have fit in. Back then I think I was one of the fittest players in the world."

Her conclusion? "I think I would have loved playing today and I believe I could have done well."

CAREER HIGHLIGHTS

Australian Championships
Singles champion 1960–66
Doubles champion 1961–63, 1965
Mixed doubles champion 1963–65

Australian Open
Singles champion 1969–71, 1973
Doubles champion 1969–71, 1973
Mixed doubles champion 1969

French Championships
Singles champion 1962, 1964
Doubles champion 1964–66
Mixed doubles champion 1963–65

French Open
Singles champion 1969–70, 1973
Doubles champion 1973
Mixed doubles champion 1969

Wimbledon
Singles champion 1963, 1965, 1970
Doubles champion 1964, 1969
Mixed doubles champion 1963, 1965–66, 1968, 1975

U.S. Championships
Singles champion 1962, 1965
Doubles champion 1963
Mixed doubles champion 1961–65

U.S. Open
Singles champion 1969–70, 1973
Doubles champion 1968, 1970, 1973, 1975
Mixed doubles champion 1969–70, 1972

Federation Cup Team Member
1963–65, 1968–70

International Tennis Hall of Fame
1979

Althea Gibson

BOUNDARY BREAKER

Althea Gibson approaches the net to make a return. Gibson was known for her athleticism and ball stalking on the court.

Postwar America was in transition. As the country boomed in population, pride and money, the geographic and political scars of World War II were largely left behind in Europe as suburbs went up, families were created and the American dream was being realized by more and more people. But underneath it all lay the ugly undercurrent of segregation; and in the United States a civil rights battle was brewing. Althea Gibson would be an inspirational figure in that movement.

In 1950, three years after Jackie Robinson broke the color barrier in Major League Baseball and five years before Rosa Parks refused to give up her seat on a bus in Montgomery, Alabama, Gibson became the first black woman to play tennis at the U.S. Championships.

Like Robinson, Gibson was such a superior athlete that there were no reasonable arguments available to defend her exclusion from elite competition. Tall and lithe at 5 foot 11, she was a star athlete growing up in Harlem, where her family moved three years after she was born in Silver, South Carolina, in 1927. Basketball was her favorite sport, but her tennis game caught the eye of Walter Johnson, a Lynchburg, Virginia, doctor who would later mentor Arthur Ashe.

History was made on August 28, 1950, when Gibson beat England's Barbara Knapp 6–2, 6–2 on a peripheral court at Forest Hills. Her next opponent was more formidable, former U.S. and Wimbledon champion Louise Brough. On a main court in front of thousands, a nervous Gibson lost the first set 6–1 before gaining her composure and taking the second set 6–3. Brough went up 3–0 in the third, but Gibson fought back to pull ahead 7–6.

With Gibson on the verge of an epic upset, the skies opened and lightning chased the players and fans from the stadium. While Gibson was subjected to a media mob, Brough was able to rest and recover, and she took the third set 9–7 the next day.

Gibson carried on her shoulders the burdens of expectation and of representing African-Americans, a heavy weight to carry on the court. But as she became a regular on the tour, it became clear she belonged with the best in the world.

In 1956 Gibson won the first major title by a black player, beating Briton Angela Mortimer 6–0, 12–10 to win the French Championships. Later that summer she made her Wimbledon debut, losing in the quarterfinal, but her powerful serve-and-volley game and her long strides were suited to the faster grass surface, and in 1957 she completed the task, beating Darlene Hard in the final.

Two months later Gibson added her own country's title, winning the U.S. Championships seven years after her groundbreaking entry with a 6–3, 6–2 victory over Brough, ending the 1957 season as the world's number one player.

After her historic summer Gibson became the first African-American woman to be named Associated Press Female Athlete of the Year, an award she won again in 1958 when she defended both her Wimbledon and U.S. titles and held on to her number one ranking.

But as an amateur, this success and notoriety did not mean riches or even a living wage, so Gibson turned pro after winning her second U.S. title. She reportedly earned $100,000 to play a series of matches against glamour girl Karol Fageros, many of them held on basketball courts before Harlem Globetrotters games. Gibson won 114 of the 118 matches.

Seeking another challenge and greater competition, Gibson joined the Ladies Professional Golf Association (LPGA), breaking yet another barrier in becoming the first African-American to do so. After some moderately successful years on tour, she decided to go back to tennis at the start of the open era in 1968, but by then she was in her 40s and didn't have the speed to keep up with the younger players.

Althea Gibson clutches the Venus Rosewater Dish, presented to her as Wimbledon champion in 1957. She is kissed by her opponent Darlene Hard, whom she defeated 6–3, 6–2 to become the first African-American to win a Wimbledon championship.

In retirement Gibson recorded an album and acted in a John Wayne movie, and later in life she was named New Jersey Commissioner of Athletics, a position she held for 10 years. She also served on both the state's Athletics Control Board and the Governor's Council on Physical Fitness.

Gibson died in 2003 at the age of 76, four years before she was honored at the U.S. Open on the 50th anniversary of her landmark victory.

"I hope that I have accomplished just one thing: that I have been a credit to tennis and my country," she wrote in her autobiography, a quote that appears on the statue of Gibson at the park in New Jersey where she taught tennis.

In a sport and nation that grew to be more inclusive because of her, she succeeded.

CAREER HIGHLIGHTS

Australian Championships
 Doubles champion 1957

French Championships
 Singles champion 1956
 Doubles champion 1956

Wimbledon
 Singles champion 1957–58
 Doubles champion 1956–58

Wightman Cup Team Member
 1957–58

U.S. Championships
 Singles champion 1957–58
 Mixed doubles champion 1957

Associated Press Female Athlete of the Year
 1957, 1958

International Tennis Hall of Fame
 1971

Suzanne Lenglen

SHOWTIME

Suzanne Lenglen, known for her dancer's grace, thrills the Wimbledon crowd as she reaches a well-placed drop shot from her opponent.

Born north of Paris in the last year of the 19th century, Suzanne Lenglen would live her life in the tumultuous center of a world rapidly changing, both shaped by it and shaping it. She would be the first female tennis superstar of the 20th century, as much for her flair for the dramatic as for her sublime talent.

Lenglen was an asthmatic child, and her father, Charles, thought tennis might make his daughter a little heartier. She first picked up a racket at age 11 and quickly developed her precision by aiming at a handkerchief on the ground on the other side of the net. Combining her accuracy with her dancer's grace, she quickly made a name for herself on the continent and beyond.

Recognizing his daughter's gift, Charles had moved the family south to Nice and became Suzanne's coach, agent and busi-ness manager. It was his idea for her to play against men, a first for women, and it paved the way to her first World Hard Court Championship when she was just 14.

With the outbreak of World War I, Lenglen didn't get to make her Wimbledon debut until 1919, when she was 20. She made it to the final with ease and faced Dorothea Lambert Chambers, the seven-time defending champion. They were a study in contrasts. Chambers was twice her age and wore an ankle-length skirt with petticoats and a corset. Lenglen ruffled the staid British tennis establish-ment with exposed calves and forearms, the freedom of movement offering her a competitive advantage as well as a sig-nature style. Eating brandy-soaked sugar cubes between sets, Lenglen dispatched Chambers in an epic battle — 10–8, 4–6, 9–7.

With that victory she became the most celebrated female athlete on the planet, and her lifestyle made her internationally famous. She was the embodiment of postwar excess and joie de vivre, known to drink and dance and have lovers. Her short hair and scandalously short skirts ushered in the flapper look, and her trademark headband, called "the Lenglen bandeau," became a trend. Lenglen introduced glamour and sex appeal to the sport.

But to focus on Lenglen's style and tabloid headlines cheapens her on-court achievements, and from 1919 to 1926 she was virtually unbeatable. Over that span she won Wimbledon and the French Championships six times and the World Hard Court Championships four times, as well as two gold medals at the 1920 Olympics in Antwerp in singles and mixed doubles. Her only loss in that seven-year period was a controversial one to U.S. champion Molla Mallory in 1921.

Lenglen had agreed to play a series of exhibition matches in America to raise money for the French villages devastated by the war. Upon arrival in the United States, she was persuaded to play in the U.S. Championships, which were being held at Forest Hills in New York for the first time. One day after she arrived by boat with whooping cough, she faced off against defending champion Mallory. After Lenglen fell behind, her illness got the better of her, and she forfeited.

Harshly criticized by the American press, Lenglen took her revenge at Wimbledon the following year, beating Mallory 6–2, 6–0. She wouldn't lose again in her amateur career, winning 182 straight matches before she turned professional.

One of her final amateur matches was against American Helen Wills Moody at a tournament in Cannes in 1926. Because Wills Moody and Lenglen were generally acknowledged as the two best female players, the match drew royalty, celebrities and countless fans without tickets who gathered on rooftops and in trees, wanting to witness history. It was a tight, tense match in front of a raucous French crowd, and Lenglen was reportedly on the verge of collapse before smelling salts and brandy propelled her to a 6–3, 8–6 victory.

Suzanne Lenglen wears her trademark headband, called "the Lenglen bandeau," around 1920.

The match made a lot of money for a lot of people, and Lenglen bristled at having to maintain amateur status while others got rich, so she turned professional.

With money dwindling and her father's health deteriorating, Lenglen accepted $50,000 from Charles "Cash and Carry" Pyle to barnstorm the United States, where she went 38-0 against former U.S. champion Mary K. Browne.

"To me it is an escape from bondage and slavery. No one can order me about any longer to play tournaments for the benefit of club owners ... I have done my bit to build up the tennis of France and of the world. It's about time tennis did something for me."

After returning from the United States, Lenglen faded from the public eye and died at 39 of pernicious anemia.

Wills Moody, who won her final Wimbledon title days before Lenglen's death, called her "the greatest woman player who ever lived."

CAREER HIGHLIGHTS

French Championships
Singles champion 1925–26
Doubles champion 1925–26
Mixed doubles champion 1925–26

Wimbledon
Singles champion 1919–23, 1925
Doubles champion 1919–23, 1925
Mixed doubles champion 1920, 1922, 1925

Olympics
Gold medalist in women's singles 1920
Gold medalist in mixed doubles 1920
Bronze medalist in women's doubles 1920

International Tennis Hall of Fame
1978

THE MAJORS

The WTA Championships for women and the men's ATP World Tour Finals are officially the season-ending tournaments for the year's top players. It's a nice purse for the winners, one last chance for fans to see the best in the game and a boon for sponsors and advertisers, but the champions are rarely remembered.

The four tennis majors, collectively known as the Grand Slam and individually as the Grand Slam tournaments, are what legacies are based on. These four tournaments are the most historic, most watched and most important to the players themselves. Many of the best players in history had a major they couldn't win, a mark against otherwise sparkling careers.

The term "Grand Slam" is derived from the card game bridge, and the origin of its use in sports is murky. It's argued that it was first used for Babe Ruth's bases-loaded home runs in the 1920s, although some say it wasn't used in baseball until 1940. Bobby Jones' biographer, O.B. Keeler, called his four major golf wins in 1930 "the Grand Slam of Golf," although the writer preferred the less catchy "Impregnable Quadrilateral of Golf." It didn't stick.

"Grand Slam" was first used in reference to tennis by Alan Gould in the Pennsylvania newspaper *The Reading Eagle* in 1933, when Jack Crawford was attempting to win his fourth major of the year. It was popularized by *New York Times* columnist John Kieran soon after.

Crawford lost the U.S. Championships, and since then only five players have earned a Grand Slam by winning each major over the course of a calendar year. Don Budge was the first, in 1938, when he set out to win "the Big Four," the national tournaments of the four countries that had won the Davis Cup. His inaugural Grand Slam made the term mainstream, and the four tournaments started calling themselves Grand Slams, although that's a misnomer that has come to be accepted as part of tennis lexicon. Technically each tournament is a major, and winning the collection of four in a single season is a Grand Slam.

After Budge, only Maureen Connolly in 1953, Rod Laver in 1962 (as an amateur) and 1969 (as a pro in the second year of open play), Margaret Court in 1970 and Steffi Graf in 1988 (who was the first to win on three different surfaces) have replicated the feat. Just 12 more players have won a career Slam — winning each title at least once over the course of their careers — and there are variations on the Grand Slam theme, such as Graf's "Golden Slam," when she also won the Olympic gold in singles the same year, and "the Serena Slam," coined when Serena Williams held all four major titles at one time, which were collected consecutively but out of order and over the course of two seasons.

In the order they're played throughout the year, the Grand Slam tournaments are the Australian Open, the French Open, Wimbledon and the U.S. Open. Each has a distinct character, a reflection of the host country and city, and each is played on its own surface. To win each one a player must master all facets of the game and be able to alter their approach and style, not to mention handle the pressure of being alone on some of the world's biggest sporting stages.

The Australian Open

The tournament was originally shared with New Zealand from 1905 to 1927 and was called the Australasian Championships. It became the Australian Championships in 1928, and in 1969 the name was changed to the Australian Open to reflect the dawn of a new era. It was the last of the majors to adopt the open policy, doing so one year after the others had changed in 1968. Women were invited to play for the first time in 1922.

Rod Laver Arena as seen at night during the 2014 quarterfinal matchup between Novak Djokovic and Stanislas Wawrinka on January 21, 2014. Wawrinka prevailed 2–6, 6–4, 6–2, 3–6, 9–7 and went on to win the tournament.

Held in Melbourne since 1972, the tournament made earlier appearances in Brisbane, Sydney, Perth and Adelaide, as well as twice in New Zealand — Christchurch in 1906 and Hastings in 1912.

In 1977 the tournament was played twice because the dates were moved from January to December, and in 1986 it wasn't held at all when the open was moved back to January, going from December 1985 to January 1987.

The Australian Open was played on the grass courts of the Kooyong Lawn Tennis Club from 1972 until 1988, when Tennis Australia decided to make changes to raise the tournament's profile (the event was sometimes derided as the poor cousin of the majors). Up to that point many of the world's top players stayed away, based on the travel required and the perception of the open as the least important of the majors.

When rumors spread that the tournament could lose its Grand Slam status, the decision was made to change the surface from grass to rubberized hard court. A sparkling new national tennis center, called Flinders Park, was also opened. It became Melbourne Park in 1998, and the main stadium was renamed in honor of Rod Laver in 1992. The Australian was the first major with a retractable roof, and in 2000 a second stadium with a retractable roof was added. In 2008 a new type of hard court

was installed, and the color was changed from green to blue.

The total prize money was increased to a record $31.1 million (U.S.) in 2013 to ensure that all the top players continue to make their way Down Under, and it's now among the most popular tournaments for players because of the amenities that have been added. The tournament has also thrived based on Asian interest (the second stadium is named Hisense Arena after a Chinese electronics company) and the strength of the Australian economy during the global financial crisis.

The championship cups are named after Australians Daphne Akhurst, a five-time champion, and 1911 winner Norman Brookes. Natives Margaret Court and Roy Emerson lead the way with 11 and six singles titles, respectively.

Played in the stifling heat of the Australian summer in January, the open is an endurance test. And while many favorites have wilted under the searing sun, the fans are holding the country's biggest party.

They flock from around the country by the thousands, dressed in bikinis and costumes and getting beer from men with kegs strapped to their backs. Tennis writer L. Jon Wertheim called it "a two-week bacchanalia masquerading as a Grand Slam tennis tournament," and "the way all big-time global sporting events ought to be."

The hosts encourage a noisy crowd and invite them to stay a while on the grounds, with plenty of bars (if the man with the keg isn't around), beanbag chairs to sit on and misters to stand in when it gets too hot. The tickets are affordable, it's on free TV, and with a country of immigrants the stadiums are awash in flags and painted faces, with every player having a support section. Tying it all together is the ubiquitous sound of the didgeridoo.

In the 2012 final Novak Djokovic beat Rafael Nadal in five hours and 53 minutes, with the match ending at 1:37 on a Monday morning. Not one fan had left Rod Laver Arena when it was all said and done; they had survived the marathon known as the Australian Open, just as the Serbian champion had.

The French Open

The French Open, formerly the French Championships, or les Championnats de France, is held in late May and early June each year at Stade Roland Garros. Played over 15 days, including three Sundays, it's the longest of the majors, and after an experiment with night tennis in 1969 it's been held solely during daylight hours.

The tournament began in 1891 for men and 1897 for women, but originally it was open only to French citizens and permanent residents. In 1925 it became international, after the 1924 Paris Olympics gave the locals an appetite for foreign competition on home soil, making it the fourth major. Rene Lacoste won the men's singles at the first international edition, beating fellow French legend Jean Borotra, and the women's singles was won by native Suzanne Lenglen, for whom the second-largest court at Roland Garros was named in 1997.

Kea Bouman of the Netherlands was the first foreigner to earn a singles title (1927), and in 1933 Australian Jack Crawford was the first non-Frenchman to win as he sought the inaugural Grand Slam (he lost the U.S. final to fall short). The first American winner was Don Budge in 1938, halfway to completing his historic Grand Slam.

Roland Garros was built to accommodate the 1928 Davis Cup after France and its Musketeers (Jacques Brugnon, Jean Borotra, Henri Cochet and Rene Lacoste) went to America and upset the United States to win the Davis Cup in 1927. The stadium seated 10,000 people and was named after a French aviator who was the first man to fly across the Mediterranean and who later died in World War I. The French Championships were held there for the first time in 1928, and soon after France defended its Davis Cup title against Bill Tilden and the Americans at their new national tennis complex.

The stadium was shut down during World War II, and a dark chapter was added to its history when French dissidents were imprisoned there. The first postwar men's winner was unseeded Frenchman Marcel Bernard in 1946, and the only Frenchman to win since is Yannick Noah, who beat Mats Wilander in 1983. On the women's side, Nelly Landry won for the home country in 1948, followed by Francoise Durr in 1967 and French-American Mary Pierce in 2000.

The men's trophy is called the Coupe des Mousquetaires. Bjorn Borg won six of them in the 1970s and 1980s, a record until Rafael Nadal surpassed him with eight titles in nine appearances through 2013. The women take home the Coupe Suzanne Lenglen, and Chris Evert leads the way with seven. Steffi Graf won six between her first in 1987 and her last in 1999.

The championship court is named after Hall of Famer Philippe Chatrier, a former player, president of the French Tennis Federation and member of the International Tennis Federation and International Olympic Committee; it holds 15,059 spectators. Court Suzanne Lenglen holds 10,076.

The French was the last to be considered a major but the first to welcome professionals, becoming the original open major in 1968. It's the lone Grand Slam tournament played on clay, a softer surface that's kinder to players' joints, which is particularly helpful to French Open king Nadal and his tender knees. The game is also slower on clay, extending rallies and matches, and the balls bounce higher. It's not conducive to hard-hitting players who like to make quick work of their opponents; Pete Sampras held the record for most major titles among men but never won in Paris.

On the downside, it can turn into a dust storm when the wind swirls, obscuring players' vision and getting in their eyes. And the red covers everything, from the players' clothing to the stadium seats.

The surface is made of limestone with a layer of crushed brick, and the consistency is dry and gritty. It's hosed between matches to keep the dust down as well as groomed and swept like a baseball infield. According to the keepers of the French Open, the red clay is for "aesthetics, player comfort, and color."

The French call it *terre battue*, meaning "beaten earth," and the press guide says it's "a subtle composition of elements, making it a unique and particularly noble surface."

Très Paris.

Rafael Nadal kisses the Coupe des Mousquetaires for the eighth time as French Open champion after defeating David Ferrer 6–3, 6–2, 6–3 in 2013.

Wimbledon

The oldest and arguably the most prestigious of the four majors, at least if you're talking to a Briton, Wimbledon upholds tradition like no other tennis tournament.

Played in southwest London at the All England Lawn Tennis and Croquet Club since 1877, it's officially called the Lawn Tennis Championships, known simply as the Championships in Great Britain. The women first played for a title in 1884.

The tournament has been at its present site on Church Road since 1922, when the club moved across the borough of Wimbledon, and has been held over the last week of June and first week of July for more than a century. The surface, as the name of the club suggests, has always been grass. It's trimmed to a height of 8 millimeters and has been 100 percent rye grass since 2000, when it changed from 70 percent rye and 30 percent red fescue.

Centre Court opened in 1922 with a capacity of 9,989, which grew to 16,000 with standing room. After standing was outlawed at sporting events in Great Britain the capacity became 15,000, and a retractable roof was added in 2009 to guard against Wimbledon's constant companion — rain.

Until 1921 the tournament followed a challenge round system, in which the defending champion played only one match, against the winner of the elimination tournament. In 1968 Wimbledon became an open tournament, and in 2007 it started to pay equal prize money for men and women. Men are given the Challenge Cup, on which "The All England Lawn Tennis Club Single Handed Championship of the World" and the names of former champions are engraved. The women are awarded the Venus Rosewater Dish, which also bears the names of the past winners.

Virginia Wade is the last British woman to win the singles title, which she did in 1977, and in 2013 Andy Murray of Scotland became the first man from Great Britain to win since Fred Perry in 1936. A statue of Perry was unveiled on the grounds in 1984 to mark the 50th anniversary of his first win.

The tennis competition at the 2012 London Olympics was held at Wimbledon, and Murray won the singles gold for the host nation.

Martina Navratilova leads all players with nine singles titles, one more than Helen Wills Moody won in the 1920s and 1930s. On the men's side Willie Renshaw won seven in the 19th century; this feat was matched by Pete Sampras, who won seven in eight years between 1993 and 2000, and Roger Federer when he won his seventh in 2012.

Wimbledon boasts the single largest catering operation at a sporting event in Europe. Over the fortnight nearly half a million people walk through the gates to drink 200,000 glasses of Pimm's and eat 28,000 kilograms (62,000 pounds) of strawberries, "usually Grade I Kent strawberries of the highest quality," served with more than 7,000 liters (1,800 gallons) of fresh cream.

Players must submit their attire earlier in the year for approval, and they can be told to change at the referees' discretion. The rules are as follows:

No solid mass of coloring

Little or no dark or bold colors

No fluorescent colors

Preference towards pastel colors

Preference for back of shirt to be totally white

Preference for shorts and skirts to be totally white

All other items of clothing including hats, socks and shoes to be almost entirely white

Rufus the hawk presides over the tournament to discourage pigeons from becoming spectators, and he's given the run of the grounds for an hour every morning before the public is let in.

Wimbledon has played host to many of the most exciting and historic matches in history, including the men's finals between Bjorn Borg and John McEnroe in 1980 and Roger Federer and Rafael Nadal in 2008, but the one match that may never be equaled had no effect on the outcome of the tournament. In 2010 John Isner of the United States and Nicolas Mahut of France played an 11 hour and five minute first-round match over three days. The final score was 6–4, 3–6, 6–7 (7–9), 7–6 (7–3), 70–68, with 980 total points played and 113 aces for Isner, who prevailed. The fifth set alone took eight hours and 11 minutes, an hour and 38 minutes longer than the previous record for an entire *match*.

The U.S. Open

In 1881, four years after the first tournament at Wimbledon, the United States held its first national championships in Newport, Rhode Island. Dick Sears won the first seven titles, and he also won six straight doubles titles starting in 1882, five of which while paired with Dr. James Dwight, who is considered the father of American tennis.

The U.S. Championships, which were also called the Nationals, were played at the Newport Casino for 34 years before settling in Forest Hills, a neighborhood in Queens, New

The roof on Centre Court is moved into place while grounds crew members attend to the grass at the All England Club during the 2012 Summer Olympics.

York City, on the grass courts of the West Side Tennis Club in 1915. In 1975 the courts were converted to clay, and in 1978 the open became a hard court tournament when it moved to Flushing Meadows, also in Queens, and the new United States Tennis Association National Tennis Center. The facility was renamed the Billie Jean King National Tennis Center in 2006, and the Newport Casino has been the home of the International Tennis Hall of Fame since 1954.

The women's tournament began in 1887 at the Philadelphia Cricket Club and stayed there until 1921, when it too moved to Forest Hills. The women's competition was contested on the calendar before the men's until they were combined in 1935. Of the four majors, the U.S. Championships was the only one played during the two World Wars.

Afraid the open concept wouldn't fly, in 1968 and 1969 the USTA held both a U.S. Open and the U.S. Championships, an amateur tournament. Arthur Ashe won both in 1968, a feat that will never be replicated, but because he was an amateur, Ashe's prize money from the open went to runner-up Tom Okker.

The winnings have been equal for men and women since 1973, the first of the majors to do this, when Australians Margaret Court and John Newcombe both won $25,000. Singles champions Serena Williams and Rafael Nadal each took home $2.6 million in 2013.

Night play began in 1975 at Forest Hills and continued at Flushing Meadows, and the tournament is famous for its midnight matches. Arthur Ashe Stadium was added to the complex in 1997, and with a capacity of 23,737, it's the world's largest tennis venue.

Molla Bjurstedt Mallory won eight singles titles in the early part of the 20th century, one more than Helen Wills Moody in the same era. More recently Chris Evert has won six, and Williams tied Court and Steffi Graf with her fifth in 2013. American legend Bill Tilden earned seven titles in the 1920s; Pete Sampras, Roger Federer and Jimmy Connors have each won five.

Connors is synonymous with the U.S. Open. His birthday falls during the tournament, and he was undefeated on that day throughout his career. He's the only player to win the event on grass, clay and hard court, and in 1991, at the age of 39, he put an exclamation mark on the end of his career with an age-defying and thrilling run to the semifinals.

The U.S. Open itself is a microcosm of New York City; it's big, loud, intimidating and thrilling. With a hint of danger.

In 1977 at the last U.S. Open held in Forest Hills, a fan was shot in the leg during John McEnroe's third-round match. Apparently fired from a nearby apartment building, the shot added another chapter to a summer that saw widespread looting during a blackout and a city living in fear of serial killer "Son of Sam."

Racism reared its ugly head at the 1977 tournament when a West Side board member suggested that Flushing Meadows was a bad choice because the neighborhood was mostly "Negro." Ashe threatened to resign from the board after the comment, but the man who made the comment did instead. There was also heated debate in 1977 about the inclusion of Renee Richards, who had been Richard Raskind until a 1975 sex change operation. After the New York State Supreme Court ruled that she should be allowed to participate, the 6-foot-1, 43-year-old Richards lost in the first round to Virginia Wade but made the final of the doubles competition with partner Betty Ann Stuart.

On the other end of the age spectrum was 14-year-old prodigy Tracy Austin, who made her debut at the 1977 U.S. Open and reached the quarterfinals before falling to Betty Stove. McEnroe also made his first appearance at the tournament that year, but Connors stole the show with his petulance, including running to the other side of the net to erase a ball mark before the judge could inspect it. He lost to Guillermo Vilas in the final but left the stadium before the trophy ceremony, which was hardly noticed as fans invaded the court and carried Vilas around on their shoulders.

Not all U.S. Opens are as turbulent and dramatic as the 1977 tournament, but no other major has the same edge.

New York is a safer city than it was in the 1970s and the U.S. Open is a little more sanitized, but the fans have remained just as raucous. They're the most vocal of all the majors, and the late-night matches give them time and reason to really commit to the summer-ending party.

Even the most casual tennis fan is familiar with these four tournaments and the unique texture and personality of each one. They amplify the rivalries and statuses of the players, the pressure and desire to win showcasing them at their most competitive and willful. It exposes them at their best — and often their worst. That's what makes the majors so compelling and why they've remained among the most popular sporting events in the world for more than a hundred years.

An American flag is unfurled on center court of Arthur Ashe Stadium during the opening ceremony of the 2010 U.S. Open.

THE
OPEN
ERA

Tennis greats from 1968 to the 2000s

Martina Navratilova smiles from behind her hand as Chris Evert ponders a reporter's question after Navratilova defeated her at the 1979 Avon Championships in straight sets, 7–5, 7–5. Navratilova and Evert had a friendly but intense rivalry that saw them face off with major implications at every Grand Slam tournament.

Andre Agassi

IMAGE WASN'T EVERYTHING

Andre Agassi makes a forehand return to Benjamin Becker at the 2006 U.S. Open. His eventual four-set loss to Becker marked the end of Agassi's professional career, as he retired following the match.

From his brash youth, when he was thrust into the spotlight by his father and a host of advertisers—all frosted hair and fluorescent clothing—to his life now as a devoted (and bald) husband, father and philanthropist, Andre Kirk Agassi grew up in front of the world.

Mike Agassi was an Iranian of Armenian descent who boxed for Iran at the 1948 and 1952 Olympics before immigrating to the United States and settling in Las Vegas. He was a tough, violent man who taught Andre to play tennis like a fighter, and he built a court and a ball machine dubbed "the Dragon" in their yard so his son could hit 2,500 balls a day. A million a year, Mike figured, would make Andre unbeatable.

At 13, Andre was sent to Nick Bollettieri's tennis academy in Florida. Bollettieri was a man only slightly more lenient than Agassi's father, and after three years of "living hell," the budding star turned pro at the age of 16 in 1986. By the end of the 1988 season he was number three in the world and had already won $2 million in prize money.

Agassi reached that milestone faster than any player in history, but he was making far more money in endorsements. A famous and fitting tagline for one Canon camera campaign was "Image is everything." With his flowing mullet, denim shorts and garish colors he was a tennis rebel, manufactured by Madison Avenue, and the public ate it up.

By 1990 Agassi was the favorite at the U.S. Open but lost to Pete Sampras in the final. He also reached the final of the French Open in 1990 and 1991 but lost each one. It seemed he was more style than substance; that his image *was* everything.

And even that was fraudulent. Agassi later admitted he started wearing a wig after his famous blond hair started falling out. It was his look—and marketers were counting on it—but he was so concerned about an embarrassing slip that it cost him the 1990 French Open final. Before the match he says he prayed "not for victory, but that my hairpiece would not fall off."

Agassi's breakthrough came at Wimbledon in 1992. He entered that year's contest as the 12th seed and beat Boris Becker, John McEnroe and Goran Ivanisevic to become one of the lowest seeds to ever win at the All England Club.

Agassi won his second major at the 1994 U.S. Open. He was over his playing weight, was ranked 20th in the world and was unseeded at the tournament after missing time for wrist surgery. His upset victory over Michael Stich made Agassi just the third unseeded man and the first since 1966 to win the tournament.

The year 1994 was also when Agassi hired coach Brad Gilbert, and by the end of that season he'd beaten every player in the top 10 to reach number two. He also freed himself of his past and the lie on his head, finally cutting off what remained of his hair. The transformation also included a healthy diet and fitness regimen and a switch to wearing more conservative attire.

It was with this new look that Agassi made his first appearance at the Australian Open in 1995. He won that tournament, dispatching defending champion Sampras in a four-set final, and claimed the number one ranking for the first time in his career. A year later in Atlanta he became the second Agassi to compete in the Olympics, and he won the gold medal for the United States. But that was the lone highlight of a down year, and in 1997 Agassi had plummeted to number 141 in the world and finished the year at 122.

A secret at the time, Agassi's precipitous drop came as a result of abusing crystal meth, which his assistant convinced him to try. Caught up in the media vortex surrounding his engagement to actress

Andre Agassi (middle) waves to the crowd after receiving his gold medal in men's singles at the 1996 Atlanta Olympics. Spain's Sergi Bruguera (left) won the silver, and India's Leander Paes (right) won the bronze.

Before the match Agassi says he prayed "not for victory, but that my hairpiece would not fall off."

Brooke Shields and after a lifetime of trying to be in control of his body, he gave in and let go. He finally had the escape he'd longed for, but it nearly cost him his career. A positive drug test that Agassi claimed was the result of a spiked drink—a lie to save his skin—was rock bottom. The Association of Tennis Professionals believed Agassi, however, and decided not to suspend him.

With a second chance, the fallen star renewed his commitment to the game, and in 1998 he was back to number six in the world. It was the biggest turnaround

Andre Agassi is celebrated prior to his 1,000th professional tennis match, a match he won against Peter Luczak at the 2003 Queen's Club Championships. Agassi would advance to the semifinal before losing to eventual champion Andy Roddick.

112th-ranked Benjamin Becker in the third round. Both matches were played through crippling pain brought on by more than 30 years of tennis and spondylolisthesis, a condition he was born with that caused one of the vertebrae in his lower back to slip out of place.

After his loss to Becker, Agassi cried, humble and grateful in his tennis whites, as the 20,000 fans at Arthur Ashe Stadium gave him a four-minute standing ovation. He was universally respected for his game and for the man he'd become.

"I was overwhelmed with how they embraced me at the end," said Agassi afterward. "They saw me through my career. They've seen me through this, as well."

Agassi retired with 870 career match wins, 60 tournament victories and 101 weeks as the top-ranked player in the world. His 224 match wins at the majors were nine behind Jimmy Connors' record, and he's the only player in the open era to win at least one ATP tournament for 18 years.

After his high-profile and tabloid-friendly marriage to Shields ended in 1999, Agassi married 22-time major winner Steffi Graf in 2001. The couple is bonded not only by their tennis successes but also by having two of the most unforgiving tennis fathers in history.

Their mothers were the only witnesses at the wedding, and four days after the ceremony their son Jaden was born. Sister Jaz joined him in 2003, and the family now lives a quiet life in Agassi's hometown, where he opened the Andre Agassi College Preparatory Academy, a free charter school in Las Vegas' most at-risk neighborhood that helps give kids a childhood that he never had.

In 2009 Agassi released *Open: An Autobiography*. In it he admits that his father made him hate the game, a feeling that returned in the latter part of his career when the pain was unbearable and he had to take seven-inch needles full of cortisone directly in his spine to play.

But ultimately there's gratitude for all that the game gave him and all it allowed him to do.

"I look at my wife and my children … and I say, thank you, tennis," said Agassi in his heartfelt and tearful Hall of Fame acceptance speech in 2011. "I look to the future, my efforts to build high-performing charter schools in inner cities across the U.S.… and I say, thank you, tennis, for making that possible."

in tennis history and the start of an unexpected and unprecedented career renaissance that saw Agassi take the 1999 Australian Open, French Open and U.S. Open. Combined with a loss to Sampras in the Wimbledon final that year, Agassi became just the second man, after Rod Laver, in the open era to reach four consecutive major finals. He also became the fifth man to win all four majors and complete the career Grand Slam, after Fred Perry, Don Budge, Laver and Roy Emerson.

Agassi claimed two more Australian titles (2001 and 2003) before retiring, giving him eight career major championships. His last matches came at the 2006 U.S. Open, where he won a grueling five-set match over world number eight Marcos Baghdatis and then lost 7–5, 6–7 (4–7), 6–4, 7–5 to

CAREER HIGHLIGHTS

Australian Open
Singles champion 1995, 2000, 2001, 2003

French Open
Singles champion 1999

Wimbledon
Singles champion 1992

U.S. Open
Singles champion 1994, 1999

Olympics
Gold medalist in men's singles 1996

Davis Cup Team Member
1988–93, 1995, 1997–98, 2000, 2005

International Tennis Hall of Fame
2011

Andre Agassi serves during his first-round match against Robbie Weiss at the 1989 U.S. Open. Agassi defeated Weiss and reached the semifinal before losing to Ivan Lendl.

Arthur Ashe

THE STOIC SOLDIER

Arthur Ashe makes a backhand return to Jimmy Connors on Centre Court of the All England Club during the 1975 Wimbledon final. Ashe won 6–1, 6–1, 5–7, 6–4 to become the first black player to win Wimbledon.

The main stadium at the Billie Jean King Tennis Center, home of the U.S. Open, is named after Arthur Ashe—a tribute to a pioneering tennis champion and builder whose heroism extended far beyond the white lines of the court.

Born in 1943 in Richmond, Virginia, deep in the American south, Arthur Robert Ashe Jr. grew up on the grounds of Brookfield Playground, a blacks-only park where Arthur Sr. was groundskeeper. After his mother, Mattie, died when he was six, Arthur Jr. was raised by his father, a disciplinarian who taught his son the value of hard work, respect and maintaining one's calm in the face of racism and inequality.

Proving his talent on the Brookfield courts despite his willowy frame, Ashe caught the eye of Ronald Charity, one of the country's top black players, who took him under his wing. By 1953 it was apparent that Ashe was ready to take the next step, so Charity introduced him to Dr. Walter Johnson, a prominent physician and tennis patron who was coaching Althea Gibson.

Limited to only black opponents and tournaments in Richmond, Ashe moved to St. Louis before his senior year of high school to expand his competition. Johnson lobbied to have him entered in the segregated U.S. interscholastic tournament, which Ashe won in 1960 and 1961.

Recruited and given a scholarship by UCLA, Ashe won the 1965 U.S. intercollegiate singles and doubles titles. A year later he graduated with a degree in business administration, the first member of his family with a college diploma.

After graduation Ashe joined the Army, and as a lieutenant he maintained his amateur status, which also made him eligible for Davis Cup play. He won the U.S. amateur title in 1968, the first black man to do so, and achieved a unique double by winning the very first U.S. Open the same year.

The American championship tournament had changed names from the U.S. Championships once professionals were allowed to participate. As the fifth seed, Ashe wasn't a favorite, but with a sharp serve-and-volley game and 26 aces in the five-set final, the amateur won the Open. He got $280 in expenses, while runner-up and professional Tom Okker got $14,000.

Ashe was the first American man to win the U.S. title since Tony Trabert in 1955 and the first black man and second black player to win a major singles title, after Gibson won the U.S. women's singles in 1957 and 1958.

It was a banner year for Ashe, who won 11 straight singles matches in the 1968 Davis Cup—a record for American men—as the country earned its first Cup in five years. He also won 10 of the 22 tournaments he entered, with a 72-10 match record.

After two years in the army, Ashe turned pro in 1969 at the age of 26. Tennis was reaching new heights of popularity in the open era, due in part to Ashe's success, but players had little control over their own careers. They weren't being treated or compensated fairly by the various federations and tournaments, so Ashe spearheaded the formation of the Association of Tennis Professionals, the first players' union, and served as president from 1974 to 1979.

Ashe was also working to raise awareness of South Africa's apartheid policy, and after years of trying he was granted a visa to play in the 1973 South African Open. Many black South Africans were against his presence, saying it legitimized government policy. But he wanted to bear witness, and he believed that the government's allowing him in was a small concession, and "small concessions incline toward larger ones."

Arthur Ashe holds the Wimbledon championship trophy after defeating Jimmy Connors in the final match of the men's singles championship at the All England Club on July 5, 1975.

"It is not the urge to surpass all others at whatever cost, but the urge to serve others at whatever cost." – Arthur Ashe

With shades of Jesse Owens at the 1936 Berlin Olympics, Ashe reached the singles final and won the doubles title with Okker.

The second major title of Ashe's career was the 1970 Australian Open, where he took out Dick Crealy in straight sets in the final, and in 1975 he won his third. Played days before his 32nd birthday, Ashe was a 10 to 1 long shot against Jimmy Connors, a man 10 years his junior, in the Wimbledon final.

Ashe meditated during changeovers and played a cerebral

The crowd applauds Arthur Ashe as he shakes hands with Jimmy Connors, the 1974 Wimbledon champion, after defeating him in the final match of the 1975 edition of the tournament.

game, changing speeds and spin and slicing serves to Connors' backhand. Taking away Connors' strengths, Ashe upset the young hothead, 6–1, 6–1, 5–7, 6–4. His record for 1975 was 108-23, he won nine tournaments and he reached the number one world ranking for the first time.

It was the high-water mark of his career, and in 1979 it was over. He had a heart attack, and it was suggested that years of swallowing his anger, his indignation and his rage had eaten him up inside. The price for his quiet dignity and tireless activism was his life as an athlete.

Ashe won 35 amateur and 33 professional singles titles and 18 pro doubles championships, he was in the world top 10 for 10 years, and in 1985 he was the first black man inducted into the International Tennis Hall of Fame. But those aren't the achievements he would want to be remembered for.

"True heroism is remarkably sober, very undramatic," according to Ashe. "It is not the urge to surpass all others at whatever cost, but the urge to serve others at whatever cost."

In retirement Ashe had time to pursue his many interests. He served as national campaign chairman of the American Heart Association; wrote for *Time*, the *Washington Post* and *Tennis* magazine; was a commentator for ABC Sports and served as captain of the U.S. Davis Cup team. He supported the United Negro College Fund, the Safe Passage Foundation, the ABC Tennis Program, and the Athlete-Career Connection, and he founded Artists and Athletes Against Apartheid. In 1988 he published *A Hard Road to Glory*, a history of black athletes, and in 1991 he returned to South Africa when apartheid fell, meeting Nelson Mandela after the newly released political prisoner said he was an Ashe fan.

And he did it all while quietly living with HIV. In 1992 *USA Today* threatened to reveal his secret, so Ashe did it for them. He had contracted the disease from a blood transfusion after a second heart attack in 1983. It was discovered when he had brain surgery in 1988 because of paralysis in his right arm.

After his condition was made public, he created the Arthur Ashe Foundation for the Defeat of AIDS and spoke at the U.N. General Assembly on World AIDS Day. In his final months he created the Arthur Ashe Institute for Urban Health, and he was also arrested outside the White House for protesting U.S. treatment of Haitian refugees. *Sports Illustrated* named him Sportsman of the Year in 1992.

Days after completing his memoir, *Days of Grace*, early in 1993, Ashe passed away at the age of 49 from AIDS-related pneumonia, leaving his wife of 16 years, Jeanne, and their six year-old daughter, Camera. He lay in state at the Virginia governor's mansion, the first person to receive the honor since Confederate general Stonewall Jackson 130 years earlier, and later that year he was posthumously awarded the Presidential Medal of Freedom by President Clinton.

On what would have been his 53rd birthday in 1996, a statue of Ashe was dedicated on Richmond's Monument Avenue, a place he wouldn't have been allowed as a child because of his skin color. The statue depicts Ashe carrying a tennis racket in one hand and a stack of books in the other. And in 1997 the United States Tennis Association named its new stadium after him.

The name Arthur Ashe will endure not just on the marquee but in the legacy he left behind, for the way he led his sport and country to a new age of inclusion and awareness.

CAREER HIGHLIGHTS

Australian Open
Singles champion 1970
Doubles champion 1977

French Open
Doubles champion 1971

Wimbledon
Singles champion 1975

U.S. Open
Singles champion 1968

Davis Cup Team Member
1963, 1965–1970, 1974, 1976, 1978

International Tennis Hall of Fame
1985

Arthur Ashe digs up some turf while serving during the quarterfinal of the 1965 U.S. Championships. Ashe received a 15-minute standing ovation after defeating Roy Emerson.

Germany's Boris Becker (left) and Michael Stich are all smiles after winning the men's tennis doubles competition at the 1992 Barcelona Olympics.

Boris Becker

POWER AND PASSION

"Tennis is an art form. I feel as if I'm performing on a stage in front of millions of people, and I was sometimes able to fascinate them for two weeks. This culminates with a Sunday final, match point, and then all the celebrations."

The gospel according to Boris Franz Becker, a guiding principle in his career and an explanation for the passion that he played with and that the fans felt for him.

Becker was born in 1967 in Leimen, Germany, and his architect father, Karl-Heinz, designed the local tennis club. He started playing competitively at age 8, but because he wasn't one of the stronger boys he occasionally practiced with the girls, including future 22-time major winner Steffi Graf. He eventually dropped out of high school to train with the West German Tennis Federation and turned pro in 1984 when he was 16, moving to Monaco to be coached by former player Ion Tiriac.

At 6 foot 3 and 180 pounds, he had gained the size he lacked when he was younger. Coupled with his shock of red hair, Becker had a powerful game and a big personality. His charisma, charm and confidence made him a fan favorite—and a favorite of the ladies.

He had a heavy serve and a strong forehand, and he threw his body around the court with reckless abandon in pursuit of points. Unlike many Europeans, he preferred faster surfaces to clay, and the French Open was the one major he didn't capture, reaching the semifinals in 1987, 1989 and 1991. He was also a gracious loser, not a common trait among male tennis players of the era.

Fellow pro Aaron Krickstein said that Becker was "our spokesman, our role model, the guy tennis players want to represent tennis."

Becker played his first Wimbledon in 1984 at the age of 16, reaching the third round before he tore ligaments in his ankle. His fortunes were better in 1985. In his third-round match, Joakim Nystrom served for the win twice in the fifth set before Becker prevailed, and in the fourth round he was trailing when he twisted his ankle. Opponent Tim Mayotte graciously allowed an extended break so Becker could receive treatment, and he went on to win in five sets.

In the final, Becker hit 21 aces to beat Kevin Curren 6–3, 6–7 (4–7), 7–6 (7–3), 6–4 and become the first German and first unseeded player to win Wimbledon. At 17 years and seven months old, he was also the youngest man to win a major. It was a thrilling and shocking win, and suddenly he was the biggest thing in tennis.

In Germany the hero worship grew when Becker brought his country to the brink of its first Davis Cup title in 1985 by beating Stefan Edberg and Mats Wilander, two future Hall of Famers, in a 3-2 loss to Sweden. Three years later Becker helped complete the Davis Cup task, taking Edberg down again as West Germany won 4-1 for the 1988 championship.

In singles tournament play, Becker defended his Wimbledon title in 1986 by beating Ivan Lendl in three sets in the final. Going for his third in 1987, Tiriac sent Becker's then-girlfriend home because she was a distraction, but he lost to Peter Doohan, a virtual unknown, in the second round.

The tabloids had a field day with it, implying that too much sex cost him the tournament. Becker simply said: "I didn't lose a war. Nobody died. Basically, I just lost a tennis match."

Becker was back in 1988, playing Edberg in the first of three consecutive finals on Centre Court, the first time in nearly a century that the same two players met in the final for three straight years. Two Edberg victories sandwiched Becker's third Wimbledon title in 1989, which was a vintage year for Becker. He won six of the 13 tournaments he entered

Boris Becker hits a forehand volley during his match against Nicolas Kiefer at the 1997 German Open in Hamburg. Becker won 7–5, 6–2.

Becker was "our spokesman, our role model, the guy tennis players want to represent tennis."
– Aaron Krickstein

and posted a 64-8 record, including his fourth major and lone U.S. Open victory, beating world number one Lendl in the final. He also beat Edberg and Wilander again, both in straight sets, as well as picking up another doubles point with Eric Jelen in a 3-2 defense of the Davis Cup title. The International Tennis Federation named him world champion in 1989.

In 1990 Becker chose not to participate in the Davis Cup, in part to focus on reaching number one but also because he felt the tournament had become too commercial and had lost meaning for the German people. His Davis Cup stance, coupled with romantic rumors about him and East German figure skating legend Katarina Witt, meant Becker continued to dominate German headlines.

Seventeen-year-old Boris Becker returns a shot at the 1985 edition of Wimbledon. He defeated Kevin Curren in the final to become the first unseeded player to win the tournament.

against top-seeded Andre Agassi in the semifinals, but he pulled out the victory before falling to Pete Sampras in the final.

At 28 and on the downside of his career, Becker dispatched Michael Chang in four sets in the final of the 1996 Australian Open for his sixth and final Grand Slam tournament victory.

Becker won 49 singles and 15 doubles titles during his career, retiring in 1999 with more than $25 million in prize money, behind only Sampras and Agassi at the time. He was in the world top 10 for 11 years and had a 22-match winning streak in the Davis Cup, the second longest in tournament history after Bjorn Borg's 33. In 2003 he was inducted into the International Tennis Hall of Fame.

A favorite of the tabloids, Becker will be remembered almost as much for his scandals as for his sport. He met model and actress Barbara Feltus in 1991 and married her in 1993. She was the daughter of a German woman and an African-American, and when their romance became public, they were subjected to racist vitriol from certain parts of his native country. Becker threatened to leave Germany if it didn't stop. By the mid-1990s, and with the birth of son Noah, attitudes had changed and they became "a symbol of the new Germany," according to Becker.

In 2000, on the 62nd anniversary of the Kristallnacht Nazi attack, Becker was part of a march through the streets of Berlin to protest Germany's increasing racist violence. Weeks later he was in the news again, this time for more lurid reasons. It was revealed that Becker had an illegitimate child with Russian waitress/model Angela Ermakova. His marriage to Barbara was troubled beforehand, and this was the final straw. The couple divorced in messy and public fashion in 2001.

Becker married Dutch model Sharlely "Lilly" Kerssenberg in 2009, and in 2010 son Amadeus was born. Today Becker channels his competitive urges on the professional poker tour, and he's a founding partner of the International Premier Tennis League—a six-team league based in Asia with a TV-friendly format that includes a draft where legends play on teams with current players.

With a new scoring system the matches will be quicker, but Becker will be back performing, 30 years and countless headlines after he fascinated the world as a tennis neophyte.

The fifth major of Becker's career was also at Lendl's expense, and it helped him achieve his goal. By beating Lendl in the 1991 Australian Open final, Becker briefly stole the top ranking from the Czech.

Later that year the first all-German final was played at Wimbledon, with Michael Stich upsetting Becker in three sets. The two joined forces the following year in Barcelona to win an Olympic gold in doubles.

For all his success at Wimbledon, Becker didn't make it back to the final until 1995. He was a set and two breaks down

CAREER HIGHLIGHTS

Australian Open
Singles champion 1991, 1996

Wimbledon
Singles champion 1985–86, 1989

U.S. Open
Singles champion 1989

Olympics
Gold medalist in men's doubles 1992

Davis Cup Team Member
1985–89, 1991–92, 1995–99

International Tennis Hall of Fame
2003

Boris Becker returns a forehand approach shot against Martin Jaite during their first-round match at the 1991 U.S. Open. The 1989 champion was ousted in the third round.

Bjorn Borg returns Victor Pecci's offering during the 1979 French Open final. Borg's four-set win marked his fourth French title and his second of four consecutive championships.

Bjorn Borg

FROM SWEDEN WITH LOVE

Born in 1956 in the Stockholm suburb Sodertalje, 9-year-old Bjorn Rune Borg was fascinated by a tennis racket his father won in a ping-pong tournament. It didn't take long before his handiwork with it put him on the radar of the Swedish Tennis Federation.

Coach and Federation scout Percy Rosburg went to see Borg play when he was 10, and by the time he was 13 he was beating the country's best under-18 players. At one national tournament Borg entered, he played nine matches over 11 hours in one day; he reached the final of five different classes.

He was already well on his way to becoming known nationally as "BjornBorg," always said as one word because it rolled off the tongue and distinguished the boy with two common names, and he already had wisdom and calm that matched a talent far beyond his years.

Lennart Bergelin, the Swedish Davis Cup captain who became Borg's coach and advisor throughout his career, encouraged the young phenom to stick with his distinct, ragged style because it was so effective, although others were trying to change his game to a more traditional approach.

After leaving school at 14 to focus on tennis, Borg joined Bergelin and the Davis Cup team in 1972 as a 15-year-old, the same year he won the Wimbledon junior title.

Borg beat New Zealand veteran Onny Parun in five sets in his Davis Cup debut, and three years later he led Sweden to the 1975 Davis Cup title over Czechoslovakia on the back of a record-setting tournament run of 19 straight match wins. The streak would reach 33 by the time he retired, a Davis Cup record that still stands.

At 17 Borg became the youngest man to win the Italian Open, taking the 1974 title by beating Ilie Nastase in a three-set final. He set the same record at the French Open two weeks later. Meeting Manuel Orantes in the final, Borg dropped the first two sets, but he stormed back and lost only two games over the final three sets to win his first major championship.

Successful and very serious, Borg was playing every match as if his life depended on it. Nastase questioned whether, having just turned 18, Borg was having enough fun.

"Tennis is my fun," responded Borg. "I have to keep thinking this is my last tournament. Not that I'll be playing 20 years from now. So I must be good right away. I have given up a lot of things for this. Ice cream, chocolates, close feelings for friends. Tennis is all I know, or want to know. It is my life."

A master of topspin, Borg's upper-body strength helped him whip the ball violently, and his two-handed backhand—adapted from the slap shots he took growing up on the hockey rink—was devastating. He was deceptively quick despite his bowlegged running style, and his endurance was exceptional. As a baseline player, Borg was at his best when he could set up long rallies and wear down his opponents.

Knowing his style didn't lend itself to grass, the right-hander spent two weeks in 1976 focusing on a serve-and-volley game. He took his first Wimbledon crown that year without losing a set, beating Nastase in the final and becoming Wimbledon's youngest male winner in the modern era, at 20 years and one month.

Borg was challenged a little more at Wimbledon in 1977, but he beat Vitas Gerulaitis 6–4, 3–6, 6–3, 3–6, 8–6 in the semifinal and Jimmy Connors 2–6, 6–2, 6–1, 5–7, 6–4 in the final to repeat as champion.

A year later he made easier work of Connors in a three-set final to become the first man since Fred Perry (1934 to 1936)

"I have given up a lot of things for this. Ice cream, chocolates, close feelings for friends. Tennis is all I know, or want to know. It is my life." – Bjorn Borg

Nineteen-year-old Bjorn Borg returns a forehand to John Alexander at the 1975 U.S. Pro Tennis Championships. Borg went on to defeat Guillermo Vilas in the final for his second straight title at the tournament.

to win three Wimbledon titles in a row; a five-set win over Roscoe Tanner in the 1979 final equaled Tony Wilding's four straight from 1910 to 1913.

Rolling in 1980, the top-ranked Borg faced world number two John McEnroe in the Wimbledon final. The fourth set had a 34-point tiebreaker in which Borg had five match points and saved six set points before dropping it. A lesser player would have wilted, but Borg's signature calm and resilience carried him and he ultimately prevailed 1–6, 7–5, 6–3, 6–7

Bjorn Borg celebrates his fifth French Open title in 1980 after beating Vitas Gerulaitis in straight-sets, 6–4, 6–1, 6–2.

(16–18), 8–6 for his fifth consecutive title at the All England Club. In 2012 author Steve Flink named it the second best match in tennis history.

Borg had surpassed Rod Laver's male Wimbledon record of 31 straight match wins, and he stretched it to 41 matches in 1981. He was also attempting to tie the record of six straight Wimbledon titles, won by Willie Renshaw (1881 to 1886) in the days the defending champion had an automatic berth in the final. Borg reached the 1981 final but lost in a rematch to McEnroe, 4–6, 7–6 (7–1), 7–6 (7–4), 6–4.

McEnroe, who had avenged his 1980 Wimbledon loss with a win over Borg in the final at the 1980 U.S. Open (another epic five-setter), met Borg again in the final at the

1981 U.S. Open. It was the pair's 14th tour meeting, and McEnroe sealed a 7-7 series split with Borg by beating him 4–6, 6–2, 6–4, 6–3 to claim his second straight American championship. After the loss, Borg ceded his number one ranking to McEnroe, ending a two-year run as the world number one. The 1981 U.S. Open also marked Borg's final major tournament appearance, but his decision to step away from the game was made after his loss on Centre Court earlier in the year.

"Here I was, in another Wimbledon final, the biggest thing you can play in, but I didn't have that sparkling feeling," said Borg years later of the 1981 match. "Of all the Wimbledon finals I played, that is the one I should have won, yet it didn't bother me when I lost. So I decided it was time to go."

Borg was just 25 at the time, in the midst of one of the most dominant stretches in tennis history, and his 11 major singles titles were just one behind Roy Emerson's men's record when he lost his motivation.

"I think Bjorn could have won the U.S. Open. I think he could have won the Grand Slam," said Arthur Ashe, a frequent victim of Borg's. "But by the time he left, the historical challenge didn't mean anything. He was bigger than the game. He was like Elvis or Liz Taylor or somebody. He'd lost touch with the real world."

Recognizing that he would have to give even more of himself to stay on top of his game and ahead of McEnroe, Borg chose to find a life outside of tennis—the game he'd played since childhood—instead.

Inducted into the International Tennis Hall of Fame in 1987, Borg, the "first rock star of tennis," still hadn't found his place in the world away from the game. After some business failures, two broken marriages and his first child, he attempted comebacks in 1991, 1992 and 1993, all of which were unsuccessful.

"I sometimes look back to those days with all the girls, but I have a great family life now and I prefer that, staying at home with the family," said Borg in a 2007 interview. "This is my third marriage. Patricia and I have been together now for seven years and I'm so happy … I have the perfect life now and I wouldn't change a thing."

And even if the hair is gray and the 64 tournament victories and 11 majors have faded from memory, his name remains on the lips and hips of fans today, both male and female, with his own line of underwear, available at bjornborg.com.

CAREER HIGHLIGHTS

French Open	**Davis Cup Team Member**
Singles champion 1974–75, 1978–81	1972–75, 1978–80
	International Tennis Hall of Fame
Wimbledon	1987
Singles champion 1976–80	

Bjorn Borg reacts after defeating John McEnroe in 1980 to win his fifth consecutive Wimbledon singles title. The match was a grueling test of will, with Borg prevailing, 1–6, 7–5, 6–3, 6–7 (16–18), 8–6.

Jimmy Connors makes a flying forehand return to Kevin Curren in their 1985 Wimbledon semifinal match. Curren defeated the two-time Wimbledon champion 6–2, 6–2, 6–1.

Jimmy Connors

THE OUTSIDER

At his best, Jimmy Connors was a left-handed baseliner with a two-fisted backhand who hit the ball hard and low and fought tooth and nail for every point he played. He ushered in the golden age of tennis in the United States with the pugnacity and personality of a prizefighter, and he captured the attention of the casual sports fan in a way no tennis star had before.

At his worst, Connors was an irascible loner known for his boorish and obscene behavior on the court and for his womanizing off it. He slammed rackets, threatened umpires and abhorred tradition.

Hard to like, James Scott Connors was even harder not to watch.

Born in 1952 in Belleville, Illinois, a blue-collar suburb just east of St. Louis, his single mother, Gloria Thompson Connors, a teaching pro, brought young "Jimbo" up on the tennis court.

"Gloria intentionally kept him separate," said former pro Trey Waltke, who knew Connors growing up. "She set up the us-versus-them mentality back when he was really young."

In 1968 Gloria took her 15-year-old son to California to be

coached by Pancho Segura, who taught Connors to hit the ball on the rise in order to return the power of his opponents.

Connors turned pro in 1972 and showed his antiestablishment streak when he refused to join the fledgling players' union, the Association of Tennis Professionals. In 1973 he won the U.S. Pro Singles title, beating Arthur Ashe, an ATP founder, in five sets and ended the year as the co–number one in the United States with Stan Smith.

But 1974 is when Connors really began to impress and impose.

He started the year by claiming his first major—the Australian Open—and later crushed legend Ken Rosewall in straight sets in the final of both Wimbledon and the U.S. Open to take three of the four majors on the year. And he could have been the third Grand Slam winner in men's history.

Connors, who also played in the professional World Team Tennis loop, was barred from the French Open because of his WTT affiliation. Connors' manager and promoter, Bill Riordan, filed lawsuits against the ATP and president Ashe as a result, and Connors boycotted Roland Garros the next three years.

Connors also struck out on his own in 1974 with the International Players Association, a new outfit created by Riordan to allow his star client to play in exhibitions against the biggest names of the day. Connors beat Rod Laver, John Newcombe, Manuel Orantes and Ilie Nastase, and he earned more than a million dollars doing it.

Even without the French, 1974 was a momentous year for Connors, who won 14 tournaments, a record for an American man, and went 99-4 for the year. He was also dating tennis sweetheart Chris Evert.

Ashe may have been Connors' first major adversary, but his talent and brusque persona gave him his fair share of rivals, champions like Bjorn Borg, Ivan Lendl and John McEnroe—and Connors had his signature moments against each player.

His matches against Borg were intense, and despite Connors being on the losing side of their all-time tour rivalry, the pair went 2-2 in the majors, with Connors taking the 1976 and 1978 U.S. Opens. The 1976 final was a classic: Connors saved four set points to win an 11–9 third-set tiebreaker on his way to a four-set victory. His victory in 1978 was even more dominant, as he beat the Swede in straight sets to take the

Jimmy Connors serves to Pat Dupre during their quarterfinal match at the 1979 U.S. Open. Connors defeated Dupre 6–2, 6–1, 6–1 but could not overcome John McEnroe in the semifinal.

"Jimmy Connors is one of the giants and an original in a game that rarely produces them."
– Brian Koppelman

first U.S. Open played on hard court at Flushing Meadows.

Czech Ivan Lendl was Connors' polar opposite in both style and personality, and the American defeated him twice in the final at the U.S. Open as well. The New York stage was made for Connors, who won five U.S. Open titles and is the only player to do so on three surfaces—grass in 1974, clay in 1976 and the last three (1978, 1982, 1983) on hard court. Lendl was the victim of his last two triumphs at the American championship, and each time Connors dropped only one set.

Jimmy Connors gets set to use his devastating two-fisted backhand to return a shot to Brian Teacher at the 1982 Cincinnati Masters. Connors won, 6–1, 7–5, to advance to the quarterfinal round.

McEnroe, the other American bad boy, was Connors' most kindred rival. The two were equally volatile, but as Brian Koppelman, director of the Connors documentary *This Is What They Want*, wrote: "While McEnroe's fury burned mostly at his own inability to transcend himself and the fools surrounding him—and always came off as genuine uncontrolled rage—Connors's anger was directed outward and had a top note of self-righteous meanness."

McEnroe, nearly six and a half years Connors' junior, got the best of the older American in their career matchups, but when McEnroe was at the height of his considerable powers, Connors trumped him in the 1982 Wimbledon final. After being 3 points from defeat in the fourth-set tiebreaker, Connors stormed back to win 3–6, 6–3, 6–7 (2–7), 7–6 (7–5), 6–4. It was his second Wimbledon title and the last time Connors would beat McEnroe in a major.

Having played hard for so many years, Connors' career

appeared to be over in 1990. Mostly because of injury, he tumbled to number 936 in the rankings. But, never the kind to go gently into the night, he had surgery on his left wrist and came back strongly in 1991.

At that year's U.S. Open, Connors celebrated his 39th birthday with a fourth-round victory over Aaron Krickstein. The two had been friends on tour, but Connors' gamesmanship put an end to that, and they "lost contact" afterward. All that mattered to Connors was winning, and in that match he came back against the 24-year-old Krickstein from 2–5 down in the fifth set to win 3–6, 7–5 (10–8), 1–6, 6–3, 7–6 (6–4). He followed that with another five-set win to reach the semifinals of the U.S. Open for the 14th time. It was a stirring and dramatic run, and Connors reveled in every moment, but it ended when he fell to Jim Courier in straight sets.

Connors set numerous modern-era male records upon his retirement, including years spent in the U.S. top 10 (20) and world top 10 (16), tournament victories (109), most tournaments played (410), most matches won (1,337) and most quarterfinal appearances (41), and before Roger Federer broke his record in 2012, he'd also played in the most semifinals at the majors (31). Pete Sampras broke Connors' record of five consecutive season-ending number one rankings in 1998, and Connors was second to Lendl at the time of his retirement but Sampras and Roger Federer have both surpassed Lendl.

The blustery American remained in the news in 2013 when he released his autobiography, *The Outsider*, in which he talked about his gambling, dyslexia, obsessive-compulsive disorder and serial infidelity. He also dropped a bombshell on the tennis world when he alleged that Evert had an abortion in 1974, ending their short-lived and tempestuous engagement.

This Is What They Want, about his run at the 1991 U.S. Open, was also released that year, and after spending time with Connors, Koppelman says there's a gentler side to the star that's rarely talked about, like when he quietly helped Vitas Gerulaitis with his cocaine addiction.

And Koppelman has a different take on Connors' antics and motivation. "It wasn't meanness. It was desperation, desire, and need that came from somewhere deep inside of him ... So as you're watching Connors stomp on another opponent's throat, almost threaten to rip an ump out of his chair, or refuse to speak to a fellow player years later, maybe it's worth folding all of it in, not to excuse him, not to glorify him, but to recognize that Jimmy Connors is one of the giants and an original in a game that rarely produces them."

CAREER HIGHLIGHTS

Australian Open
  Singles champion 1974

Wimbledon
  Singles champion 1974, 1982
  Doubles champion 1973

Davis Cup Team Member
  1975, 1981, 1984

U.S. Open
  Singles champion 1974, 1976, 1978, 1982–83
  Doubles champion 1975

International Tennis Hall of Fame
  1998

Jimmy Connors celebrates his 39th birthday with a marathon victory over Aaron Krickstein at the U.S. Open on Monday, September 2, 1991. Connors' behavior during the match soured his relationship with Krickstein.

Jim Courier

"CHARLIE HUSTLE"

Jim Courier, in his trademark baseball cap, makes a return shot to Mark Philippoussis at the 1997 Monte Carlo Open.

To get accepted to Nick Bollettieri's famous academy — the Hogwarts of the tennis world — money helps, but talent, above all else, is what really matters. Good thing for James Spencer Courier, who was born and raised in Florida by parents Jim and Linda, who weren't poor by any stretch, but elite-level tennis schools were not in the household budget.

Young Jim, who began his path to tennis stardom by taking lessons from his great-aunt and former UCLA women's coach Emma Spencer, earned his way into the top tennis program by playing hard — just like his idol, Pete "Charlie Hustle" Rose.

Although Courier was already playing tennis as a 7-year-old in 1977, he was a big baseball fan as a kid, specifically of Rose and the Cincinnati Reds' Big Red Machine. It showed on the court; his backhand resembled a two-handed swing of the bat, and he usually wore a baseball hat when he played.

Growing to be 6 foot 1 and strong, Courier was a heavy hitter from the baseline and was known to backpedal to get the ball on his powerful inside-out forehand, a common move now, but one that Courier first perfected. In baseball terms he was a slugger — he wasn't hitting for average.

Industrious, down to earth and professional, Courier was also known as a grinder who got the most out of his talent. And he never gave up on a match.

"He won't quit even if he's down five-love in the final set," said Australian Mark Woodforde. "No one on the tour has more tenacity or a stronger will to win."

Before reaching Bollettieri's academy, 11-year-old Jim went to the tennis school of Harry Hopman, the legendary coach of the powerhouse Australian Davis Cup teams in the 1950s and 1960s. After seeing his young pupil smash the ball, Hopman let him stay at the school for free.

In 1985 after reaching the final of the Orange Bowl junior championship, Courier got a scholarship to Bollettieri's school. While he was there he lived with Andre Agassi briefly and lost to him frequently. Although Courier won the Orange Bowl title in 1986 and 1987, the first back-to-back winner since Bjorn Borg, Agassi was always Bollettieri's prize pupil.

After deciding against college and turning pro in 1988, Courier announced his arrival on tour by beating fifth-ranked Agassi at the 1989 French Open. The eventual winner at Roland Garros that year was 17-year-old American Michael Chang, who was coached by Spaniard Jose Higueras. Courier, who dropped Bollettieri as his coach in 1990, took on Higueras, and the onetime world number six taught him variety and patience.

It paid off in a match in early 1991 against Agassi; after losing the first set 6–2, Courier realized he had no hope trading forehands from the baseline and decided to alter his angles and speeds. He won the last two sets and the match, saying it was the first time he won using his brain and not just his brawn.

Agassi was victimized again at the 1991 French Open final. It was the first time two Americans had met in the final at Roland Garros since 1954, and the match was played through rain and a dust storm. Agassi was up one set and 3–1 in the second before Courier took over and won his first major title in five sets. Afterwards he charmed the crowd by giving his victory speech in French.

"There was one life-changing match for me," said Courier when he was inducted into the International Tennis Hall of Fame in 2005. "That was winning the French Open in 1991. Winning that match certainly put me on a path to here."

Courier opened the 1992 season with a win over Stefan Edberg in the Australian Open final, leapfrogging the Swede to become the first American since John McEnroe in 1985 to be ranked

Jim Courier serves during his 6–1, 7–6, 6–3 victory over Jeff Tarango in the third round of the 1997 Australian Open. The two-time Australian Open champion was unable to advance past the fourth round.

"He won't quit even if he's down five-love in the final set. No one on the tour has more tenacity or a stronger will to win."
– Mark Woodforde

number one in the world. It was a phenomenal rise for a player who started the 1991 season ranked 25th.

Courier defended his 1991 French Open title with a victory over Czech Petr Korda in straights sets in the 1992 final; the win made Courier the first American to hold the Australian and French Open titles simultaneously.

Jim Courier stretches to return Karol Kucera's shot in their third-round match of the 1996 French Open. Courier ultimately lost a five-set scorcher in the quarterfinal to Pete Sampras, 7–6 (7–4), 6–4, 4–6, 4–6, 4–6.

1993 started like 1992, with Courier again dispatching Edberg to win his second straight Australian Open. Continuing with his hot hand, the American headed into Paris looking for a three-peat at Roland Garros. In the final, facing Spain's Sergi Bruguera, Courier was up a break in the fifth but couldn't hold on and lost 4–6, 6–2, 2–6, 6–3, 3–6. Despite the loss, Courier became the first American to make it to three straight French Open finals, and by winning the Italian Open in 1992 and 1993, he became the only American man to win the French and Italian Opens twice each.

Unfortunately for Courier, his hustle wasn't enough to get him over the hump at either the U.S. Open or Wimbledon, appearing only once in the final of each major. His shot at the American title came in 1991, a straight-sets loss to Edberg, 6–2, 6–4, 6–0; his lone shot at Wimbledon was against compatriot Pete Sampras in the 1993 final, a four-set scorcher that twice went to tiebreaks. However, with appearances in all four major finals, Courier became just the third American to achieve that feat, after Don Budge and Agassi, and the sixth man of the open era.

Courier was also a member of six Davis Cup teams, his determination and hustle helping the Americans win in 1992 and 1995. In 1992 he clinched the Cup with a win over Switzerland's Jakob Hlasek, and three times he won decisive fifth matches to take a series, a record for U.S. players.

Courier retired in 2000 after winning 23 singles and 13 doubles titles. He was in the world's top 10 in 1991, 1993 and 1995, to go with his top ranking in 1992, which he held for 58 weeks. He was the first of the American phalanx of Agassi, Chang and Sampras to win two Grand Slam tournaments and the first to reach number one. When he retired, he was fourth among active players in tournament victories, behind Sampras (62), Agassi (45) and Chang (33).

"It was a gradual feeling where my enthusiasm to train and prepare started waning," said Courier when he announced his retirement. "I was not enthusiastic when I was getting ready to play the matches. I was to the point where I was almost going to start going through the motions ... There was a transition where tennis was my life and somewhere along the way, life became more important than the tennis."

Today Courier is still very involved in the sport that gave him so much. He sits on the board of the Gullikson Foundation, for brain tumor patients and their families, and First Serve, which "promotes positive values, healthy habits and education through tennis." He also created the Raymond James Courier's Kids inner-city youth tennis program as well as InsideOut Sports + Entertainment, his event production company that puts on tennis exhibitions and fantasy camps—all with a charitable fund-raising component.

In 2010 he married Susanna Lingman, a former Harvard tennis player, and was named 40th captain of the U.S. Davis Cup team. And Courier still finds time to do some tennis commentary in the United States and Down Under, where he's become a fixture every January at the Australian Open as the official on-court postmatch interviewer.

Although he's witty and knowledgeable, Courier has confessed he was much more comfortable out there with a racket in his hand instead of a microphone. It's a performance, he says, "live without a net."

CAREER HIGHLIGHTS

Australian Open
Singles champion 1992–93

French Open
Singles champion 1991–92

Davis Cup Team Member
1991–92, 1994–95, 1997–99

International Tennis Hall of Fame
2005

Jim Courier works his way to a victory over John McEnroe during their fourth-round match at the 1992 U.S. Open. Courier, who had won both the Australian Open and the French Open in 1992, lost in the semifinal of the tournament.

Stefan Edberg

A THINKING
MAN'S GAME

Stefan Edberg returns to Jim Courier during their match at the 1991 U.S. Open. Edberg defeated Courier in straight sets, 6–2, 6–4, 6–0, to capture his first American title.

Stefan Edberg was born in Vastervik, a small town on Sweden's Baltic coast, in 1966 and first played tennis when his parents, Bengt and Barbro, sent him to sports camp at age 6. When his best friend quit the camp a year later, Stefan wanted to leave too. But the tennis coach saw something in him and persuaded him to stick around.

Fast forward to 1982 and 16-year-old Edberg is quitting school to pursue the game full time, with his father putting their house up as collateral so he could pay for the coaching and lessons. One year later Stefan won the junior Grand Slam, and he remains the only player to do so.

Unlike fellow Swedes Bjorn Borg and Mats Wilander, who were baseliners, Edberg was a net player with a wicked serve and a flowing volley, especially on his one-handed backhand. He was a master of positioning and angles, had a deft and gentle touch, and was a cerebral sort who didn't do a lot of talking.

Order and organization were Edberg's constant companions, and if there was a knock against him it was that he was too bland, lacking the fireworks of a Borg or Boris Becker. The complaint extended to his style of play.

"I play tennis the simple way," he explained in 1991. "Don't wait for the other guy to make mistakes—just outplay him and finish the point off yourself. Try not to make tennis too difficult: It's difficult enough. Don't complicate it: Just hit the ball where the opponent is not."

In 1984 Edberg made his Davis Cup debut as an 18-year-old and became the youngest winner in tournament history when he and Anders Jarryd stunned the American doubles team of Peter Fleming and John McEnroe, who hadn't lost any of their 14 previous Cup matches.

The following year Edberg proved his international success was no fluke when he won a decisive fifth match over Michael Westphal, as Sweden beat Germany 3-2 to defend their title.

It was also the year there was a changing of the Swedish guard. At the 1985 Australian Open, Edberg beat two-time defending champion Wilander in straight sets in the final to win his first major.

Edberg retained the title in 1987 (there was no Australian Open in 1986 because the tournament had moved from December to January), downing hometown hero Pat Cash in a five-set final, the last time the tournament was played on grass courts.

Always admired for his grace, class and composure, his placid demeanor still led people to question his competitiveness. His critics were answered at Wimbledon in 1988.

Edberg had moved to London because he appreciated the relative privacy it afforded him, and he connected with English coach Tony Pickard, who worked on Edberg's self-belief just as much as his serve. The talent was always there; the confidence and body language weren't.

Down two sets to none in the 1988 semifinal against Miloslav Mecir, Edberg fought back to win three straight and set a date in the final with tournament favorite Becker. After dropping the first set, Edberg won 4–6, 7–6 (7–2), 6–4, 6–2 for his third major and first Wimbledon title. It was a rain-delayed match that started on Sunday and ended on Monday. In both matches Edberg avoided "the droops," as Pickard called them, his tendency to drop his head and capitulate when things were going against him.

"Obviously, the rain delay after playing just a few games on the Sunday was a bit frustrating," said Edberg. "I was hitting the ball beautifully on Sunday and started off not as good on the Monday. But the change really came in the tiebreak in the second set. From then on I never looked back.

Stefan Edberg leaps to return a shot at Wimbledon, where he was champion twice: 1988 and 1990.

"Try not to make tennis too difficult: It's difficult enough. Don't complicate it: Just hit the ball where the opponent is not." – Stefan Edberg

I was flowing around the court and doing the things that I wanted to do. It was a great day."

Becker won the rematch on Centre Court in straight sets in the 1989 final, and the two faced off once again with the 1990 title on the line. Edberg won the first two sets, dropped the next two and won the fifth for his second Wimbledon crown and fourth major championship.

Edberg's four majors had all come on grass, and although he made it to three more Australian Open finals, he didn't

Stefan Edberg drives a serve in the late 1980s to early 1990s.

had his breakthrough and a resounding victory. Facing American Jim Courier in the final, he held serve throughout the match and won his first U.S. Open title, 6–2, 6–4, 6–0. He was just the second man to win the tournament after losing in the first round the year prior.

Edberg's 1992 defense of the title was more difficult but equally impressive. He outlasted Michael Chang in the semifinal, a five-hour and 26-minute match that set a tournament record for length and ended 6–7 (3–7), 7–5, 7–6 (7–3), 5–7, 6–4. Somehow he had enough energy to finish the job against Pete Sampras in four sets in the final.

Winning twice each at Wimbledon and the Australian and U.S. Opens in singles, Edberg couldn't complete the career Grand Slam to go with his junior one. Despite being raised on clay courts, he never won the French Open—the closest he came was in 1989 when he lost to Chang in a five-set final.

The 1993 Australian Open was the last major final Edberg appeared in, a loss to Courier, but in 1994 he won his third Davis Cup, saving match point and beating Russia's Alexander Volkov 6–4, 6–2, 6–7 (2–7), 0–6, 8–6 in Moscow as Sweden won the final 4-1.

Realizing he was in the twilight of his career, Edberg announced that the 1996 season would be his last. He went out with his head held high, reaching the quarterfinals at the French Open and Wimbledon, the 25th time he'd been that far in a major. Overall he made a record 53rd consecutive appearance in a Grand Slam tournament, dating back to Wimbledon in 1983.

Calm and consistent, Edberg was ranked in the top 10 for 10 years and was number one in 1990 and 1991. He won 41 singles tournaments, for a .749 winning percentage, and added 18 doubles titles. He also won a doubles bronze for Sweden with Jarryd at the 1988 Olympics in Seoul.

"Stefan Edberg is the perfect example of a champion," said Courier when Edberg retired. "But people think he's boring. He is a great example of what we want for the next tennis generation."

Edberg was inducted into the International Tennis Hall of Fame in 2004, and the ATP Sportsmanship Award, which he won five times during his career, was renamed after him. The Stefan Edberg Sportsmanship Award is presented to "the player who, throughout the year, conducted himself at the highest level of professionalism and integrity, who competed with his fellow players with the utmost spirit of fairness and who promoted the game through his off-court activities."

win any once the tournament was moved to hard court, a surface that seemed to flummox the Swedes. Borg had been to 10 U.S. Opens—a tournament that had also made the switch to hard court—without a title, and it seemed Edberg would follow his lead.

In 1990 Edberg was ousted in the first round of the U.S. Open, but in 1991, on his ninth trip to Flushing Meadows, he

CAREER HIGHLIGHTS

Australian Open
Singles champion 1985, 1987
Doubles champion 1987, 1996

Wimbledon
Singles champion 1988, 1990

U.S. Open
Singles champion 1991–92
Doubles champion 1987

Olympics
Bronze medalist in men's doubles 1988

Davis Cup Team Member
1984–96

International Tennis Hall of Fame
2004

Stefan Edberg reaches to return the ball toward Ivan Lendl during their 1992 U.S. Open quarterfinal match. Edberg defeated Lendl and went on to win the championship.

Ivan Lendl

MECHANICAL DELIGHT

Ivan Lendl serves to Steve Denton in quarterfinal play of the 1983 World Championship Tennis Finals. Lendl, who won three straight WCT Finals, finished as runner-up to John McEnroe.

"Emotions don't help you," Jiri Lendl told his son Ivan when he threw tantrums on the tennis court as a child. "Never show your opponent that you are upset."

"If you're going to cry," warned his mother Olga, "go home."

Jiri and Olga were both nationally ranked tennis players in Czechoslovakia. Ivan, their only child, was born in Ostrava in 1960. Too small and shy to play soccer or hockey with his classmates, Ivan turned to the family business and became a national tennis champion in his age group when he was 11. He still couldn't beat his mother until he was 14, however, and she certainly wasn't going to let him win so he could feel better about himself. She instilled her competitive will and values to her son on the court.

"Ivan's father was ready to bow when he was met by a stronger opponent, but I never did," said Olga. "My adversary had to exhaust me totally and win."

Few people would be able to exhaust the 6-foot-2 Lendl. His preparation was meticulous, and he was a fitness fanatic whose work ethic in the gym allowed him to play a marathon schedule. Lendl was obsessive about his rackets and made a point of understanding the bounce of every court he played and the balls being used; he worked to find and exploit his opponents' every tendency and weakness. A baseliner with a pioneering inside-out forehand and heavy topspin, Lendl was relentless but betrayed little emotion.

As he played and lived, even Lendl's defection was quiet. He had his first taste of America and freedom when the Czech Tennis Federation sent him to Florida in 1975 when he was 15, and when he settled in the United States in 1984 he didn't announce it, he just stopped playing for Czechoslovakia after the 1985 Davis Cup tournament. He had always been at the mercy of the Federation because his father was a board member, and later president, and Ivan had grown tired of the demands. His decision to leave the country allowed him to break free of his parents' grip and become his own man. In 1992 he became an American citizen.

After winning the boys' singles titles at the French Open and Wimbledon in 1978, Lendl, the number one ranked junior player in the world, turned pro. He led Czechoslovakia to its lone Davis Cup triumph in 1980, winning two singles and a doubles match in a 4-1 win over Italy, and between 1980 and 1983 he appeared in 101 tournaments on the pro tour. (He appeared in 32 tournaments in 1980, the second most anyone has ever played in a single season.)

In 1982 Lendl had a match record of 107-9, winning 15 of the 23 tournaments he entered while stringing together the third-longest winning streak of the open era that year with 44. He also had a 66-match winning streak indoors at one point, where his play and preparation weren't affected by the whims of weather.

However, in the days of Jimmy Connors, John McEnroe and Ilie Nastase — the bad boys of the tour — it was their colorful personalities that dictated what the public thought a top tennis player should look and act like. Lendl was at the entire opposite end of the spectrum when compared with those three. He was a human version of gray communist architecture, an automaton who didn't let the public see what was behind his own iron curtain.

So in spite of all his success up to that point, the public didn't embrace Lendl. He was "a chilly, self-centered, condescending, mean-spirited, arrogant man with a nice forehand," according to *Time*.

And critics thought he couldn't dig for the same passion and fire displayed by the Big Three when the stakes were highest, especially after losing to Connors in the

Ivan Lendl gets set for a backhand return to Brad Gilbert at the 1986 U.S. Open. Lendl prevailed over Gilbert and went on to win the championship, his second of three consecutive American titles.

He was a human version of gray communist architecture, an automaton who didn't let the public see what was behind his own iron curtain.

1982 and 1983 U.S. Open finals. In particular, in the 1983 final it appeared Lendl simply gave up, meekly going down without a fight in the 6–0 third set.

However, Lendl showed in the 1984 French Open final that his icy demeanor could win him the big ones. Down two sets to none to McEnroe, Lendl took advantage of one of the American's classic meltdowns and won the next three sets and the match, 3–6, 2–6, 6–4, 7–5, 7–5, for his first major victory. There was

Ivan Lendl reaches to return Stefan Edberg's offering during their semifinal Wimbledon match in 1987. Lendl defeated Edberg 3–6, 6–4, 7–6, 6–4, to advance to the final.

no questioning his fight when, because of heatstroke, he vomited while waiting for the trophy presentation and nearly lost consciousness in the locker room afterward.

The match drained Lendl, and when he was slow to recover he consulted Dr. Robert Haas, who also helped defected Czech Martina Navratilova reach the top of the women's game. Like Navratilova, Lendl's diet upon arriving in the United States consisted heavily of fast food. On his doctor's advice, he became fanatical about what he ate, and his game and moods both improved.

Lendl won his second major at the 1985 U.S. Open, beating McEnroe again to take the number one ranking from him.

CAREER HIGHLIGHTS

Australian Open
Singles champion 1989–90

French Open
Singles champion 1984,
1986–87

U.S. Open
Singles champion 1985–87

Davis Cup Team Member
1978–85

International Tennis Hall of Fame
2001

Lendl held it for 157 straight weeks, just three shy of Jimmy Connors' open-era record.

After winning the U.S. Open again in 1986 and 1987, a loss to Mats Wilander in five sets in the 1988 final put an end to Lendl's 27-match winning streak at Flushing Meadows, second to Bill Tilden's 42 wins between 1920 and 1926. That appearance in the 1988 final equaled Tilden's record of eight straight U.S. Open finals (1918 to 1925), but the loss cost him his top ranking. His 1987 U.S. Open title would be his last at the American championship.

The year 1987 was also the last time Lendl won the French Open, which, like the U.S. Open, he had won three times. But after a barren 1988, he won his first Australian Open title in 1989, dismissing Czech Miloslav Mecir in straight sets and returning to number one in the world.

Lendl defended the title in 1990, beating Stefan Edberg for his eighth and final major championship. The 1991 Australian Open was his last major final, a four-set loss to Boris Becker.

Despite 14 trips to the All England Club and two to the final (1986 and 1987), Lendl couldn't complete the career Grand Slam with a Wimbledon victory. He had a .774 winning percentage at the tournament, but he never mastered the serve-and-volley game required to win the whole thing.

A bad back hampered Lendl at his last Wimbledon in 1993 and forced him out of the 1994 U.S. Open, after which he retired at the age of 34. He won 94 professional singles titles in his career, second only to Connors' 109 in the open era, and spent a total of 270 weeks as world number one over the course of 13 years in the top 10 between 1980 and 1992.

In late 2011 Lendl took his first top-flight coaching job, agreeing to mentor Andy Murray. After a painful loss for the young Briton in the 2012 Wimbledon final, Lendl's quiet strength helped Murray through intense pressure to triumph in 2013 and become the first British man to win at home in 77 years.

Murray said he hoped the historic victory would give his coach some Wimbledon closure and satisfaction.

"I know where you're heading," Lendl said to reporters before they could even ask. "This is really all about Andy and helping him achieve his goals and dreams. My job is to help Andy win as many majors as possible. It is not about how I feel about it."

Ivan Lendl duels with Stefan Edberg on Centre Court at Wimbledon in 1987. Lendl bested Edberg but could not overcome Pat Cash in the final. Wimbledon was the one major Lendl never won.

John McEnroe, the defending Wimbledon champion, stretches to reach a shot by Wally Masur during their third-round match at Wimbledon in 1984. McEnroe defeated Masur and went on to win the championship.

John McEnroe

PETULANT PERFECTION

A military brat born on a U.S. Air Force base in Wiesbaden, Germany, in 1959, John Patrick McEnroe Jr. had neither the discipline nor hairstyle associated with the armed forces, and that rebellious nature served him well on the tennis court.

McEnroe was raised in Douglaston, in the New York City borough of Queens, after his family moved back and John Sr. became a lawyer. It's where John Jr. first picked up a racket at age seven, and where he became a turnstile-jumping ruffian at a Manhattan private school.

He also became an embodiment of the Big Apple itself — tough, gritty, creative and competitive. He was a dichotomy: a perfectionist who was never concerned with his diet and who never found the benefit of practice, famously stating, "[I've] never spent more than a couple hours a day practicing in my life."

An *enfant terrible* with a petulant look on his face, the left-hander with the unruly mop of curls was famous for his racket-throwing tantrums and wild-eyed, gesticulating arguments with the officials. But behind that was an authentic and all-consuming drive to win, or more specifically, to avoid losing, which he despised.

But "Superbrat" and "McNasty" was also known for his gentle touch with the ball and the purity and artistry of his game. He attacked with an unorthodox serve and masterful volley, and he never stopped.

"Against [Jimmy] Connors and [Bjorn] Borg you feel like you're being hit by a sledgehammer," explained Arthur Ashe. "But McEnroe uses a stiletto. He just slices you up; a nick here, a cut there, pretty soon you've got blood all over and you're bleeding to death."

His first taste of major success came with childhood friend Mary Carillo as the two took the mixed doubles title at the French Open in 1977 when McEnroe was 18. Later that year the New Yorker had to win a qualifying tournament to earn a singles spot at his first Wimbledon. He won the qualifier and then made it all the way to the semifinal before being stopped by Jimmy Connors in four sets. It was the deepest into a Grand Slam tournament that a qualifier had ever gone. It was also the first time he threw a fit in front of a crowd, getting booed for kicking his racket in his quarterfinal match.

At 20, McEnroe won his first major singles title by beating Vitas Gerulaitis in three sets in his own backyard to win the 1979 U.S. Open. That year he set open-era records with 27 tournament victories (10 singles, 17 doubles) and 177 match victories.

McEnroe won the U.S. Open again in 1980 and 1981, both times in dramatic fashion over Bjorn Borg, the latter victory being one of the motivating factors in hastening Borg's retirement.

The McEnroe–Borg rivalry was one for the ages, but they faced each other only 14 times—each winning seven—and McEnroe rarely acted up in their matches, the theory being that he respected Borg and that there was enough drama already inherent in their meetings.

Wimbledon's All England Club was the duo's grandest stage. Their 1980 Wimbledon final is arguably the best match ever played. McEnroe fought off seven match points, including five in the fourth-set tiebreaker alone, before losing 1–6, 7–5, 6–3, 6–7 (16–18), 8–6. The following year, McEnroe got his revenge, beating Borg 4–6, 7–6 (7–1), 7–6 (7–4), 6–4 to win his first Wimbledon title and snap Borg's five-year, 41-match winning streak at the tournament.

"[McEnroe] slices you up; a nick here, a cut there, pretty soon you've got blood all over and you're bleeding to death." –Arthur Ashe

John McEnroe celebrates a second-round victory at the U.S. Open over Martin Laurendeau in straight sets, 6–3, 6–4, 6–2. McEnroe retired in 1992.

McEnroe also had an intense rivalry with Ivan Lendl, his exact opposite in terms of comportment. McEnroe beat him in three sets to win his last U.S. Open title in 1984; a year later Lendl won the rematch and vaulted past McEnroe to become world number one, a perch McEnroe had occupied for four years and 170 weeks in total.

Lendl also kept McEnroe from winning the French Open in 1984 as the Czech kept his composure while McEnroe, up two sets, wilted after an outburst about extraneous noise. Lendl won 3–6, 2–6, 6–4, 7–5, 7–5.

John McEnroe hoists the Wimbledon championship trophy after defeating Jimmy Connors, 6–1, 6–1, 6–2, in the 1984 final for his second straight Wimbledon title.

His temper also bit him at the Australian Open in 1990. McEnroe was up in his fourth-round match two sets to one against Mikael Pernfors when he unraveled. A smashed racket and a stream of expletives and insults toward officials earned McEnroe three code violations. He was tossed from the match and became the first person disqualified from a major since 1963.

Despite the histrionics and singles success, McEnroe was a good teammate and always answered when his country called. Joining the Davis Cup team fulfilled a promise to his mother and revived interest in the tournament after Connors and other Americans had given it a pass.

Patriotism must have rubbed off on McEnroe in his military youth because he brought his best to the tournament,

where he represented the United States on 12 occasions between 1978 and 1992, helping win the Cup as a 19-year-old rookie in 1978 and again in 1979, 1981, 1982 and 1992. In doing so he set American records for years played (12), series (30), singles wins (41) and total wins (59). He also set the record for match length in 1982 when he and Sweden's Mats Wilander battled for six hours and 22 minutes in a 9–7, 6–2, 15–17, 3–6, 8–6 McEnroe victory.

With his career winding down, McEnroe turned back the clock in 1992. At 33 years old he entered Wimbledon as an unseeded player and advanced to the semifinal against Andre Agassi. Reaching the semi brought his career full circle, his last major ending at the same stage as his Wimbledon debut 15 years earlier.

McEnroe didn't leave the 1992 Wimbledon tournament empty-handed, however. Paired with Michael Stich he made the doubles final, which was suspended for darkness with the fourth-set tiebreaker at 13–13. McEnroe and Stich closed it out the next day, winning 5–7, 7–6 (7–5), 3–6, 7–6 (7–5), 19–17, in a record-setting time for a doubles final of five hours and one minute.

It was his final major title, eight years after his last, and his fifth Wimbledon doubles win. When McEnroe said goodbye in 1992 he had a total of 17 major championships in all disciplines, held the open-era record of 155 tournament victories (77 singles, 78 doubles) and was third behind Connors (109) and Lendl (94) in singles titles.

In retirement McEnroe penned his autobiography, *You Cannot Be Serious*, the phrase he famously screamed at an official that's still repeated back to him. In the book he was open about his stormy eight-year marriage to actress Tatum O'Neal, which ended in 1994. McEnroe was given custody of their three children while O'Neal battled addiction and drug charges. He now lives with his wife, singer and fellow New Yorker Patty Smyth, and their two daughters, Anna and Ava.

Mellowed a bit by time and family, McEnroe still speaks his mind as a respected tennis elder and commentator, and he retains some of his competitive zeal on the senior tour, with the fire that always drew fans to him.

"Part of why I believe people look at me in a slightly favorable way is because they can see my frustrations in themselves, and live it a little, vicariously, if you like. I had the nerve to do it, to confront the boss, even if I did get fined. Of course, I was luckier because when you get really good there's not a whole lot [the boss] can do about it."

CAREER HIGHLIGHTS

French Open
Mixed doubles champion 1977

Wimbledon
Singles champion 1981, 1983–84
Doubles champion 1979, 1981, 1983–84, 1992

U.S. Open
Singles champion 1979–81, 1984
Doubles champion 1979, 1981, 1983, 1989

Davis Cup Team Member
1978–84, 1987–89, 1991–92

International Tennis Hall of Fame
1999

John McEnroe argues with umpire George Grimes over a call during his 1981 Wimbledon semifinal match. McEnroe was charged a penalty point and was given a public warning, but he went on to win the match. He defeated Bjorn Borg in the final to win the championship.

Ilie Nastase

NASTY BOY

Ilie Nastase, the reigning French Open champion, extends for a return to Harold Solomon. Solomon ended Nastase's bid at repeating at Roland Garros, defeating him in the quarterfinal.

There was never a dull moment when Ilie "Nasty" Nastase was on the tennis court. He once had an opponent jump over the net and try to choke him, but when he was in control of his emotions—a rarity—he had the raw talent to beat anyone.

Nastase was gifted with exceptional speed and athleticism, he had a tricky serve and he was one of the first players to master the topspin lob on both his forehand and backhand. He was also one of the original bad boys of tennis.

"He is a nonpareil showman, an utterly exasperating games-man, a pouting, crying genius with a racquet in his hand and a curse on his lips," wrote Curry Kirkpatrick in 1972. "He is a magnificent enfant terrible any self-respecting sport would be glad to call its own. At a given moment Nastase will out-charisma Ali, out-sex Namath, out-temperament [Bobby] Fischer and out-bad anybody you care to suit up."

Nastase was born in Bucharest, Romania, in 1946, on a day with a yellow sky his mother says she had never seen before, which she believes made him a sickly and moody child. Growing up he played soccer in the streets from morning until night, and his family lived on the grounds of the Progresul Sports Club.

"I was thin and raggedy, nobody bothered with me much, a restless soul," says Nastase. "I had a chest like chicken and legs like matchsticks in the cartoons. The tennis racquet was always too heavy for me. And I always think more about soccer than tennis anyway."

An older brother and uncle convinced Nastase to practice his tennis game, and he says he knew he was "lucky to grow up with sound of balls hitting racquets, smell of freshly sprinkled courts at four in morning, I learn everything by looking."

In 1959 Nastase won the national junior title and served as a ball boy for the senior championship the next day, which was won by Ion Tiriac, an intimidating professional hockey player from Transylvania who played in the 1964 Innsbruck Olympics.

Tiriac was the Romanian tennis champion for eight years in a row, until Nastase broke his streak in 1966, the same year he made his Davis Cup debut. Tiriac took Nastase under his wing, and together they thrust their country into the international tennis spotlight by making the Davis Cup final three times, in 1969, 1970 and 1972, after the country had won only nine series in the history of the tournament.

The 1972 final was the third time Romania faced the Americans, and after two losses in the United States, Tiriac petitioned to have the games played in Romania. The United States Lawn Tennis Association agreed, and it was the first time the final was played outside a Grand Slam host country, and the first final in Europe since 1937.

It was in Nastase's hometown, on the courts of Progresul he grew up on, and he had all the advantages; it was on clay, which suited his game, and the officiating was comically partisan. "We cannot lose at home," he claimed, and after Nastase's 19 straight singles wins and 13 consecutive victories for Romania in Bucharest, it didn't seem like bragging.

The final was also played amidst heavy security. Weeks prior terrorists had killed 11 Israeli athletes at the Munich Olympics. Jewish players on the American Davis Cup team had received threats. But with an inspired performance Stan Smith upset Nastase 11–9, 6–2, 6–3, and Smith and Erik van Dillen beat Nastase and Tiriac 6–2, 6–0, 6–3 as the United States defeated Romania once again.

Nastase played in 18 Davis Cup tournaments between 1966 and 1985, and at the end of his career he was second to

"Nastase will out-charisma Ali, out-sex Namath, out-temperament [Bobby] Fischer and out-bad anybody you care to suit up." – Curry Kirkpatrick

Italy's Nicola Pietrangeli in total matches (146), wins (109), singles wins (74) and doubles wins (35).

A few months before their Davis Cup clash, the disciplined Smith and mercurial Nastase met in the 1972 Wimbledon final. They were opposing personalities and the first and second seeds at the tournament.

Ilie Nastase, in the first round of the 1974 French Open, returns to native son Maurice Claitte in a straight-sets victory.

Ilie Nastase, known for his antics, takes shelter from the sun under a linesman's chair at Wimbledon in 1975 during his first-round match. Nastase defeated Temuraz Kakulia in straight sets, 6–2, 6–4, 6–2.

Nastase beat Jimmy Connors in the quarterfinal and Manuel Orantes in the semifinal, both in straight sets, and took the first set of the final. But after losing the next two sets he looked confused and ready to implode, as he was prone to do. With Smith serving for a 5–3 lead in the fourth set, Nastase found his groove and started playing with confidence and flair, winning the set to force a fifth. At 4–4 in the fifth Smith got a lucky bounce off the frame of his wooden racket

to win a point that turned the match, which he won 4–6, 6–3, 6–3, 4–6, 7–5. It would be named one of the 30 best matches of all time in 2012.

"The better competitor beat the better tennis player today. Stan won this one with character," said former player Jack Kramer on BBC television.

There was some consolation for Nastase in the 1972 U.S. Open. He was the only foreigner in the final four, and after beating Tom Gorman in the semifinal he faced Arthur Ashe in front of a record-setting crowd of 14,696.

Nastase threw a couple of tantrums early in the match, spitting, swearing and berating linesmen, but he gathered himself, coming back from 2–4 in the fourth set to beat the national hero 3–6, 6–3, 6–7 (1–5), 6–4, 6–3. The win made Nastase the first U.S. champion from Eastern Europe.

"He is a great player and someday he will be a better one if he learns to control his temper," said Ashe at the trophy presentation ceremony.

Nastase must have heeded the advice because he beat Smith to win the season-ending Masters in Barcelona in another five-set match and then followed that with his best year in 1973. He won 15 of the 31 tournaments he entered (with a match record of 118-17), and he added eight doubles titles as well. His combined total of 23 titles in one year matched Rod Laver's open-era record.

The 1973 Italian Open final was a walk for Nastase, 6–1, 6–1, 6–1 over Orantes, and he then won his second major title at the French Open, beating Nikola Pilic with ease in the final, 6–3, 6–3, 6–0. In the first year of computer rankings, he ended the season number one in the world.

"The Bucharest Buffoon" was in the top 10 every year from 1970 to 1977, and he won his last prominent title by beating Bjorn Borg at the Masters in Stockholm in 1975, one of four times he was tournament victor. In 1976 he reached the Wimbledon final again, losing to Borg in three sets, and became the first European to earn more than $1 million in career prize money. By the end of his career, he was one of five players to win more than 100 professional tournaments—57 in singles and 51 in doubles.

In retirement Nastase was president of the Romanian Tennis Federation, was inducted into the International Tennis Hall of Fame in 1991 and ran for mayor of Bucharest in 1996, which he lost.

"Probably a very good thing for him and Bucharest," said Tiriac.

CAREER HIGHLIGHTS

French Open
   Singles champion 1973
   Doubles champion 1970

Wimbledon
   Doubles champion 1973
   Mixed doubles champion 1970, 1972

U.S. Open
   Singles champion 1972
   Doubles champion 1975

Davis Cup Team Member
   1966–77, 1979–80, 1982–85

International Tennis Hall of Fame
   1991

Ilie Nastase raises the U.S. Open championship trophy after dispatching Arthur Ashe, 3–6, 6–3, 6–7, 6–4, 6–3, to earn his first major championship.

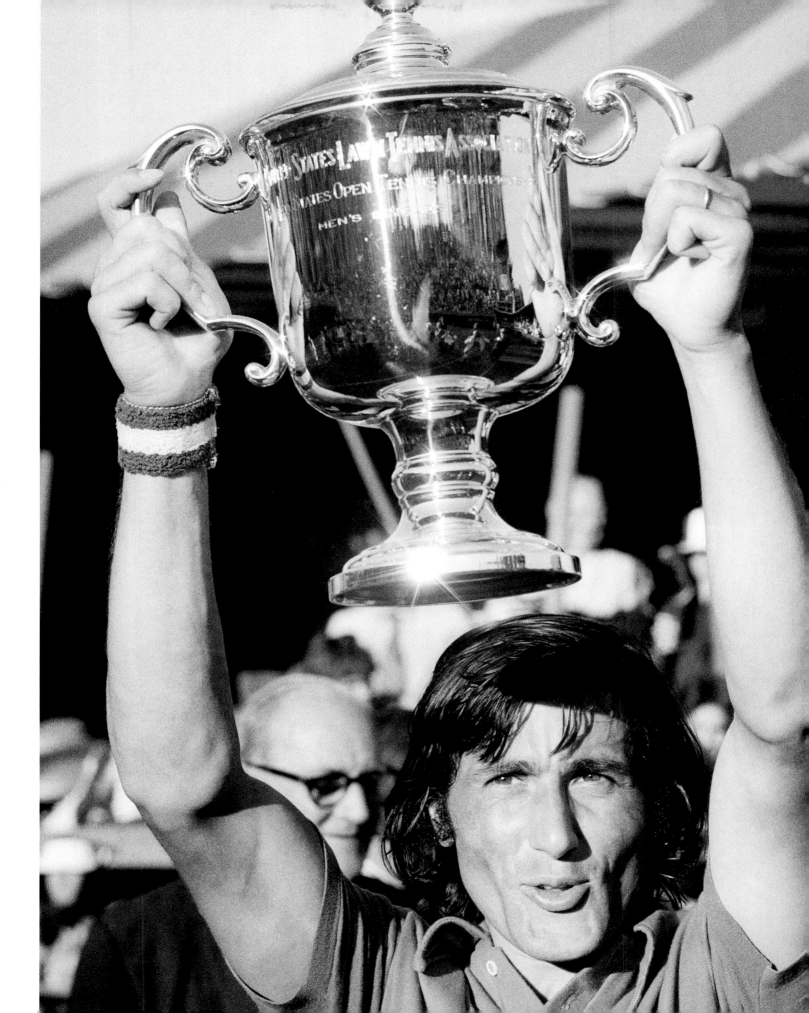

Pete Sampras

PLAIN OLD PERFECTION

Pete Sampras tracks his return shot to Alex Calatrava at the 2001 Hamburg Masters. Sampras didn't advance in the clay-court tournament — clay being one of his weaker surfaces.

Rod Laver won all four majors in a calendar year twice, the only player with two Grand Slams. His second Slam and the last of his 11 major titles was in 1969, two years before Pete Sampras was born, yet that's who Sampras chased his whole life.

Born in a Washington, D.C., suburb to Greek immigrants Sam and Georgia, Sampras started playing tennis when he was 7. The family moved to Palos Verdes, California, soon after, where Sampras met Dr. Peter Fisher, a retired pediatrician and tennis aficionado. He would have a monumental impact on the young player, setting one of tennis' all-time great careers in motion.

Fisher taught Sampras to serve and volley instead of playing from the baseline—which, as a technique, had been gaining popularity thanks to the likes of American Jimmy Connors—and convinced him to use a traditional one-handed backhand, counter to the common two-hander. He also made his young charge use an antiquated wooden racket so he would develop a better stroke.

The doctor encouraged Sampras to mimic Laver, both in style and in his respect for the game, and drilled into him that the only things really worth pursuing were Laver's records.

Fisher, a bit of a perfectionist, almost had perfection in Sampras' complete arsenal of skills. His first and second serve combination was devastating. The first was as precise as it was fast, regularly topping 120 miles per hour from an early age and with tremendous topspin; if that missed his second wasn't much slower, and it was deadly accurate. Sampras' running forehand was also nearly unstoppable, he moved on the court with uncommon grace, and as he got older he also improved his conditioning, strategy, backhand and service return.

"I have played him on different surfaces, and I've experienced something I didn't experience with the likes of [John] McEnroe or [Ivan] Lendl or even [Bjorn] Borg," said Boris Becker. "He's able to adapt on different surfaces in a way no one has done before. He's able to play very aggressive tennis even on a clay court or a slow hard court. And his tennis doesn't have any flaws. He's probably better than anybody who ever played the game."

Sampras dropped out of high school to pursue his tennis dreams, turning pro when he was 16 in 1988 and winning his first tournament that year in Philadelphia. At his second U.S. Open, in 1989, he made a name for himself by beating defending champion Mats Wilander in five sets in the third round. He then took control of his life by relieving Fisher of his duties after a dispute over his position and compensation. The two didn't speak again for three years.

At the start of the 1990 season Sampras was ranked 81st in the world, but he took that year's U.S. Open by storm. With a barrage of aces he beat former champions and future Hall of Famers Lendl in the quarterfinals and McEnroe in the semifinals. In the final he dismissed Andre Agassi in three sets and 106 minutes to become the youngest man to win the U.S. Open, at 19 years and one month.

Without Fisher, however, Sampras wasn't being spurred on, and he seemed satisfied with his place in the tennis world. But after losing the 1992 U.S. Open final to Stefan Edberg something changed; the loss haunted him, and he realized he wasn't satisfied with only one major victory. Suddenly, the inspiration came from within.

Sampras won the first of his three straight titles at the All England Club in 1993 and took his first Australian Open in 1994.

In 1996 his coach and friend Tim Gullikson, a former pro, died of brain cancer. Sampras played gamely following the

Pete Sampras serves to Adrian Voinea at the 1997 Australian Open. Sampras won the match and went on to win his second Aussie title, defeating Carlos Moya in straight sets.

"I shouldn't have to apologize for the way I am, I could be a jerk and get a lot more publicity, but that's not who I am." – Pete Sampras

funeral, making it to the semis of the French Open — the only major he never won — but he was emotionally drained and later lost in the Wimbledon quarterfinals. He embarked on a new streak at Wimbledon in 1997, winning four in a row through the 2000 tournament.

A tennis historian, Sampras, who'd already surpassed

The Duke and Duchess of Kent applaud as Pete Sampras celebrates winning Wimbledon in 1997. Sampras was a French Open away from winning the Grand Slam that year.

Laver's 11 majors, was well aware that with his seventh Wimbledon title in 2000 (and 13th major overall), he had eclipsed Roy Emerson's male record of 12 major championships. Emerson, on the other hand, didn't even know he held the record until he was told that Sampras had beaten it.

The 13th was far from easy; the Centre Court final against Pat Rafter was delayed twice for rain, and in the interim, the cortisone shot Sampras received before the match to mask the intense pain of a leg injury wore off. He considered dropping out but he gritted his teeth and beat Rafter in four sets.

That Wimbledon title also tied Willie Renshaw's 100-year-old record of seven victories between 1881 and 1889. Seeking

his eighth in 2001, Sampras lost to 19-year-old Roger Federer.

In 2002 Sampras was winless in 33 tournaments, including an opening-round loss at the French Open and a second-round loss at Wimbledon, both to virtual unknowns. When the U.S. Open began, few gave the 31-year-old a chance, despite his past success at Flushing Meadows and having reached the final in 2000 and 2001.

But 17th-seeded Sampras turned back the clock and dismissed Agassi in the final, just as he did 12 years earlier to win his first major. It was Sampras' fifth U.S. Open, 14th major title and his last competitive match. He left the game the way he played it—on top and with little fanfare.

His low-key approach to the game meant he was never fully embraced by casual fans or advertisers. He was too quiet, too nice and too introverted. Despite sponsoring both players, Nike made Agassi the focus of its tennis campaigns when Sampras was regularly beating him, and tennis tyrant and Hall of Famer Jimmy Connors famously called him "vanilla."

"I shouldn't have to apologize for the way I am," responded Sampras to the criticism. "I could be a jerk and get a lot more publicity, but that's not who I am."

Sampras excelled because he was in control, and he simply let his achievements do the talking. He held the year-end number one ranking for six straight years, a record he took from Connors and still holds. He was also named ATP Player of the Year six times, the most since the award was first handed out in 1975, spent a total of 12 years in the world top 10, won 64 singles titles and two in doubles, had an overall winning percentage of .776 (including a record of 203-39 in the majors for an .839 winning clip), and won 14 of the 18 major finals he played in.

What made his feats even more remarkable was that Sampras was dealing with thalassemia minor, also known as Mediterranean anemia, a genetic disease that makes it difficult for the body to make healthy red blood cells and carry oxygen.

Sampras is secure with his legacy and happy with his low-profile life in California, where he and wife Bridgette Wilson, an actress, are raising their two sons, Christian and Ryan. But he did make a rare confession when Federer was on the verge of winning his 15th major title in 2009, saying he wished his record had held up a little longer.

"But I can honestly say I don't have an issue with Roger passing me. He gets the job done and does it with class.

"I won 14," he added. "Which is 14 more than I ever thought I'd win."

And three more than Laver.

CAREER HIGHLIGHTS

Australian Open
Singles champion 1994, 1997

Wimbledon
Singles champion 1993–95, 1997–2000

U.S. Open
Singles champion 1990, 1993, 1995–96, 2002

Davis Cup Team Member
1991–92, 1994–95, 1997, 1999–2000, 2002

International Tennis Hall of Fame
2007

Pete Sampras serves to Thomas Enqvist in the fourth round of the 1993 U.S. Open. Sampras dismissed Enqvist 6–4, 6–4, 7–6 (7–4) and went on to claim his second U.S. crown.

Stan Smith

ALL-AMERICAN CHAMPION

Stan Smith returns Roy Emerson's offering at the 1970 U.S. Open during their fourth-round match. Smith advanced to the quarterfinal but was vanquished by eventual champion Ken Rosewall. Smith would win his first American title the next year.

Like Rene Lacoste and Fred Perry and their eponymous clothing lines, Stan Smith is probably more known now for his signature shoes than for his Hall of Fame tennis career.

Born in Pasadena, California, in 1946, Smith grew up playing baseball and basketball, the latter he called his "first love," and at a lanky 6 foot 4 he had the build for it. It wasn't until he was in his teens that he started playing tennis with any regularity, but Perry Jones, a tennis coach and bigwig in southern California, saw him play and said he could make him a champion.

It wasn't an easy decision for Smith, though; he cried when he called his basketball coach in his senior year of high school to tell him he was focusing on tennis. But almost immediately he was a champion, winning the U.S. juniors in 1964 and earning the only tennis scholarship available at the University of Southern California.

During his sophomore year at USC, coach George Toley noticed how Smith held the racket too tightly on his forehand and completely remade his stroke. What had been a weakness became a strength, an additional weapon to add to the heavy serve he already had.

With his reach and fitness, Smith was also tireless in retrieving balls, and he had a calm about him that was especially helpful during tiebreakers, of which he won the vast majority over the course of his career.

Smith was also known for having a character as strong as his game. He was universally respected for being "deeply religious, God-fearing, temperate and disciplined, a true sportsman, a respectful loving son and a self-made champion whose 'corny dream' is to build and manage his own YMCA," according to a *Sports Illustrated* profile in 1972.

While at USC Smith met Bob Lutz, his polar opposite in terms of personality but his perfect match on the court. They won the U.S. intercollegiate doubles crown in 1967 and 1968, and Smith, a three-time All-American, also won the singles in 1968.

It was a very good year for Smith; he won his very first Davis Cup match to clinch the title for the United States, the country's first in five years, and he earned his first major championship—the 1968 U.S. Open doubles with Lutz. They stuck together and became one of the dominant teams of the era, winning the Australian Open doubles in 1970 and the U.S. Open again in 1974, 1978 and 1980.

Smith joined the Army in 1971, at a time when Americans weren't particularly fond of the military and its intervention in Vietnam, and was assigned to the Sports Program Office and the U.S. Army Recruiting Command. As a shaggy-haired private, Smith won his first major singles title that year, beating Jan Kodes in the first U.S. Open final to end in a tiebreaker—3–6, 6–3, 6–2, 7–6 (5–3).

"I know I'm being used as a kind of Army soft-sell," Smith said in 1972. "But I feel I'm performing a service for my country. Maybe I'm more patriotic than most kids my age. But I've represented the United States in Davis Cup play, I've stood there and felt pride as they played the national anthem before matches. And I've traveled around the world. I've been able to compare. I think we have a tremendous system. Oh, I'd like to see some changes. I'd like us to get out of Vietnam."

Smith played for his country in the Davis Cup on 11 occasions between 1968 and 1979, securing the Cup-clinching victory a record six times and winning the tournament seven times, which tied Bill Tilden's U.S. record.

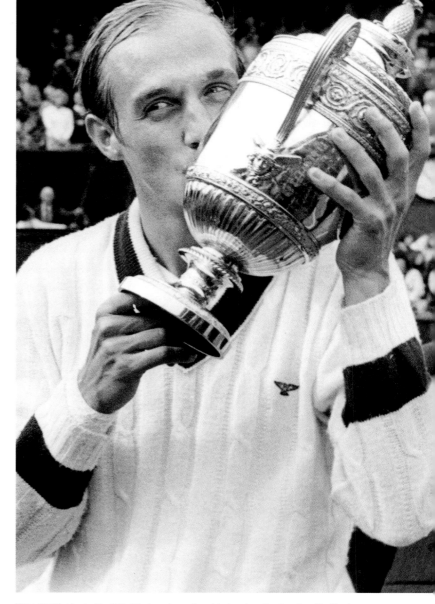

Stan Smith kisses the Wimbledon championship trophy after besting Ilie Nastase for the 1972 title. It would be Smith's third and final major singles championship.

"I feel I'm performing a service for my country ... Oh, I'd like to see some changes. I'd like us to get out of Vietnam." – Stan Smith

In their Davis Cup swansong, Smith and Lutz also played a small role in helping the United States win in 1981, beating the Czechoslovakian team of Ivan Lendl and Tom Smid in the quarterfinal.

Smith's most historic Davis Cup series was in Bucharest, Romania, in 1972, battling a hostile crowd and homer line judges to win seven of eight singles matches and five doubles matches with Erik van Dillen. He beat two of the giants of tennis on their home turf, world number three Ilie Nastase in three sets and Ion Tiriac in five sets, as Romania

Stan Smith celebrates his advancement to the 1972 Wimbledon final after defeating Jan Kodes 3–6, 6–4, 6–1, 7–5.

was looking to avenge losses to the United States in 1969 and 1971.

Smith had already beaten Nastase at Wimbledon in 1972, in a final that's considered one of the tournament's great matches. In the fifth set Smith fought off two break points in the fifth game, which had seven deuces, and Nastase saved a match point at 4–5 and another at 5–6 before hitting an easy backhand into the net to give Smith the 4–6, 6–3, 6–3, 4–6, 7–5 victory and his second major singles title.

There was no defense of his Wimbledon title in 1973; Smith was one of the players who boycotted the tournament

in solidarity with Croatian player Nikola Pilic, who was banned for choosing not to play in the Davis Cup. For Smith, unfortunately, his game began to slide that year. He lost an important Davis Cup match to Australia's John Newcombe and was ousted in the first round of the U.S. Pro Tennis Championships in straight sets by Jimmy Connors.

Smith lost to Connors again at the year-end Grand Prix Masters, blowing two match points in the process. Afterward the normally affable and easygoing Smith left the court alone instead of walking off with his opponent, as tradition dictates.

"There were three billion people standing around him," explained Smith. "I decided I wasn't waiting any longer."

Not himself physically or emotionally, Smith went in for a physical. He was sluggish and underweight, but the doctor found nothing wrong. He diagnosed burnout and prescribed a break from tennis. Smith didn't play in the Davis Cup in 1974 and put down his racket for a month at the end of the year while he honeymooned with new wife Margie, a former Princeton player.

After reuniting with coach Toley in Mexico in early 1975, Smith returned to the tour, but his best days as a singles player were behind him. He remained successful in doubles and the Davis Cup and became one of only five "centurions"—players who've won at least 100 professional tournament victories, hitting the mark exactly with 39 in singles and 61 in doubles. He was the top-ranked player in the United States four of the five years between 1969 and 1973, and from 1969 to 1974 he was in the world top 10, reaching number one in 1972.

Smith retired in 1985 but stayed close to the game by coaching, playing exhibition matches and becoming president of the International Tennis Hall of Fame and Museum in September 2011. He also opened a tennis academy near his home in Hilton Head Island, South Carolina.

If his students aren't impressed by his playing resume, they are certainly captivated when he appears with Snoop Dogg in an animated Christmas story by Adidas, or when his namesake shoes are mentioned in a Jay-Z song.

The first all-leather tennis shoe released by Adidas was originally named the Haillet in 1964, after French player Robert Haillet. The simple white sneaker with the green tendon protector on the back became the Stan Smith in 1971 when Adidas wanted to break into the American market. In 2012 Sneaker Report named it the 13th most influential footwear sponsorship in sports history.

Many have worn Stan Smiths over the last 40 years; very few have filled them.

CAREER HIGHLIGHTS

Australian Open
Doubles champion 1970

Wimbledon
Singles champion 1972

U.S. Open
Singles champion 1971
Doubles champion 1968, 1974, 1978, 1980

Davis Cup Team Member
1968–73, 1975–79, 1981

International Tennis Hall of Fame
1987

Stan Smith makes a desperate backhand stab to keep the rally alive against Ilie Nastase in the 1972 Wimbledon final. Smith prevailed 4–6, 6–3, 6–3, 4–6, 7–5 to become the first American since 1963 to take the title.

Mats Wilander

FOR THE FUN OF IT

Mats Wilander, in his second year entering the U.S. Open, serves to Glenn Michibata in first-round play at the 1984 edition of the tournament. Wilander advanced to the quarterfinal before being ousted by Pat Cash.

In the world of tennis, Mats Wilander was an original; he could run forever without training hard, he was a number one who didn't strive for the top, and he was a man with many passions outside the lines of the court, one of which was sleep.

"I could fall asleep during a changeover," he once said.

Born in Vaxjo in southern Sweden in 1964, Wilander said that Swedes get very used to doing nothing because of the cold and darkness.

Young Mats picked up a racket when he was six, and in the warmer months, he started playing in the parking lot of the factory where his dad, Einar, worked. Einar painted lines on the asphalt and made a net out of chicken wire. He spent his lunch hours playing with Mats, who would then challenge anyone who came along until his dad finished work and dragged him home.

Wilander won the under-12, under-14 and under-16 national titles, giving up hockey along the way to focus on tennis because he liked being in complete control of who won the match. He also said his tennis coaches didn't push him too hard, otherwise he would have quit.

The right-hander with a two-fisted backhand was fleet of foot and wore opponents down from the baseline. Wilander also exuded class and uncommon grace under pressure, but his demeanor was often confused with indifference, and John McEnroe accused him of being complacent.

"I play tennis to play tennis," said Wilander in response. "It's strictly an American attitude to think that if you're not the best, you're a failure. I want to have fun, make a living and have good friends. Being number one is somewhere down the line."

Wilander started down the path to the top in his first French Open in 1982. Unseeded and just 17, he reached the semifinal against the heavily favored Jose-Luis Clerc and had match point when Clerc's shot was called out. Wilander, however, approached the umpire, who had already left his chair, and told him that Clerc's ball had landed in, so the point was replayed. Wilander won the match (for the second time) and then beat former champion Guillermo Vilas 1–6, 7–6 (8–6), 6–0, 6–4 in the final to become the youngest male winner in major history, unseating Swedish legend Bjorn Borg.

Many compared the two Swedes, who had similar looks and games, but they weren't close personally. Oddly, Wilander's role models were Jimmy Connors and Ilie Nastase, two of the more colorful individuals in tennis history.

In 1984 Wilander dismissed Connors in three sets as Sweden upset the United States to win the Davis Cup. At the next year's tournament he won two singles and a doubles match as Sweden beat Germany in Munich, and in 1987 he was part of a 5-0 dismantling of India for his third Davis Cup triumph.

Showing his stamina, two of Wilander's Davis Cup matches were among the most drawn out in tennis history. In 1989 he lost to Austria's Horst Skoff 6–7 (5–7), 7–6 (9–7), 1–6, 6–4, 9–7 in six hours and four minutes, and in 1982 he battled McEnroe for six hours and 22 minutes before falling 9–7, 6–2, 15–17, 3–6, 8–6. It was the longest match in any competition until it was surpassed at the 2004 French Open.

Wilander won his second French Open in 1985, beating Ivan Lendl, the efficient and single-minded Czech, in a four-set final, but for the next three years Lendl won all their meetings, including two extended chess matches at the 1987 French and U.S. Opens.

Around this time Wilander started to develop an attacking game, taking opponents by surprise when the baseliner suddenly started approaching the net. He

Mats Wilander serves to Todd Nelson in the first round of the 1986 U.S. Open. Wilander had a disappointing singles tournament, falling in a fourth-round loss to Miloslav Mecir after a semifinal appearance the year before.

"I play tennis to play tennis. It's strictly an American attitude to think that if you're not the best, you're a failure." – Mats Wilander

also added a one-handed backhand to his repertoire.

The work paid off, and in 1988 Wilander came very close to winning a Grand Slam, taking three of the four majors. He started the year by beating Australian hero Pat Cash in five sets over four hours to win the Australian Open, his third major Down Under. It was the first Australian Open played on hard court, and Wilander was just the second man, after Connors, to win majors on grass, clay and hard.

In the French Open final Wilander beat Henri Leconte,

Reigning Australian Open champ Mats Wilander follows through on a backhand stroke at the 1984 U.S. Open. Wilander made it as far as the quarterfinal, his farthest ever in the American championship to that point.

another native son, in straight sets, missing only two of his 74 first serves and committing just one unforced error in the final two sets.

After winning the first two majors of 1988, Wilander was at the top of his game and even admitted he might be the best in the world, a rarity for modest Mats. But the following month he was tripped up in the Wimbledon quarterfinals by Miloslav Mecir.

Rebounding at the U.S. Open, Wilander faced Lendl in a rematch of the 1987 final, which Lendl had won in four sets.

CAREER HIGHLIGHTS

Australian Open
Singles champion 1983–84, 1988

French Open
Singles champion 1982, 1985, 1988

Wimbledon
Doubles champion 1986

U.S. Open
Singles champion 1988

Davis Cup Team Member
1981–90, 1995

International Tennis Hall of Fame
2002

At four hours and 55 minutes, the 1988 final was the longest in U.S. championship history, with Wilander prevailing 6–4, 4–6, 6–3, 5–7, 6–4 to make him the first man to win three majors in a year since Connors in 1974. In the process he also unseated Lendl after the Czech had spent the previous three years at the top of the world rankings.

Finally reaching number one seemed to satisfy Wilander, however, and he faded from that point.

"It was such a special win that nothing else in tennis seemed important," said Wilander of his 1988 U.S. Open victory, the seventh and last major victory of his career. "I thought, 'What am I working for now?' It was weird. I had trained for years to reach the top, and when I finally got there I realized I'd have to work even harder to stay there. All I really wanted was to take a holiday."

His reign at the top lasted only four months, and in December of 1988 he lost to journeyman West German Carl-Uwe Steeb on home soil in a Davis Cup match. It was the first time in his career he lost a five-set match after taking the first two, and when West Germany took a 3-1 lead, Wilander decided not to bother playing the meaningless fifth match for his country.

"He's extremely content in his private life," suggested his wife, Sonya, in 1989. "I think he's just bored with tennis."

Wilander, an avid guitarist who celebrated his 1988 U.S. Open win by jamming with the Rolling Stones' Keith Richards, also spent more time in the recording studio of his Greenwich, Connecticut, home than on the practice court.

The last of Wilander's 33 career titles came in 1990, and after taking a break from the game he made a modest comeback in 1993. He climbed to number 45 in the world in 1995 and was named to the Swedish Davis Cup team one more time, losing a doubles match to Americans Andre Agassi and Pete Sampras in the 1995 semifinal.

True to his wandering spirit and originality, Wilander now drives his 29-foot Winnebago to local tennis clubs around North America to give lessons. All you have to do is ask. His workouts are punishing, although Wilander can still do them without breaking much of a sweat, because, as he says, "tennis is a running game, not a hitting game—it's not golf." Afterward the Hall of Famer, who was inducted in 2002, might sit down for dinner with you and sleep in the parking lot of the club.

"It's—it's just weird," says George Bezecny, the tennis pro at Fisher Island in Miami, where Wilander put on two clinics in 2011. "He doesn't have to do this. It's amazing that he does."

Mats Wilander, in his first U.S. Open final, reacts after forcing Ivan Lendl into a third-set tiebreaker in their 1987 match. Lendl would prevail over Wilander, but the Swede would have the last laugh, defeating Lendl in their rematch in the 1988 U.S. final.

Tracy Austin

PINT-SIZED PERFECTION

Fourteen-year-old Tracy Austin returns the ball to fourth-seeded Sue Barker in their third-round match of the 1977 U.S. Open. Austin rolled over Barker and then did the same to Virginia Ruzici before falling to Betty Stove in the quarterfinal.

Tennis' popularity was soaring in the United States in the 1970s. Chris Evert and Martina Navratilova were taking over tournaments and headlines, but their dominance also threatened the sport by robbing it of intrigue. Then along came a precocious and homegrown teen—bouncing onto the scene in pigtails and braces—to tilt the tennis axis.

Born outside Los Angeles into a tennis family in 1962, Tracy Austin was a transcendent talent, a prodigy whose star burned briefly but brightly.

Austin's mother, Jeanne, was the pro shop manager at the Jack Kramer Club in Rolling Hills Estates, California. She brought Tracy to work, putting her in a tennis program when she was 2. Austin's older sister and two older brothers all went on to professional tennis careers as well, but none were like their younger sister.

"I knew very early, almost immediately, that she was special," said her father, George Austin. "She started at two when she picked up a sawed-off racquet and knocked lamps over in the living room. She held the racquet very well even then. There was nothing else she wanted to do in preference to playing tennis."

Her father wasn't the only one who thought she was special. Austin was on the cover of *World Tennis* magazine when she was 4, won the American junior championship when she was 10 and earned her first *Sports Illustrated* cover at 13.

In 1977, less than a month after turning 14, Austin won a professional tournament in Portland, Oregon, and she became the youngest woman to ever play at Wimbledon that summer, losing to defending champion Chris Evert in the second round. She also made it to the quarterfinals of the 1977 U.S. Open as an unseeded amateur, setting another age record and earning a phone call from President Jimmy Carter. She was already ranked fourth in the United States and earning plenty of postmatch Baskin-Robbins ice cream from her parents.

Only 5 feet tall and 90 pounds at the time, Austin looked every bit her age and played nothing like it. On her way to the U.S. quarterfinals, she beat two French Open champions before losing to Wimbledon finalist Betty Stove.

Two years later Austin won the 1979 Italian Open, snapping Evert's 125-match winning streak on clay in the process. Evert had a chance to avenge the loss in the U.S. Open later that year when they met in the final.

Evert had won the U.S. Open four years in a row and came in fit and determined. She'd beaten Austin in a tune-up tournament and blew through the field, flattening Billie Jean King, 6–1, 6–0, in the semifinal to extend her U.S. Open women's record to 31 consecutive victories.

Austin beat world number two Navratilova 7–5, 7–5 in the other semifinal, but even her coach, Robert Lansdorp, put his pupil's chances of winning at "about a 40%" and had promised to give up smoking if she won.

Now 5 foot 4 and 110 pounds, Austin held him to his vow after dispatching Evert in the final, 6–4, 6–3, to become the youngest U.S. Open winner, male or female, at 16 years, nine months — three months younger than Maureen Connolly when she won in 1951.

To celebrate, Jeanne brought Tracy to McDonald's. "I was still in my tennis dress," she says. "Some people recognized me and looked at me kind of strangely."

"I thought Tracy might be intimidated by the thought of winning a major tournament, but she wasn't," said Evert after the match. "She treated the final just like any other tennis match. If nerves don't get her, she'll be number one in the next year or two."

"That might be my biggest regret. Imagine a top player today missing a major because she wanted to do well in social studies!" – Tracy Austin

Sixteen-year-old Tracy Austin smashes a backhand return in her 6–4, 6–2 triumph over reigning Wimbledon champion Martina Navratilova in the final of the 1979 Wells Fargo San Diego Open.

Evert was right; after Austin beat Navratilova in two straight finals in 1980, she wrestled the number one ranking from her and at 17 became the youngest person to ever hold it, while also breaking Evert's and Navratilova's six-year grip on the top spot.

In the same year Evert got so frustrated after losing three matches in two weeks to Austin that she took a brief hiatus from tennis. Austin, in her short career, had a 9-8 record against Evert, the woman with the highest winning percentage of any tennis player in history.

Tracy Austin (left) and Billie Jean King after the completion of their 1979 Wimbledon quarterfinal match, in which the 16-year-old Austin defeated the six-time champion King. In the semifinal Austin lost a tough battle to eventual champion Martina Navratilova.

After playing all that tennis, Austin decided to sit out the 1980 French Open so she could finish the school year.

"That might be my biggest regret," said Austin in 2006. "Imagine a top player today missing a major because she wanted to do well in social studies!"

Austin didn't skip Wimbledon, however, and she and her brother John became the first siblings to win the mixed doubles title. 1980 was also the year Austin became the youngest player of either gender to earn over a million dollars in prize money, breaking the barrier before her 18th birthday.

Evert dispatched Austin in the semifinal of the 1980 U.S. Open in three sets, but the following year Austin was back in the final.

After beating Evert 6–1, 6–4 to win the 1981 Canadian Open, Austin sailed into the final of the U.S. Open without much trouble before losing the first set 6–1 to Navratilova, who'd beaten Evert in the semifinal. Austin gathered herself and won the next two sets, both in tiebreakers, with Navratilova double-faulting on championship point to end a record-setting U.S. Open women's final at two hours and 42 minutes. It was Austin's second U.S. title—and she was still only 18.

But back injuries began to take their toll on the petite Austin, forcing her to take long layoffs and limiting her mobility, and by 1983, at the age of 20, her career was in serious jeopardy.

Like her style on the court her rehabilitation was relentless, but after a serious car accident in 1989 Austin's right knee had to be rebuilt using bone from her hip, derailing her attempts at a comeback. Even in retirement she set a record by becoming the youngest player to be inducted into the Tennis Hall of Fame when she was 29.

One more short-lived return to the court in 1994 did earn Austin another distinction; she was the first player to win a major singles match after being named to the Hall, which she accomplished at the Australian Open. It was her first appearance at the tournament in 13 years, and it lasted two rounds before she retired for the last time.

As David Foster Wallace wrote in his 1992 essay "Tracy Austin Broke My Heart," she was the first of the "now-ubiquitous nymphet prodigies ... beautiful and inspiring."

Austin now lives in Rolling Hills, California, with her husband Scott Holt and three sons—Dylan, Brandon and Sean. A tennis writer and TV analyst, she holds a celebrity pro–am tournament for charity and sees herself in a slightly less glamorous fashion.

"I'm Tracy Holt who manages to fit in three games [a week] while chauffeuring her sons around."

Asked if she would encourage any of her children to follow in their mother's footsteps, she said: "I know what it takes to become number one, and unless the drive is there, burning inside that kid, then it's never going to happen. It can't come from the parents, and that's the mistake many make."

CAREER HIGHLIGHTS

Wimbledon
Mixed doubles champion 1980

U.S. Open
Singles champion 1979, 1981

Wightman Cup Team Member
1978–79, 1981

Federation Cup Team Member
1978–80

International Tennis Hall of Fame
1992

Tracy Austin, 14, at the 1977 U.S. Open. In two years she would be American champion and the Associated Press Female Athlete of the Year.

Jennifer Capriati

MAKING WAVES

Jennifer Capriati stretches for a ball from Julia Schruff during their third-round match at the 2004 German Open in Berlin. Capriati advanced all the way to the semifinal before falling to eventual champion Amelie Mauresmo.

Jennifer Capriati wasn't the first tennis prodigy to burn out early, just the first to do it so publicly in the tabloid age. Hers is a cautionary tale, but also one of redemption and second chances.

Capriati was born in New York City in 1976. Her father was a boxer, soccer player and stuntman turned tennis coach, and her mother was a flight attendant who played tennis the day before Jennifer was born. They let their toddler daughter roam the courts of the Long Island tennis club they belonged to, and before long the family moved to Florida so she could train all year under Jimmy Evert, father of tennis legend Chris. At 10 she was beating grown men, and by 13 Capriati made her professional debut after rules prohibiting players under the age of 14 from competing in pro tournaments were relaxed to allow 13-year-olds to play in the month of their 14th birthday. Her first tournament was the Virginia Slims in March 1990, and she made it all the way to the final before she was stopped by world number three Gabriela Sabatini. In doing so she became the youngest player to reach a tour final.

Capriati made it to the final in two of her first three events, and in 1990 after she'd turned 14, she was the youngest semifinalist in French championship history, losing to eventual champion Monica Seles. She was also both the youngest player and match winner in Federation Cup history, helping the United States win the 1990 title.

Still just 14, Capriati finished the year ranked eighth in the world. The next season she became the youngest Wimbledon semifinalist in history at 15 when she upset defending champion Martina Navratilova in the quarterfinal. It was Navratilova's earliest exit at the tournament in 14 years.

Capriati won the Olympic gold medal in Barcelona in 1992 when she was 16, beating second-seeded Arantxa Sanchez Vicario in the semifinal and top-seeded, reigning gold medalist and world number one Steffi Graf in the final. By this time Capriati was already feared for her power and had earned a reputation as a scrapper, playing her best with her back against the wall, which she did to beat Graf for Olympic gold: 3–6, 6–3, 6–4.

Carefree and vivacious when she exploded onto the tennis scene, Capriati slowly started to become fond of black nail polish, piercings, grunge music and monosyllabic answers. Her teen angst might not have been unusual for the average adolescent, but she was anything but ordinary.

Rebelling against the parents who drove her career and the ever-expanding circle of people who depended on her success, Capriati was navigating the perils of high school while also dealing with the stress of professional tennis and being a teenage millionaire.

"I think it would be important to have more of a mental coach to help you make sure you don't get twisted your perceptions of who you are," mused Capriati years later. "So many things that go on in your head are not normal."

With her psychological health deteriorating, Capriati withdrew from tennis in 1993 after a first-round loss at the U.S. Open.

"When I looked in the mirror I actually saw this distorted image. I was so ugly and fat I just wanted to kill myself," said Capriati. "At the end of a match, I couldn't wait to get off the court. Mentally, I'd just lost it. I wasn't happy with myself, my tennis, my life, my coaches, my friends."

The next time Capriati made headlines it was for all the wrong reasons. She was arrested for shoplifting and marijuana

Fifteen-year-old Jennifer Capriati volleys with her third-round opponent, Patricia Hy, at the 1991 U.S. Open. Capriati made a remarkable run, losing to eventual champion Monica Seles in the semifinal.

"Who would have thought I'd ever make it here after so much has happened? If you believe, dreams do come true." –Jennifer Capriati

possession in a very public meltdown, and there were allegations of heroin and crack use and several stints in rehab.

After a life focused on her tennis career and then battling her demons, Capriati was forced to deal with events she had absolutely no control over. Her parents were divorcing and her mother was fighting cancer. This adversity bred maturity and perspective, and with it a renewed focus and love of tennis.

Capriati came back, after a few stuttering attempts, and won two minor tournaments in 1999 and reached the fourth

Sixteen-year-old Jennifer Capriati (left) shows off her Olympic gold medal in tennis singles. Capriati defeated Steffi Graf (right) 3–6, 6–3, 6–4 for the title.

"I never thought I'd be standing here 11 years later, after playing my first time here when I was 14 years old," Capriati said to the crowd. "Really, I'm just waiting to wake up from this dream."

The year ended with Capriati ranked number one in the world for the first time in her career, and she was named Associated Press Female Athlete of the Year.

The defining game of Capriati's comeback came at the 2002 Australian Open final. Down 6–4, 4–0 against Hingis in stifling heat, she fought off four championship points in the second set, the most ever in a major women's final. With both players seeking any shade and ice they could find during breaks, Hingis sagged in the third set and Capriati won 4–6, 7–6, 6–2.

Tennis magazine named it one of the 10 best matches of the decade, and Capriati won an ESPN ESPY Award for Comeback Player of the Year, beating basketball's Michael Jordan and hockey player Mario Lemieux, who had returned to the NHL after beating cancer.

In 2003 Capriati became the first defending Australian Open champion to bow out in the first round, and later that season she lost in one of the best U.S. Open matches of all time. She came within 2 points of a semifinal victory 11 times before losing five straight games and a third-set tiebreaker to Justine Henin—4–6, 7–5, 7–6.

It would prove to be the last great match of her career. An injury to her right shoulder in 2004 and three subsequent surgeries ended her comeback, and her life in tennis was over at the age of 28.

"I know she still wanted to play," said Navratilova. "But the body didn't let her. It's a shame when the body tells the athlete to stop, instead of the heart."

Capriati maintained a private life after her retirement but was in the news in 2010 after she was hospitalized for an overdose of prescription drugs. In 2012 Capriati was inducted into the International Tennis Hall of Fame, giving a heartfelt and emotional speech, an enshrinement lauded by the tennis community.

"She was an immense talent, was put under stifling scrutiny, and ended up accomplishing so much that she is a very deserved Hall of Famer," wrote former coach Justin Gimelstob. "The way she worked through adversity, persevered, and what she achieved was remarkable. I have nothing but the utmost respect for her."

round of the French Open. In 2000 she finished the year ranked 14th in the world, the highest she'd been since she was ninth in 1993.

She entered the 2001 Australian Open as the 12th seed and became the lowest-seeded player to win the singles title, her first major, beating defending champion Lindsay Davenport in the semifinal and world number one Martina Hingis 6–4, 6–3 in the final. With her dad in the crowd she leaped around the court after the shocking win, years of pent-up emotion released.

"Who would have thought I'd ever make it here after so much has happened?" asked Capriati. "If you believe, dreams do come true."

At the French Open that year Capriati was seeded fourth and beat Serena Williams and Hingis to reach the final. She overcame Kim Clijsters in dramatic fashion—1–6, 6–4, 12–10—for her second major in a row, making her just the fifth woman to win the Australian and French in the same year.

CAREER HIGHLIGHTS

Australian Open
Singles champion 2001–02

French Open
Singles champion 2001

Olympics
Gold medalist in women's singles 1992

International Tennis Hall of Fame
2012

Jennifer Capriati returns the offering of Italy's Francesca Schiavone during the 2003 German Open. Capriati's bid for the title ended in the semifinal to eventual runner-up Kim Clijsters.

Chris Evert

AMERICA'S SWEETHEART

Chris Evert uses her patented two-handed backhand to return a challenge from her rival Martina Navratilova during their 1988 Wimbledon semifinal match. Ultimately, Evert was unable to fend off Navratilova.

In 1970 Margaret Court was the best player on the women's tour. She was the undisputed number one who had just completed the Grand Slam (winning all four major tournaments in a single year) when she entered a small tournament in North Carolina and was shocked by a 15-year-old, losing 7–6, 7–6.

Serving notice that she'd arrived on the scene was Christine Marie Evert, and those who weren't convinced became believers the following year when she made it to the semifinals of the U.S. Open as a 16-year-old. Evert lost to eventual champion Billie Jean King, but on the way she won a thriller on national TV against Mary-Ann Eisel. Down 6–5 and 40–0 in the second set, Evert fought off six match points to win the set in a tiebreaker, and she took the final set 6–1.

The fortitude Evert showed became one of her trademarks, as did her two-handed backhand, which she developed as a youngster when she wasn't strong enough to hit with one hand. Her father, Jimmy, a former professional himself, had hoped she would develop a more traditional approach. But the two-hander was such a successful shot that she stuck with it, and for a generation that followed in her footsteps, Evert's signature shot became the only way.

With her powerful backhand and accurate groundstrokes from the baseline, shots and victories became automatic. Evert was a fiery competitor who hated losing, but she was always gracious with fellow players and the media.

The one player who kept Evert from running away with all the records was Martina Navratilova, a contrasting character and a fierce but friendly rival. Their careers ended with identical major singles titles of 18, behind only Court, Steffi Graf and Helen Wills Moody.

But Evert has them all beaten with the longest streak of majors, winning at least one for 13 consecutive years from 1974 to 1986. Her last of that epic run, at the age of 33, was a three-set upset of Navratilova at the French Open, when the younger Navratilova was at the peak of her powers and Evert was in the twilight of her career. Early in their rivalry Evert had dominated Navratilova, but as the years passed Navratilova won more often. The pair's final head-to-head record of 43-37 is in Navratilova's favor.

Evert performed particularly well on the clay courts of the French Open, given that she had cut her teeth on clay in Fort Lauderdale, Florida, where she was born in 1954. Evert enjoyed so much success at the French Open that she holds the women's record of seven French Open titles. And until 2013 when Rafael Nadal won his eighth title, Evert was the all-time French Open winner. On clay, she recorded 125 straight victories from 1973 through 1979.

But Evert proved that her game could also work on hard courts and grass. It is true that she won her first three U.S. Open titles on clay—the only three years the tournament was played on the surface—but she won three more once the tournament moved to the hard courts of Flushing Meadows. She was also Wimbledon champion three times and twice won the Australian Open, which was played on grass courts at the time.

Evert was the first player to win more than 1,000 matches and 150 tournaments, and she was the third after Court and King to win 100 matches in a season, with 103 wins and seven losses in 1974, the year she set an open-era record for men and women with 55 straight victories.

It was also the year that America's tennis sweethearts were sweet on each other, with Evert and Jimmy Connors dating and both winning their first Wimbledon singles titles. They were the king

Chris Evert is seen in action on clay in 1974, one of her 125 straight victories on the surface from 1973 through 1979.

"Looking back, I'd rather be in love any day, but that's twice love cost me Wimbledon. I just wish I had been a little tougher." –Chris Evert

and queen of the court, and it brought tennis to the tabloids.

Evert was only 19 when the two got engaged, but it was a tumultuous affair and tennis' golden couple didn't last. Connors spoke bitterly about it in his 2013 memoirs, making headlines almost 40 years after the fact by accusing Evert of having an abortion without telling him.

Soon after her relationship with Connors ended she met

Christ Evert hoists the Venus Rosewater Dish after defeating Olga Morozova, 6–0, 6–4, for the 1974 Wimbledon crown. It was her second career major title, and her second of the year.

English player John Lloyd, and in 1979 she became Chris Evert Lloyd.

Her relationship with John started to crumble in 1986, and Evert needed a break. By that time she and Navratilova

had become close, and Navratilova invited Evert to Aspen for Christmas, where she met Olympic skier Andy Mills.

Evert's divorce became final in 1987, and later that year she wed Mills. Their marriage lasted 18 years and they had three children together, but it came to an end and put her back in the gossip columns when she left Mills for his friend, Australian golf legend Greg Norman. Evert and Norman married in 2008 and divorced in 2009.

Evert admits that her emotions got the better of her during her career, with relationship problems costing her matches and tournaments.

"Looking back, I'd rather be in love any day, but that's twice love cost me Wimbledon. I just wish I had been a little tougher."

Evert's last major was the 1989 U.S. Open. It was her 19th appearance at the U.S. championship tournament, and she beat Monica Seles to advance to the quarterfinals. It was her 101st match there, both of which set records.

Having accomplished everything she could in the game of tennis and wanting to start a family with Mills, Evert's decision to retire was easy. But even though she was at peace with her decision, she did have a request before her final U.S. Open: "Don't remind me it's the last one. I hate any tone of finality. I've never had to deal with endings. Even winning the tournament won't necessarily make the ending happy. Giving up tennis will leave a void in my life forever."

Zina Garrison eliminated Evert in the quarterfinals, and after the victory Garrison broke down in tears and apologized for ending the legend's career.

Before 1989 ended and Evert officially retired, she played in the Federation Cup one last time, winning all five of her singles matches en route to an American victory. At the end of her career she'd won 90 percent of her matches, a ridiculous winning percentage that tops all players, male or female.

In 1991 Evert had the first of her three sons, Alexander. Nicholas followed three years later in 1994, and Colton came in 1996. She also stayed active in tennis, starting a tennis academy in Boca Raton, Florida; publishing a tennis magazine; running a pro–am tournament to combat drug abuse and child neglect in Florida; and commentating for ESPN at the four Grand Slam tournaments.

"For those first 10 years every morning felt like vacation," said Evert in 2006 of her life after tennis. "I hadn't realized how much pressure had built up inside me. I got my life back."

CAREER HIGHLIGHTS

Australian Open
Singles champion 1982, 1984

French Open
Singles champion 1974–75, 1979–80, 1983, 1985–86
Doubles champion 1974–75

Wimbledon
Singles champion 1974, 1976, 1981
Doubles champion 1976

U.S. Open
Singles champion 1975–78, 1980, 1982

Wightman Cup Team Member
1971–73, 1975–82, 1984–85

Federation Cup Team Member
1977–82, 1986–87, 1989

International Tennis Hall of Fame
1995

Chris Evert whips a two-handed backhand return at the 1986 French Open. Evert would win the event, marking her seventh and final French title, by defeating longtime foil Martina Navratilova, 2–6, 6–3, 6–3.

Evonne Goolagong

"SUNSHINE SUPERGIRL"

Evonne Goolagong makes a return to Chris Evert during the final match of the 1978 Virginia Slims Boston tournament. Goolagong defeated Evert 4–6, 6–1, 6–4.

Decades before the Williams sisters came out of the wrong side of Los Angeles and changed the lily-white tennis establishment, Evonne Fay Goolagong was an equally unlikely star with even fewer advantages.

A Wiradjuri (indigenous Australian), Goolagong was born in 1951 and grew up in the country 265 miles west of Sydney, Australia, in the small town of Barellan, New South Wales. One of eight children in the only Aboriginal family in the community, she excelled at rugby, cricket and soccer when she wasn't climbing silos, swimming in irrigation canals or running from any cars she and her siblings didn't recognize.

The latter was a game to them but also a way to keep the family together. Until 1971 the Australian government forcibly removed what they considered half-caste Aboriginal children from their families and put them in camps to re-educate them and integrate them into white society.

To say Goolagong's beginnings were humble would be an understatement. Her father, Kenny, a sheep shearer, carved her first racket out of a wooden fruit crate, and her mother, Linda, made her a tennis dress from a sheet.

"She never cared for dolls. All she wanted to play with was an old tennis ball. It was her constant companion," said Linda. "She would hold it in her hand and squeeze it all day long. Later she would bounce it and catch it and hit it with a broomstick. She was never without it."

The Goolagong home, an abandoned newspaper office, was located near the Barellan War Memorial Tennis Club, where Bill Kurtzman saw Evonne watching through the fence. He invited her in to play, and it didn't take long to recognize a natural talent with speed and reflexes.

Kurtzman took Goolagong and her parents to her first tournament in nearby Narrandera, but when they arrived they realized it wasn't a children's tournament as Kurtzman had thought. Ten-year-old Evonne entered with the adults anyway and won the women's singles.

Word got out to renowned coach Vic Edwards, and he saw Goolagong's burgeoning game firsthand after the townspeople of Barellan pooled their money to send her to his tennis camp in Sydney. At age 13 Goolagong moved to Sydney to live with Edwards and his family.

"We left everything to Mr. Edwards," said her father. "We know that whatever he decides will be in Evonne's best interests."

Five years later, when Goolagong was 18, it was decided that she would make her major debut. Playing against professionals, Edwards' star pupil was ousted in the first round of the 1970 edition of Wimbledon.

But Goolagong and Edwards kept working, and on February 1, 1971, she gave notice she had arrived by beating her idol, Australian legend Margaret Court, at the Victorian Championships in Melbourne. Later that year the whole tennis world knew her name.

After joining forces to help Australia beat Great Britain to win the 1971 Federation Cup, Goolagong lost a hard-fought match to Court (2–6, 7–6, 7–5) in the Australian Open final. The win was Court's sixth consecutive major title. The pair tangled shortly after at the South African Open, and while Court again got the better of Goolagong, the up-and-coming star was still the center of attention. Her participation at the South African Open marked the first time a non-white had competed during apartheid.

Goolagong went on to win the 1971 French Open at age 19, beating another Aussie, Helen Gourlay, 6–3, 7–5 in the final. Goolagong was the first player since Althea Gibson in 1956

Evonne Goolagong at the 1979 U.S. Open. The U.S. Open was the only major Goolagong failed to capture, finishing as runner-up for four consecutive years, from 1973 to 1976.

"When I was 19, I didn't appreciate it. But in '80, I had a child and nobody expected much. That was amazingly sweet." —Evonne Goolagong

to win the French championship on her maiden trip there.

A month later Goolagong and the top-ranked Court met in the Wimbledon final after the youngster downed second seed Billie Jean King 6–4, 6–4 in the semifinal. Wearing a dress specially made for her by tennis designer Ted Tinling, which he sent with a good luck message sewn in, Goolagong won 6–4, 6–1 to win the title on her second appearance at the All England Club. With her second major title of the year, Goolagong earned the number one ranking at the end of the season.

Evonne Goolagong makes a running forehand return to Patti Hogan at Wimbledon in 1973. Goolagong advanced all the way to the semifinal, losing to eventual champion Billie Jean King.

From 1971 to 1976 Goolagong went to the finals in 16 of the 24 Grand Slam singles tournaments, winning five of them, and she won the Australian Open for four consecutive years starting in 1974. Her game was based on finesse and angles, not on power.

"She was such a pretty player," according to Martina Navratilova. "She didn't serve-and-volley; she would sort of saunter-and-volley."

In 1975 Goolagong married English tennis pro Roger Cawley, and in 1977 she gave birth to daughter Kelly. During her pregnancy she kept up a rigorous fitness regimen and

gained just 14 pounds, returning five pounds lighter than her previous playing weight. And in 1980 she became the second mother to win a major in the open era, beating friendly rival Chris Evert to earn her second Wimbledon title.

"When I was 19, I didn't appreciate it. But in '80, I had a child and nobody expected much. That was amazingly sweet."

In total Goolagong won seven major singles titles and six doubles crowns, but unlike Venus and Serena, Goolagong's rise to the top wasn't fueled by slights and marginalization. She was a gentle soul with a smile as sweet as her backhand, but media in her native Australia suggested her demeanor and occasional lapses in concentration cost her a few major titles.

Goolagong lost four consecutive U.S. Open finals from 1973 to 1976, once each to Court and King and twice to Evert, preventing her from capturing the one major that eluded her and completing a career Grand Slam. But her graceful play and gracious manner made her a favorite of fans and fellow players alike, with the English press dubbing her "Sunshine Supergirl."

She could bare her teeth though. Early in her career she was sensitive to questions about her roots, suggesting to one member of the media that she would "point the bone at him" if he asked her any more questions about it. In Aboriginal culture, to point the bone at someone is an omen of death.

Goolagong did grow to embrace and celebrate her heritage. After retiring in 1983, she lived in South Carolina and Florida, but after attending her mother's funeral in 1991 she decided Australia was where she belonged, and she moved back in 1992.

Since returning, Goolagong has held government posts in Aboriginal affairs, and she now runs the Tennis Australia Evonne Goolagong Cawley Getting Started Program and the Goolagong state and national development camps. With her two endeavors she is paying forward what Kurtzman and Edwards gave her and is fostering the development of Aboriginal youth.

"I just have such a passion for this. It's not political. It's about educating, about sharing my experiences with my people. And the best part is, I'm learning so much from them too."

In 2009 Barellan celebrated its centenary with "the Big Tennis Racquet," an Evonne Goolagong signature Dunlop statue, as a tribute to the community's favorite daughter, who still considers Barellan home. It's where she was married and where her parents were laid to rest. The kid with the oversized talent and smile now has a monument to match.

"They've done such a great job on the racquet. And don't forget the ball. It's a bloody big ball."

CAREER HIGHLIGHTS

Australian Open	Wimbledon
Singles champion 1974–77	Singles champion 1971, 1980
Doubles champion 1971, 1974–77	Doubles champion 1974
	Associated Press Female Athlete of the Year
French Open	1971
Singles champion 1971	
Mixed doubles champion 1972	**International Tennis Hall of Fame**
Federation Cup Team Member	1988
1971–76, 1982	

Australia's Evonne Goolagong in action at Wimbledon in 1971. Goolagong defeated compatriot and childhood hero Margaret Court, 6–4, 6–1, in the final to claim her second major title.

Steffi Graf

GRAND SLAM GODDESS

Steffi Graf serves at the 1986 U.S. Open. The German star lost in the semifinal to eventual champion Martina Navratilova. She'd take her first of five American titles two years later in 1988.

Owner of "the Fraulein Forehand," one of the most devastating and effective strokes in history, Steffi Graf dominated tennis in the 1980s and 1990s the way few players ever have.

Born in Bruhl, Germany, in 1969, Stephanie Maria was raised by her father, Peter, to be a champion. He taught her a forehand more powerful than that of most men, and her quickness and footwork were a genetic blessing she sharpened through countless hours spent on the court.

Tall, slim, powerful and focused, by 1982 Graf was already a professional at the age of 13, losing her only pro match that year to Tracy Austin. When she was 16 she beat Chris Evert—the woman with the best winning percentage in history—in the 1986 Family Circle Cup final for her first tournament victory.

Just two years later the confluence of talent and timing led to possibly the greatest year for one player in tennis history.

Graf's record in 1988 was 73-3, and she won 11 of the 14 tournaments she entered, including all four of the majors. The season ended in Seoul, where tennis was being contested at the Olympics for the first time since 1924. Graf beat

Argentina's Gabriela Sabatini 6–3, 6–3 to cap the year with a gold medal.

"The Golden Grand Slam" was a historic first, and Graf was only the third woman and fifth person to win a Grand Slam—holding all four majors in a calendar year.

Yet somehow her 1989 campaign might've been more impressive. Graf won 14 of 16 tournaments and 86 matches. One of her only two losses that year was against Arantxa Sanchez Vicario in the French Open final, which prevented her from becoming the first person to win two consecutive Grand Slams.

But winning Olympic gold and seven of eight majors in a culture increasingly enamored with celebrity meant more exposure than the private Graf was comfortable with. She retreated from the media and the public eye whenever possible, relishing the anonymity New York City offered at her Manhattan condo and the respect the people of her hometown gave her.

It also meant serious earning power, and Peter Graf saw his daughter as a commodity and cash machine. Peter was arrested for fraud and tax evasion in 1995 and imprisoned in 1997. Steffi remained steadfastly loyal to him despite whispers on tour and from tabloids about his addiction and infidelity, as well as her presumed complicity in the financial crimes.

Steffi was cleared of any knowledge or wrongdoing, but she was facing a low point in her career, and it was the first time she wouldn't be able to turn to her father for support.

She persevered with quiet dignity and determination, the same qualities that got her through previous hardships. There was the calf injury in 1995 that kept her from defending her Australian Open title and foot surgery that prevented her from entering the tournament in 1996. She also dealt with back and knee problems that meant she couldn't represent Germany at the Atlanta Olympics in 1996. But all those disappointments paled in comparison to what had happened in 1993, the year a deranged fan stabbed the only player who could stop Graf.

Graf had won her first major title a day before she turned 18, beating Martina Navratilova 6–4, 4–6, 8–6 in the 1987 French Open final. The victory helped her knock Navratilova from her perch as world number one, a position Graf held for a record 186 consecutive weeks until Monica Seles took it in 1991.

Seles had already stopped Graf's 66-match winning streak, the second-longest in history, in 1990 and beat her in a dra-

Stefi Graf, fresh off her first major victory at the 1987 French Open and a final appearance in Wimbledon, plays at the 1987 U.S. Open. She advanced to the final but lost to Martina Navratilova, to whom she also lost Wimbledon.

"There is so much joy in being on the court and winning when it is so much more difficult because of all the circumstances." – Steffi Graf

matic Australian Open final in 1993. The tennis world was enjoying the clash of two of history's best as they struggled for supremacy.

But dangerously obsessed with Graf and upset that she had lost her number one ranking, Guenther Parche shocked the tennis world three months later when he leaped from the stands at a tour-

Steffi Graf (second from left) celebrates her Olympic gold medal in women's singles competition. By the conclusion of the year, Graf would become the only player, male or female, to win an Olympic gold medal and all four major tournaments in one calendar year.

nament in Hamburg and stabbed 19-year-old Seles in the back. The attack happened during a changeover, and the knife narrowly missed Seles' spine and lung.

Graf regained top spot five weeks after the disturbing attack and won the next four Grand Slam tournaments, but the guilt she felt over the stabbing, which was carried out ostensibly in her honor, took a heavy emotional toll. It also opened up debate about the ranking system and whether Seles' spot should have been frozen.

After being out of the game for more than two years, Seles made it to the final of the 1995 U.S. Open, where she faced Graf. It was a welcome reprise of their rivalry and an intense and emotional match that Graf won 7–6 (8–6), 0–6, 6–3.

After the match Graf fled the press conference in tears. The trials she faced had exposed a vulnerable side of her, which she had previously kept hidden, that the public embraced. Graf also found an emotional strength she didn't know she had.

"There is so much joy in being on the court and winning when it is so much more difficult because of all the circumstances," said Graf in 1996. "I treasure these moments so much more than I ever did. When you're 17, you win and you win and you just accept it. Winning [then] was so much more natural than it is now. Maybe my heart wasn't so much in it as it is today. It's nicer to have these feelings. This joy!"

The tennis court was always Graf's refuge, and the surface was irrelevant to her. She halted Navratilova's run of six consecutive Wimbledon titles and 47 straight victories by beating her in the 1988 final. And she beat clay-court specialist Sanchez Vicario in the French Open final in 1996. Graf is the only player, male or female, to win each major at least four times.

Her last major title was the 1999 French Open over 18-year-old Martina Hingis, just before she turned 30. Later that summer she lost to Lindsay Davenport at Wimbledon in what was her 31st major final. She decided to retire soon after.

By the end of her career Graf had earned 107 singles titles and just under $22 million in prize money. Her 22 major singles titles—seven Wimbledon, six French, five U.S. and four Australian—are second all-time to Margaret Court's 24.

And though he won a measly eight majors during his tennis career, Graf married Andre Agassi in 2001. Together they have potentially the greatest mixed doubles pair of the future in son Jaden and daughter Jaz.

Jaden and Jaz have some mighty big tennis shoes to fill if they wish to follow in their parents' footsteps, but Graf won't push her children into tennis. And when games are played on the backyard court at their home in Las Vegas, she'll be much gentler on them than on the countless opponents she overwhelmed with that dreaded forehand.

CAREER HIGHLIGHTS

Australian Open
Singles champion 1988–90, 1994

French Open
Singles champion 1987–88, 1993, 1995–96, 1999

Wimbledon
Singles champion 1988–89, 1991–93, 1995–96
Doubles champion 1988

U.S. Open
Singles champion 1988–89, 1993, 1995–96

Olympics
Gold medalist in women's singles 1988
Bronze medalist in women's doubles 1988
Silver medalist in women's singles 1992

Federation Cup Team Member
1986–87, 1989, 1991–93

Fed Cup Team Member
1996

International Tennis Hall of Fame
2004

Steffi Graf returns the ball to Marcella Mesker during the second round of the 1986 French Open. Graf advanced to the quarterfinal before being ousted by Hana Mandlikova.

Billie Jean King

EQUAL TO THE TASK

Billie Jean King is seen at Wimbledon in 1974. King, a favorite at the tournament, was ousted in the quarterfinals after having won the previous two years. She rebounded to win again in 1975.

Looking around the local tennis courts of Long Beach, California, Billie Jean King noticed that not only were all the clothes white, but so were the faces. Once she read the autobiography of Althea Gibson, the first woman of color granted entry into a major tennis competition (and the first to win a major), an activist was born.

Born in 1943, Billie was named after her father, Bill, a firefighter and renowned sportsman, and theirs was a family of athletes. Her brother Randy went on to pitch for the San Francisco Giants, and by the time she was 11 she knew that tennis was her future.

By 1960 King was ranked fourth in the United States, and in 1961 she teamed with fellow 18-year-old Karen Hantze to shock the tennis world as the pair won the Wimbledon women's doubles title, beating Australians Margaret Court, the all-time leader in major titles, and Jan Lehane in the final.

Over the course of her career, King would make the home of tennis tradition and all-white attire hers. She won a total of 20 Wimbledon championships in her career—six singles, 10 doubles and four mixed doubles—to set a tournament record.

She won her 20 championships in 19 tournament appearances, taking all three titles—the singles, doubles and mixed doubles—at Wimbledon in 1967 and again in 1973. (She also achieved this rare feat at the U.S. Championships in 1967.)

King paired with Martina Navratilova to win her 20th Wimbledon crown in 1979, and the friends were also partners for King's final major victory at the 1980 U.S. Open. In 2003 46-year-old Navratilova paired with India's Leander Paes to tie King's Wimbledon wins record.

Although she was most successful on the doubles court, King was also a formidable singles player. Her most memorable Wimbledon match may have been her loss to Court in the 1970 singles final, a record 46-game match that ended 14–12, 11–9.

Of her 39 major victories, third in history among women behind Court and Navratilova, 12 were in singles play—she won six Wimbledon titles, four U.S. titles and one each at the Australian and French, giving her the career Grand Slam.

In 1971 King became the first woman to win more than $100,000, earning it with 38 titles and 192 total match victories, but she was well aware that her prize money was far below that of the men. Adding insult, the men were planning to launch a players' association without the women.

King decided she would start her own tour, which got her suspended by the U.S. National Lawn Tennis Association, costing her entry into Wimbledon and the U.S. Open. Undaunted, she and eight other women went their own way and eventually gathered 62 players to form the Women's Tennis Association.

At the same time, she was lobbying politicians for equal opportunities for female athletes, leading to what became Title IX. Passed in 1972, Title IX states that "no person in the United States shall, on the basis of sex, be excluded from participation in, be denied the benefits of, or be subjected to discrimination under any education program or activity receiving federal financial assistance."

Since Title IX, female participation in sports at the collegiate level has gone up more than 600 percent, and now tennis is one of the few professional sports in which women earn the same amount as men.

"It's not about the money, it's about the message we send," said King. "We are sending the equality message out that this is the right thing to do. Yes, the men are better than us in some ways. Yes,

Billie Jean King displays the Venus Rosewater Dish after dismissing Chris Evert in the 1973 Wimbledon final. The win marked King's fourth Wimbledon crown.

"We are sending the equality message out that this is the right thing to do ... Don't you want to share in this world? I do."
–Billie Jean King

we're better in some ways. It doesn't matter. Don't you want to share in this world? I do."

King had something to say about equality in 1973 in her most famous match, an exhibition against 55-year-old former Wimbledon champion and proud chauvinist Bobby Riggs dubbed "the Battle of the Sexes."

Billie Jean King pursues a shot from 16-year-old Chris Evert during their semifinal match at the 1971 U.S. Open. King won, 6–3, 6–2, and went on to defeat Rosemary Casals to claim her first U.S. Open and second American championship.

Riggs, a man who used to bet on himself when he played, wanted to make some money and a statement about gender. Calling King "the sex leader of the revolutionary pack," Riggs challenged King to a match. She declined, and Riggs approached several top female players. Margaret Court agreed to play Riggs, and after he beat her easily in what was known as "the Mother's Day Massacre," King relented.

Watched by a record crowd of more than 30,000 at Houston's glitzy new Astrodome and more than a hundred million more on TV, a loss by King to Riggs would have done untold damage to Title IX, the fledgling women's tour and players' association, and the momentum of the women's movement.

King was carried to the court by four shirtless men, while Riggs was carried by his "bosom buddies." They exchanged gifts at center court before the match began—he gave King a lollipop and she gave him a piglet. She then beat him 6–4, 6–3, 6–3.

By that time King had been secretly seeing a woman, but it wasn't until 1981, the same year Martina Navratilova came out, that it became public after a palimony suit was filed by her former partner. Now King fights equally as hard for LGBT equality as she did for feminism, calling it the civil rights movement of the 21st century.

An icon off the court and a mentor on it, King partnered with 13-year-old prodigy Jennifer Capriati to win a match in 1990 at the age of 46, and she coached Lindsay Davenport, Monica Seles and Venus and Serena Williams to Olympic medals.

In 2006 the United States Tennis Association opened the newly renamed Billie Jean King National Tennis Center, and in 2009 she was awarded the Presidential Medal of Freedom.

The WTA celebrated its 40th anniversary in 2013 with the "40 Love" ad campaign. The ad campaign featured current stars and the retired players who led the way, with the tagline "Forty years of breaking barriers. Thank you for inspiring us."

And it's not just tennis that owes King a debt of gratitude. Every day, in every part of the United States, a girl is given a chance to pursue her love of sports, regardless of her background and socioeconomic status, thanks to Billie Jean King.

That's just one reason why Frank Deford wrote in *Sports Illustrated* in 1975 that it's "very likely Billie Jean Moffitt King will go down in history as the most significant athlete of this century."

CAREER HIGHLIGHTS

Australian Championships
Singles champion 1968
Mixed doubles champion 1968

French Championships
Mixed doubles champion 1967

French Open
Singles champion 1972
Doubles champion 1972
Mixed doubles champion 1970

Wimbledon
Singles champion 1966–68, 1972–73, 1975
Doubles champion 1961–62, 1965, 1967–68, 1970–73, 1979
Mixed doubles champion 1967, 1971, 1973–74

U.S. Championships
Singles champion 1967
Doubles champion 1964, 1967
Mixed doubles champion 1967

U.S. Open
Singles champion 1971–72, 1974
Doubles champion 1974, 1978, 1980
Mixed doubles champion 1971, 1973, 1976

Wightman Cup Team Member
1961–67, 1970, 1977–78

Federation Cup Team Member
1963–67, 1976–78

International Tennis Hall of Fame
1987

Defending champion Billie Jean King plays at Wimbledon in 1968. King advanced to the final where she repeated as champion, defeating Judy Tegart for her third consecutive championship at the All England Club.

Hana Mandlikova

CAPRICIOUSNESS OF YOUTH

Hana Mandlikova returns a strong baseline drive to Martina Navratilova at the 1985 U.S. Open. Mandlikova defeated Navratilova to win the American championship, her third of four major singles titles.

Born in 1962, Hana Mandlikova remembers the Soviet tanks rolling into her hometown of Prague, Czechoslovakia, when she was 6. For someone growing up under communist rule, one of the few ways to escape the country and see the world was through sports.

A tomboy and natural athlete, Mandlikova played any sport she could find growing up, usually with her older brother Vilda. She showed enormous promise in tennis, and at the age of 12 she was a ball girl for national icon Martina Navratilova.

Like many aspiring tennis players in the country, Mandlikova idolized the champion and patterned her game after Navratilova's serve-and-volley style. Very few were good enough to be allowed to leave the country, however, and even fewer went on to beat their heroine.

Mandlikova's father, Vilem Mandlik, was an 11-time national 100-meter champion who represented Czechoslovakia at the 1956 and 1960 Olympics, but leery of steroids he steered his daughter away from the track. Instead he carved her a wooden racket and let her practice against the living room wall when her mother wasn't home.

While her father's connections got her the best tennis coaching in the country, Mandlikova was driven from within, not by parental pressure. She was a prodigy with passion, which her parents and teachers indulged, often letting her skip classes to hit the court.

"I was very lucky to have my father and certain teachers who would let me practice," said Mandlikova in 1985. "I was spoiled, but in a good way, I think. But I know in some ways it makes me young for my age."

In 1978, when she was 16, Mandlikova was the best junior player in the world and was allowed to travel to tournaments in the United States. But she wasn't always in control of her emotions on the court. She had a terrific serve-and-volley game and was a relentless attacker, but she was erratic.

"Magnificent talents blown by capricious winds" is how former player and writer Ted Tinling described Mandlikova.

Early in her career she earned a reputation for being prickly and somewhat arrogant, two traits highlighted by her exit from Wimbledon in 1984. After proclaiming that she'd meet Navratilova in the final, a motivated Chris Evert beat her 6–1, 6–2 in the semifinal. Mandlikova left the court without congratulating Evert and barely acknowledged Princess Diana in the Royal Box.

The British tabloids had a field day with it, and Navratilova spoke out against her. "There will be no love lost for Hana by the other players. Hana has no respect for anyone, and she needs to start showing some."

Realizing there is a gracious way to lose and better expressions of confidence, Mandlikova apologized to Navratilova two months later at the U.S. Open.

But the young Czech was still confident and had the talent to back up her sometimes brash words. In 1985 she beat Navratilova and Evert on her way to victory at the U.S. Open, becoming the first player to dispatch both legends at the same major tournament.

And while Mandlikova won less than a third of her career matches against Navratilova (seven wins to 30 losses), she did win four of their 10 career meetings at Grand Slam tournaments, beating her idol twice at the U.S. Open and once each at Wimbledon and the Australian Open.

The win in Australia ended Navratilova's 58-match winning streak, a 7–5, 7–6 (7–2) final that earned Mandlikova the 1987 championship, her second title there and the last one played on grass at the Australian Open.

It was the second time Mandlikova ended an epic

"Magnificent talents blown by capricious winds."
– Ted Tinling

Navratilova run; in 1984 she put a stop to a 54-match streak. At an indoor tournament in 1985 she beat her in straight sets, one of which was 6–0, the first time in three years that Navratilova went love for a set.

Their most historic match, however, came during the Federation Cup in 1986, played in Prague after Navratilova defected.

Hana Mandlikova drops to her knees after upsetting Martina Navratilova, her childhood hero, 7–6 (7–3), 1–6, 7–6 (7–2) at the 1985 U.S. Open.

Reigning Australian Open champ Hana Mandlikova returns the offering of Chris Evert during the final of the 1980 U.S. Open. Evert defeated Mandlikova 5–7, 6–1, 6–1.

Mandlikova had led Czechoslovakia to three straight Federation Cups from 1983 to 1985, but with Navratilova playing for the Americans, the crowd in Prague was conflicted.

Mandlikova welcomed her graciously in both Czech and English, and at the start of the match the fans seemed to be

pulling for Navratilova. As the match wore on the sentiment swung back to Mandlikova, with the realization that the host country needed the point to retain the title.

Navratilova took the match and the Americans won the Cup, but Mandlikova may have had other things on her mind. Two days prior she had snuck away to marry Czech-Australian restaurateur Jan Sedlak in the Old Town Square. The marriage took the tennis world and local media by surprise. While she insisted it wasn't a visa card marriage, it lasted only two years, ending soon after she became an Australian citizen in 1988.

Toward the end of her career Mandlikova softened a little, becoming happier and more comfortable with her fellow players and the media. The contentious relationship she had with the media — which saw her do things like hide from reporters in the women's washroom instead of answering questions about the fine she incurred for swearing at the chair umpire during the 1987 U.S. Open — was becoming a thing of the past. And as for her old adversary, Navratilova, the pair made up. In fact, Mandlikova partnered with Navratilova to win the doubles title at the 1989 U.S. Open — Mandlikova's last major championship.

Citing burnout, injuries and the desire to have children, Mandlikova left the game in 1990 at the age of 28. In retirement she took up coaching and achieved what she couldn't as a player, guiding Jana Novotna to the Wimbledon title in 1998; Mandlikova was a finalist in 1981 and 1986.

Mandlikova was enshrined in the Tennis Hall of Fame in 1994, becoming the third-youngest player to be so honoured, after Tracy Austin and Bjorn Borg, and she achieved her dream of starting a family after becoming pregnant by a friend whose identity she chose to keep secret.

"I don't find our arrangement extraordinary. I am sure that lots of others have done the same — you simply don't hear of it. After all, this is the 21st century and women have the right to make choices."

In 2002 she gave birth to twins Elizabeth and Mark and is raising them in Boca Raton, Florida, with partner Liz Resseguie in the same upscale community as Evert, Novotna and Steffi Graf.

It was a long journey from communist Czechoslovakia, and the freedom to choose where she lives, whom she spends her life with and how to start a family was something Mandlikova could only dream about as a child.

CAREER HIGHLIGHTS	
Australian Open	**U.S. Open**
Singles champion 1980, 1987	Singles champion 1985
French Open	Doubles champion 1989
Singles champion 1981	**International Tennis Hall of Fame**
Federation Cup Team Member	1994
1978–87	

Second-year pro Hana Mandlikova plays at Wimbledon in 1979. Mandlikova made it to the fourth round before being defeated by seventh-seeded Billie Jean King.

Martina Navratilova

NO-NONSENSE PERFECTION

Martina Navratilova celebrates her first major singles victory after besting Chris Evert 2–6, 6–4, 7–5 at Wimbledon in 1978. She would win the championship at the All England Club a record nine times.

While Babe Didrikson Zaharias and Jackie Joyner-Kersee mastered multiple sports and endeared themselves to millions, neither can boast the longevity and complete dominance of one single sport the way Martina Navratilova can. A magnificent tennis player in all disciplines, it could be argued that Navratilova is the greatest female athlete of all time.

Some of Navratilova's records in the game of tennis are untouchable, and she was a natural at any game she dabbled in, but her story goes beyond sports to the impact of her beliefs on a changing world.

First the numbers: Navratilova won 355 titles in singles, doubles and mixed doubles over her professional career, earning a title at an astounding 48.6 percent of the tournaments she entered. Her career winning percentage is .877, and she holds singles records in tournaments and matches played (389 and 1,661, respectively) and tournament victories (168).

Between 1975 and 1991, Navratilova never fell below fourth in the Women's Tennis Association rankings and was at the top for seven years, including four straight from 1983 to 1986. Her tally in the majors includes 18 singles, 31 doubles and 10 mixed doubles titles, and she holds Wimbledon records for consecutive singles titles (6), overall singles titles (9), consecutive finals appearances (9), most matches (279), singles wins (119), doubles wins (80) and overall wins (243).

Navratilova also tied Billie Jean King's record with her 20th Wimbledon title in 2003 at the age of 46 when she captured the mixed doubles title with Leander Paes.

After announcing her first retirement in 1994 at the age of 37, Navratilova returned to singles competition with appearances at the 2004 French Open and Wimbledon. Her comeback was in preparation for the Athens Olympics, where she became the oldest Olympic tennis competitor in history at 48.

And Navratilova wasn't finished yet; in 2006 she paired with Bob Bryan to win the mixed doubles crown at the U.S. Open when she was less than two months shy of turning 50, 32 years after winning her first major. It was her 59th major title, and she may not be finished stalking Margaret Court's all-time record of 62.

As Navratilova said, "The ball doesn't know how old I am."

Navratilova's biggest hurdle at the majors was the U.S. Open singles, which she didn't win until her 11th tournament in 1983. She'd go on to take the title four times and win only the third triple of the open era with all three titles—singles, doubles and mixed doubles—at the 1987 tournament.

The only thing Navratilova couldn't add to her glittering resume was a singles Grand Slam, coming up one tournament short in both 1983 and 1984. In that stretch her record was a remarkable 254-6, and her only loss of the 1983 season was an upset by unseeded 17-year-old Kathleen Horvath at the French Open. That year Navratilova won 16 of the 17 tournaments she entered and posted an 86-1 record.

She did win a doubles Grand Slam in 1984 as part of one of tennis' truly great teams. She and Pam Shriver won 20 majors and 79 tournaments and had an unmatched streak of 109 victories between 1983 and 1985. Individually, Navratilova set the career mark for doubles titles (177) and matches won (747).

Navratilova's distinguished career spanned tennis generations, from early matches against Margaret Court and Billie Jean King; through long-time foil and friend Chris Evert, over whom she holds a 43-37 edge in head-to-head competition; and into the primes of Steffi Graf, Monica Seles and Jennifer Capriati.

It also saw a sea change in her life and in the Western world.

"I've always had this outrage against being told how to live, what to say, how to act, what to do, when to do it."
—Martina Navratilova

Martina Navratilova reacts after winning a point against Zina Garrison during their 1990 Wimbledon final. Navratilova would ultimately win, earning her ninth Venus Rosewater Dish. It was her last major singles championship.

Born in Prague in 1956 in what was then communist Czechoslovakia, Navratilova was coached by her mother and won the national title as a 16-year-old. She turned professional when she was 17, and at 18 she defected at the 1975 U.S. Open when she heard that the government planned to limit her travel for fear she was becoming too Western.

With her machine-like efficiency and icy demeanor on the court, the 5-foot-7, 140-pound Navratilova fit the stereotype of the Eastern Bloc athlete, but she would come to embrace a new culture and homeland.

After leading Czechoslovakia to a Federation Cup title in 1975, Navratilova returned to Prague in 1986 as an American citizen to play for her new country. In a match against rising Czech star Hana Mandlikova, Navratilova was welcomed warmly by the crowd. But soon after, the audi-

Martina Navratilova (left) and Billie Jean King — both prodigious doubles players — celebrate their 1979 Wimbledon doubles championship. The win marked King's 20th Wimbledon title among all disciplines. Navratilova matched King in 2003.

ence's support swung to the native daughter playing for the host country. At the end of the second set—which Navratilova won 6–1 to take the match and help the Americans win the Cup—the locals, disappointed at the country's loss, still showed their appreciation for Navratilova. While the Czechoslovakian prime minister and party officials beat a hasty retreat afterward, the fans recognized the excellence of the prodigal daughter who had been theirs but was lost because of politics.

CAREER HIGHLIGHTS

Australian Open
Singles champion 1981, 1983, 1985
Doubles champion 1980, 1982–85, 1987–89
Mixed doubles champion 2003

French Open
Singles champion 1982, 1984
Doubles champion 1975, 1982, 1984–88
Mixed doubles champion 1974, 1985

Wimbledon
Singles champion 1978–79, 1982–87, 1990
Doubles champion 1976, 1979, 1981–84, 1986
Mixed doubles champion 1985, 1993, 1995, 2003

U.S. Open
Singles champion 1983–84, 1986–87
Doubles champion 1977–78, 1980, 1983–84, 1986–87, 1989–90
Mixed doubles champion 1985, 1987, 2006

Wightman Cup Team Member 1983

Federation Cup Team Member 1975, 1982, 1986, 1989

Fed Cup Team Member 1995, 2003–04

International Tennis Hall of Fame 2000

As Navratilova later said in her autobiography: "I honestly believe I was born to be an American. With all due respect to my homeland, things never really felt right until the day I got off the plane in Florida."

Navratilova's new patriotism wasn't limited to the court. She cheered for the Dallas Cowboys and helped raise money to restore the Statue of Liberty. She also discovered fast food and her weight ballooned, but after coming under the tutelage of former professional basketball star Nancy Lieberman, she became a paragon of fitness and the first female player with proudly defined muscles. At the same time she hired Renee Richards as her coach to sharpen her serve-and-volley game. A left-hander with a one-handed backhand, Navratilova was aggressive and frequently played at the net.

And communism wasn't the only belief system Navratilova fought. She was an early advocate of animal rights and environmental awareness, and she refused to hide her homosexuality when it made the mainstream uncomfortable and cost her endorsements. In 1981, nine days after becoming a U.S. citizen, she came out, against the wishes of the WTA.

"I've always had this outrage against being told how to live, what to say, how to act, what to do, when to do it," explained Navratilova.

While the press wrote lurid headlines and compared her unfavorably with the more outwardly feminine Evert, Navratilova said she "felt free," which led to the most successful period of her career. In the season after she revealed her secret, she became the first female athlete to win over $1 million in prize money in a year.

As one of the world's first openly gay athletes, Navratilova spent her career battling prejudice and vocally supporting the LGBT community. In retirement she continues to be a high-profile advocate, fighting for equal rights and same-sex marriage in her adopted country.

Only in 2013 did gay men slowly start to emerge in North American team sports. One of the first to do so was NBA player Jason Collins, who called Navratilova his role model and inspiration, and she was one of the first to get in touch with him after he made the announcement.

There are still no openly gay tennis players on the men's tour more than 30 years after Navratilova loudly and proudly declared her sexuality and dared anyone to make it an issue. Those opponents, like the ones she faced on the tennis court, were quickly vanquished.

A male sportswriter once asked, "Martina, are you still a lesbian?"

Her response? "Are you still the alternative?"

Martina Navratilova at the 1986 French Open. After beating Chris Evert for the 1984 French crown, Evert bested Navratilova for back-to-back championships in 1985 and 1986. Of Navratilova's 18 major singles titles, only two came at the French Open.

Arantxa Sanchez Vicario

V FOR VICTORY

Arantxa Sanchez Vicario eyes her volley to Monica Seles in the final of the 1998 French Open. Sanchez Vicario defeated Seles 7–6 (7–5), 0–6, 6–2 for her third French crown.

Born in Madrid in 1971, Aranzazu "Arantxa" Sanchez moved to Barcelona with her family when she was 2. Living near the prestigious Real Club de Tenis, each of the four Sanchez children took up the game. Her sister Marisa played at Pepperdine University, and both older brothers, Emilio and Javier, played on the professional tour and on Spain's Davis Cup team.

The youngest of the brood, Arantxa was given a racket to keep her occupied while her older siblings practiced.

"Arantxa never played with dolls," says Emilio. "Slazenger was her closest friend."

The friendship was a fruitful one, and the racket never left her side: she took it to bed with her, it sat next to her at dinner and every spare moment was spent on the clay courts at the Real Club de Tenis, playing against the wall if she couldn't find an opponent. With Emilio coaching her, Sanchez was already Spain's top-ranked female player by age 13, and she turned professional before her 14th birthday.

In 1988, at the age of 16, Arantxa added her mother's maiden name of Vicario so both sides of the family could see their name in the paper, which they did when she beat seven-time winner Chris Evert at the French Open that year in the third round.

At the 1989 edition of the tournament, Sanchez Vicario made it to the final as the seventh seed. Few gave the young player a shot to win the French Open. Across the net was Steffi Graf, winner of five straight majors, reigning Olympic gold medalist and winner of 117 of her previous 121 matches. Sanchez Vicario had won only two tournaments in her career and had been soundly beaten by Graf in their three previous meetings.

But Sanchez Vicario had youthful confidence and exuberance and was not easily intimidated. "Everybody else lose to Steffi in their head before they step on court. I say, 'I beat her. It is possible, no?' They say, 'Arantxa, you crazy.' I say, 'No, it is all in the mentality. I come to play her, not pray to her.'"

And she did. Sanchez Vicario played to Graf's vaunted forehand, which seemed counterintuitive, but it opened up her weaker backhand. She also used her boundless energy to run down Graf's shots, winning the first set in a tiebreaker before losing the second and falling behind 5–3 in the third. With Graf serving for the match, Sanchez Vicario won 16 of the last 19 points to take the third set 7–5 and become the first Spanish woman to win a major and the youngest French Open champion.

Sanchez Vicario won the French Open two more times, in 1994 over Mary Pierce and in 1998 over Monica Seles.

Adding a chapter to their rivalry with another grueling battle of wills, Sanchez Vicario put an end to Graf's 36-match winning streak in 1994 at a tournament in Graf's native Germany, beating her 4–6, 7–6 (7–3), 7–6 (8–6) in the final. Graf had lost only two sets the entire year up to that point.

"I'm disappointed beyond measure at the way I lost the match," an emotional Graf said afterward. "I just can't allow myself to give away a match like that."

Sanchez Vicario rubbed salt in the wounds by beating Graf in three sets in the 1994 U.S. Open final. The victory vaulted Sanchez Vicario to a number one world ranking in 1995.

Graf got her revenge by preventing Sanchez Vicario from adding a Wimbledon title to her career resume by beating her in both the 1995 and 1996 finals. In 1995 the 11th game of the third set took 20 minutes to play and had 13 deuces, with Sanchez Vicario losing the last 6 points and the match 4–6, 6–1, 7–5.

It was the same result for the two combatants in the French Open final the same two years, with Sanchez Vicario serving

Arantxa Sanchez Vicario plays in the opening rounds of the 1992 U.S. Open. Sanchez Vicario, in her fourth U.S. Open appearance, made it all the way to the final before being ousted by defending champion Monica Seles.

"Arantxa never played with dolls. Slazenger was her closest friend."
– Emilio Sanchez

for the championship in 1996 at 5–4 and 7–6 before losing 6–3, 6–7 (4–7), 10–8 in a match that took more than three hours to play.

Sanchez Vicario also lost in the final of the Australian Open in 1994 and 1995 (the first to Graf, 6–0, 6–2, and the second to Pierce, 6–3, 6–2). Even with the loss, Sanchez Vicario claimed something; she's one of only 14 women to make the final of all four majors.

The Spanish team of Conchita Martinez (left) and Arantxa Sanchez Vicario receive their Olympic bronze medals in women's doubles at the 1996 Atlanta Olympics.

Sanchez Vicario won 29 singles titles, including her four Grand Slam tournament wins, as well as six major victories in doubles and four in mixed doubles. But some of her best tennis wasn't at the big four tournaments.

A Catalan who never failed to represent Spain, Sanchez Vicario played in the Federation Cup for 16 years, winning it all with Conchita Martinez five times to make them the most successful duo in tournament history.

On her own Sanchez Vicario holds the Federation Cup records for years played, series (58), total matches (100), wins (72) and singles wins (50).

Sanchez Vicario also participated in five Olympic Games. At the 1992 Olympics in her hometown, she won the bronze medal in the women's singles and silver in doubles with Martinez. Four years later in Atlanta she flipped it, taking bronze with Martinez and silver in singles after losing the final to Lindsay Davenport. Her four Olympic tennis medals are second all time to the five won by Kitty McKane of Great Britain in the 1920s.

Outwardly carefree and expressive on the court, Sanchez Vicario's golden smile and jewelry hid a fire inside. Even her nickname "Rabbit"—given to her by her coach for her energy and the ball holder she wore around her waist that looked like a bunny tail—didn't hint at the passion she played with.

A lover of the game, Sanchez Vicario never tired of practicing and often led the tour in matches played because she loved doubles, winning 67 titles in her career. But she knew when to refocus her energy.

"The time has come for me to think about myself," she said at the press conference in Barcelona in 2002 to announce her retirement at the age of 30, attended by the two dogs she was given as gifts when she won her first French Open. "It hasn't been an easy decision, but I believe the moment has arrived for me to dedicate my time to my personal life."

It turned out to be a tumultuous retirement. The Sanchez Vicarios were inseparable on tour—mother Marisa cleaned clothes and cooked meals at tournaments—but they didn't remain close. In 2012 Arantxa published a book that alleged several members of the family, including her mother, cost her millions of dollars in career earnings through mismanagement.

Sanchez Vicario says her parents "made me suffer a lot" and opposed her 2008 marriage. Now estranged from her family, she has her own with husband Jose Santacana and two children—Arantxa and Leo.

Sanchez Vicario played her last serious tennis at the 2004 Athens Olympics, and in 2007 she became the first Spanish woman named to the Tennis Hall of Fame. She has also returned to the scene of some of her proudest moments, being named captain of Spain's Fed Cup team in 2011.

CAREER HIGHLIGHTS

Australian Open
Doubles champion 1992, 1995–96
Mixed doubles champion 1993

French Open
Singles champion 1989, 1994, 1998
Mixed doubles champion 1990, 1992

Wimbledon
Doubles champion 1995

U.S. Open
Singles champion 1994
Doubles champion 1993–94
Mixed doubles champion 2000

Olympics
Bronze medalist in women's singles 1992
Silver medalist in women's doubles 1992
Silver medalist in women's singles 1996
Bronze medalist in women's doubles 1996

Federation Cup Team Member
1986–94

Fed Cup Team Member
96–98, 2000–02

International Tennis Hall of Fame
2007

Arantxa Sanchez Vicario returns the offering of Kristin Godridge in their second-round match at the 1991 U.S. Open. Sanchez Vicario would fall in the quarterfinal but would win it all in 1994.

Monica Seles returns the ball to Anke Huber at the 1995 U.S. Open. Seles beat Huber 6–1, 6–4 but fell in the final to Steffi Graf.

Monica Seles

CHEATED BUT NOT DEFEATED

It may never be known whether Monica Seles' career was violently derailed because she was blessed with otherworldly talent or because of her ethnicity. The sad certainty is that the tennis world will never know what could have been.

When Seles burst onto the tennis scene in the late 1980s, she possessed a rarely seen skill. As a natural left-hander, Seles used a double-fisted swing for both her forehand and her backhand. The swings were almost equally powerful and effective, and when combined with her powerful grunt—another unique trait—she stunned competitors and delighted fans. She also inadvertently created a legacy that lives and thrives with most of today's top female players.

With Hungarian and Serbian heritage, Monica Seles was born in 1973 in Novi Sad, in the former Yugoslavia. Father Karolj, a cartoonist, drew faces on the balls that young Monica hit, and when she started doing so with a freakish skill, he and mother Esther decided to move Monica to Florida and Nick Bolletieri's renowned tennis academy in 1986.

Three years after moving to Florida, 15-year-old Seles signaled a changing of the guard by beating legend Chris Evert in 1989 in what proved to be Evert's last career final, 3–6, 6–1, 6–4 in Houston.

Seles made her major debut as an unseeded player at the 1989 French Open, reaching the semifinal and putting a scare into Steffi Graf. The holder of "the Golden Grand Slam" and winner of five consecutive majors needed three sets to beat the teenager.

A year later Seles returned to finish the job, becoming the youngest French Open winner in history at 16 years, six months by beating Graf 7–6 (8–6), 6–4 in the 1990 final. It was Graf's 13th straight major final, and she held a 6–2 lead in the first-set tiebreaker before Seles ran off 6 straight points.

Seles won her second major at the Australian Open in 1991, the first of three straight Down Under, and she won the last major of the season by beating Martina Navratilova, who was twice her age but showed no signs of slowing down, 7–6 (9–7), 6–1 in the U.S. Open final.

Navratilova got a small measure of revenge the following summer when she complained about Seles' shrieking at Wimbledon. Seles won their match but was warned to stay quiet in the final. Robbed of the guttural encouragement she added to each stroke, she went down easily in the 1992 final, 6–2, 6–1, to Graf.

But Seles followed that up by winning the U.S. Open in 1992 to become the youngest woman in history with seven major titles, beating Maureen Connolly by three months. She added her eighth major at the 1993 Australian Open, beating Graf 4–6, 6–3, 6–2 in a dramatic final.

After her first major victory in Paris in 1990, Seles won seven of the eight majors she played in from 1991 to 1993, with a combined 55-1 match record. She also reached the final in 33 of 34 tournaments from January 1991 to February 1993, winning 22 times.

Still only 19, she was ranked first in the world and seemed poised to become the greatest of all time.

But three months later, on April 30th in Hamburg, Germany, Guenther Parche changed the course of tennis history.

While Seles was seated courtside during a changeover in a quarterfinal match against Magdalena Maleeva, Parche ran down from the stands, leaped over the barrier and plunged a nine-inch knife into Seles' back.

Parche was infatuated with Graf and wanted Seles out of the picture so she could return to the top of women's tennis. There was also speculation that politics were a motivating

Monica Seles celebrates winning the 1996 Australian Open after defeating Anke Huber, 6–4, 6–1. It was her first and only major championship after her return to the game from her stabbing.

"We got cheated, Monica got cheated, everyone got cheated."
—Martina Navratilova

factor. The war in Yugoslavia was raging, and although Seles tried to distance herself from the ethnic conflict, she had received death threats because of her Serbian roots.

Mercifully, the knife missed her spine and lung, and the wound was relatively minor. The psychological impact was deeper; Seles became depressed, started overeating and stayed off the court for more than two years.

"Even 10 minutes of walking was torture. I just didn't want to do it," Seles wrote in her autobiography. "What was wrong with me? There was a problem that no CAT scan or MRI readout could diagnose. Darkness had descended into my head. No matter how many ways I analyzed the situation, I couldn't find a bright side."

Monica Seles returns the challenge of Gigi Fernandez during their quarterfinal at the 1991 U.S. Open. Seles defeated Fernandez and went on to win the championship, her third Grand Slam win that season.

number one after the Women's Tennis Association restored her status when she returned. They were nearly as equal on the court, but Graf prevailed 7–6 (8–6), 0–6, 6–3 and took over top spot.

Seles rebounded in Australia, where she had never lost. There in 1996 she faced down match point against Lindsay Davenport to win a tournament in Sydney and then won the Australian Open, beating Anke Huber 6–4, 6–1 in the final, for her ninth and last major title.

If Seles' comeback in 1995 and early 1996 was driven by adrenaline and emotion, she ran out of gas as the 1996 season wore on. She was dealing with knee and shoulder injuries and her conditioning suffered. She lost in the French Open quarterfinals to Jana Novotna, breaking her streak of 25 straight wins in Paris, and lost in the second round at Wimbledon.

At the U.S. Open Seles started to look like her old self, reaching the finals to face Graf once again. Graf played a quicker, more attacking game and wore Seles down, winning 7–5, 6–4. Seles was also dealing with her father's fight with cancer, a battle he lost in 1998.

Having gained U.S. citizenship in 1995, Seles returned to Sydney in 2000 to represent the United States at the Olympics. She reached the podium in women's singles after losing to eventual gold medalist Venus Williams in the semifinal and beating Australia's Jelena Dokic in the bronze-medal match.

The last of Seles' 53 singles titles was the 2002 Madrid Open. She stopped playing in 2003, although she didn't formally announce her retirement until 2008. She was inducted into the Hall of Fame a year later for a stellar career that was on a trajectory to being the best of all time.

"We got cheated, Monica got cheated, everyone got cheated," says Navratilova.

But Seles doesn't dwell on that. Now writing a series of young adult novels based at a tennis academy, she says that life is "just really about living in the present."

"She's a very well-adjusted woman, smart, caring, one of the best women I know," says Mary Joe Fernandez, a former player, commentator and close friend of Seles. "She's considerate and a really good person, which shows her character and reflects her upbringing by great parents. She has been able to move on and create a great life for herself. [The attack] is something that will always be there, unfortunately, but Monica is strong like she always has been."

Adding to the trauma was the fact Parche received just a suspended sentence and probation, and in a cruel twist he got what he wanted when Graf went on to win the next four majors and regain her number one ranking. Seles would never be alone at the top again.

Seles returned in August 1995 in impressive fashion, topping Martina Navratilova in an exhibition match and then blowing through the Canadian Open without losing a set, beating Amanda Coetzer 6–0, 6–1 in the final.

Seles was just as merciless in getting to the final of the U.S. Open later that month, setting up a match with Graf, her co-

CAREER HIGHLIGHTS

Australian Open
Singles champion 1991–93, 1996

French Open
Singles champion 1990–92

U.S. Open
Singles champion 1991–92

Olympics
Bronze medalist in women's singles 2000

Fed Cup Team Member
1996, 1998–2000, 2002

International Tennis Hall of Fame
2009

Monica Seles serves during her quarterfinal victory over Iva Majoli, 6–1, 6–2, at the 1996 Australian Open. Seles would knock off Chanda Rubin and Anke Huber to take the title.

Virginia Wade

"OUR GINNY"

Virginia Wade defeats Rosemary Casals in two sets, 6–4, 7–5, in the quarterfinal of the 1968 U.S. Open. Wade dispatched Ann Jones and Billie Jean King to earn her first major title.

When Andy Murray ended decades of national sporting angst in 2013 by becoming the first British man to win the Wimbledon singles title since 1936, the media and public were forgetting a significant player and accomplishment.

The triumphant headlines following Murray's win were celebrating the wrong 77. It wasn't the number of years between Fred Perry's and Murray's victories, it was the year a Brit last won it all at the All England Club.

Virginia Wade, OBE, won the Wimbledon women's title in 1977, one of her three Grand Slam singles victories and seven overall.

Born in Bournemouth in 1945, Wade was a year old when her father became the Archdeacon of the Episcopal Church in Durban, South Africa. Her life in tennis began when she was 9, after finding a racket when cleaning out a closet. After that she says she played "every single minute I wasn't obliged to do something else." A quick study, she was soon unbeatable.

Wade's family moved back to England when she was 15, and in 1962 the 16-year-old was invited to play at Wimbledon because she was the best junior player in the country.

The morning after winning her first match Wade woke up to a surprise. "I was coming down the stairs and my father was reading the newspaper and said, 'Oh, you're playing on Centre Court today,' and I nearly fell down the stairs. I had to phone up and say I couldn't go to school that day."

Wade lost that match but would appear at the All England Club 26 times, tying a 72-year-old women's record when she made her 20th and final appearance in singles in 1985.

Although she spent most of her youth in South Africa she was a proud Briton, representing her country and setting records for participation among all players in international tournaments such as the Federation Cup (17 years) and the Wightman Cup (21 years). She also holds British records at the Federation Cup for total wins (66), singles wins (36) and doubles wins (30), and her 99 matches played set a record that Arantxa Sanchez Vicario eventually surpassed by one.

A tall, glamorous and elegant player who would later become friends with Princess Diana, Wade admitted to playing with grace instead of a killer instinct. "I would rather play beautiful tennis than win. In fact, if I'm really playing well, really hitting the ball, I can lose track of the purpose behind it all."

But she had a powerful serve and could play with ferocity, when it needed to be summoned, as well as precision.

Wade won the first tournament of the open era, the 1968 British Hard Court, in her hometown. Although professionals were now competing with amateurs, her prize money was an expense check for $120 because she retained her amateur status as a student. After graduating from Sussex University with a degree in math and physics, she turned professional.

Playing in the newly named U.S. Open as a pro five months later, 23-year-old Wade beat tournament favorite, defending champion and world number one Billie Jean King in the final, 6–4, 6–2, to win her first major title. This time she took home $6,000.

At the end of the 1968 season Wade was ranked second in the world, the second year of 13 straight that she was in the top 10.

In 1972 Wade won her second major, the Australian Open, defeating national sweetheart Evonne Goolagong 6–4, 6–4 in the final. It was a year that was dominated by King, who won the other three majors while losing only one set, to Wade in the Wimbledon quarterfinals.

Wade also helped Australian Margaret Court become the overall leader in major titles by teaming with her to win the

Virginia Wade participates in the 1968 Wightman Cup. She defeated American Mary-Ann Eisel, 6–0, 6–1, to give Britain a 2-1 lead. Britain ultimately prevailed 4-3, with Wade winning in both singles and doubles.

U.S. Open doubles title twice and the Australian and French once each. She remains the only British woman to win a title at each major tournament.

"Our Ginny," as she was known in her homeland, won Wimbledon at a very auspicious time; it was the centenary of the tournament, and Queen Elizabeth II, in her Silver Jubilee year, was presenting the winner's plate for the first time in a quarter-century.

Most assumed it would be given to defending champion Chris Evert. It was Wade's 17th tournament and she was just

"If I'm really playing well, really hitting the ball, I can lose track of the purpose behind it all." – Virginia Wade

Virginia Wade is all smiles as she holds the Venus Rosewater Dish in 1977. Wade defeated Betty Stove of the Netherlands 4–6, 6–3, 6–1 for the Wimbledon championship, the first by a Briton since Ann Jones in 1969.

shy of her 32nd birthday, so her window was rapidly closing. Her past failures, including two semifinal losses in the three years prior, had led the tabloids to dub her "Ginny Fizz."

Even her partner had questioned her moxie. "Virginia is a brilliant player," said Court. "She should have won so many more tournaments than she has. When she's on, she is hard to beat. But she is on and off."

But with the weight of the nation on her shoulders, Wade showed she was made of sterner stuff.

"To become the mistress of the situation here you must balance the determination with the tension," she said leading up to the 1977 tournament. "If I am determined enough, I can forget about the tension. I want to show that people's opinions about me are out of date. I've got the willpower and the guts to win this tournament. If I can just stop dreaming and get on with it, I will win."

Wade beat the powerful Evert in the semifinal, 6–2, 4–6, 6–1, before overcoming Betty Stove 4–6, 6–3, 6–1 in the final, causing the jubilant Centre Court crowd to serenade her with "For She's a Jolly Good Fellow" as the Queen descended from the private box and handed her the trophy.

"It was like a fairytale, with everyone cheering for the Queen and for me," said Wade.

As former All England Club chief executive Chris Gorringe wrote in his book *Holding Court*, "When she won the final point, she yelped with joy, but the sound was lost under the noise of every man, woman and flag-waving child leaping up and cheering and clapping. The Duchess of Kent leapt up too and gave a clenched-fist victory salute as everyone was carried away on a sea of emotions—a mix of joy and relief that Virginia had finally done it."

King was more succinct: "This script was written in heaven."

Wade played her last singles match at Wimbledon a week before her 40th birthday in 1985, losing to fifth-seed Pam Shriver in the third round, and her last appearance was in mixed doubles in 1987, the same year she was named to the Order of the British Empire.

As a professional she won 55 singles titles, eighth all-time, and a total of 839 matches, the fourth-highest total in women's tennis history.

Wade currently splits her time between London and New York, providing tennis commentary for the BBC and several American networks.

While still in the public eye, somehow their Ginny got lost in British history. As writer Chloe Angyal tweeted in response to the headlines declaring the end of the 77-year drought, "Murray is indeed the first Brit to win Wimbledon in 77 years unless you think women are people."

Virginia Wade serves the ball to Ann Jones in an all-British semifinal at the 1968 U.S. Open. Wade defeated her compatriot and went on to claim the championship.

PASSING SHOTS

An examination of some of the finer points of tennis

Surfaces

The official rules of tennis have very specific guidelines about equipment and court measurement but little about the actual surface the game is played on. The International Tennis Federation recognizes more than 160 types of tennis court, including wood, gravel, carpet and fake grass.

In the early years of tennis, after the game moved outdoors, it was played almost exclusively on grass. But in climates where grass didn't thrive, and in places it couldn't be maintained, players got creative.

The three main surfaces, if only because the majors are played on them, are hard court, clay and grass. This surface variability has a profound effect on the outcome of any given tournament. Many of history's greatest players have had a surface that proved to be their kryptonite, as players constantly need to make adjustments as the surfaces change, from tournament to tournament and from point to point.

Hard Court

The Australian and U.S. Opens are played on hard court, a more consistent surface than clay or grass but one that is less forgiving and harder on players — and not every hard court is made equal.

The Australian Open is played on a surface called Plexicushion Prestige, which consists of a cushioned layer made of latex, rubber and plastic particles on an asphalt base, topped by a Plexipave surface that "provides consistent and uniform bounce, long lasting color, and allows speed of play specification," according to the manufacturer.

While the Plexicushion remains constant throughout a tournament, it does retain and reflect heat, and when the sun beats down on Melbourne it has been known to get sticky.

The U.S. Open is the only major that's had all three surfaces.

After being played on grass from 1881 to 1974 and clay from 1975 to 1977, the U.S. Open has made DecoTurf its hard court of choice since 1978. It has a cushioned layer topped by an acrylic surface and is known to produce a lower bounce than other hard courts.

The amount of friction, and therefore how much the ball slows down when it hits the court, depends on the amount of sand in the paint of the acrylic layer. The Australian Open is slightly slower than the U.S. Open, but both do have the potential to speed up as the surface is worn smooth by players' shoes over the course of the tournament.

Clay

Clay is the slowest of the surfaces. Most famously seen in Paris at Roland Garros, home of the French Open, and also at the Italian Open in Rome (a key tune-up for the French Open), clay is what many players in Europe and Latin America grow up on. It was once more prevalent in the United States, but when the U.S. Open made the move to Flushing Meadows and the USTA switched to hard courts for the tournament, there was a seismic shift in American tennis. In 1977 there were 11 professional tournaments played on clay in the United States; today there is one. The lack of experience on the surface is one of the theories why, beyond Venus and Serena Williams, the United States hasn't produced any recent champions. The backcourt style of today's game suits those who learned their craft on clay, and young Americans are rarely exposed to it.

The signature deep-red clay surface at the French Open is just the very thin top layer of many. At the bottom is two feet of large stone, then an inch of gravel and five inches of clinker, which is residue from volcanic rock that absorbs and retains water. The top two layers are a strata of limestone topped with crushed brick or tile, which comes from the quarries of Saint-

A stadium worker wipes the clay off the lines in between sets of the second-round match featuring Rafael Nadal and Pablo Andujar at the 2011 French Open.

Maximin that were used to build much of Paris in the 19th century. Although there is only 2 millimeters of the brick, each court requires a ton. The French call it *terre battue*, which translates to "beaten earth," but it was English players who first crushed brick to cover a court in Cannes in 1878 because the climate wasn't right for their familiar grass.

Clay is softer than hard court and kinder to the players, with the loose surface allowing for sliding stops that are far less jarring than abrupt ones. The courts at the French Open are submerged in water for 15 minutes every night and regularly hosed down between matches. This keeps them from becoming too dusty and creates a constant evaporation and a cooler playing surface in the summer. The loose brick also causes friction and slows the momentum of the ball, which produces more spin and higher bounces, leading to longer rallies and matches.

According to the French Open media guide: "These materials, shaped by the teams at Roland Garros, become a playground whose qualities are limitless—land reserved for the giants of tennis. This work done, the artists can enter into alliance with the Earth. Modern players can express their inner Vulcan while giving the yellow ball trajectories that possess arabesque foolishness. For us mere mortals, it is simply the emotion of seeing this meeting between man and the beaten earth."

Grass

The sport of tennis was born on grass and is still played on this surface at the granddaddy of the majors—Wimbledon.

Cut to exactly 8 millimeters, the grass at Wimbledon is 100 percent perennial rye grass, which is more durable than the mixture of 70 percent rye and 30 percent Barcrown creeping red fescue that had been used until 2000.

The courts had been much softer before the change, rewarding players with fast serves because the ball would skid along the surface. The new grass creates higher bounces, making it more like a hard court.

Underneath the grass is a clay-based soil that can crack when it dries out. A staff of 20 groundskeepers irrigates and mows the 19 game and 22 practice courts at Wimbledon, and an independent turf consultant measures the surface's hardness, its chlorophyll index and its live grass content.

Familiar brown patches appear on the baselines as the tournament progresses, the result of thousands of serves and hours of players patrolling the backcourt. They can't be reseeded until the competition is over, so they become part of the match, with players forced to adapt the deeper they go. Smart ones will aim the ball at the bald patches, hoping for a strange bounce to throw off the opponent, and the only thing the groundskeepers can do at that point is vacuum the area with "the Billy Goat" to remove any extra debris. By the time the finals begin, the grass will cover about 75 percent of the surface but only about 10 to 15 percent of the baseline.

There have been calls to change the grass courts of Britain to clay because the upkeep of grass is too much for many small clubs to bear, and a poorly maintained surface doesn't help young players learn. The courts can also be unplayable for long stretches of the year. Some say it's an antiquated surface because of modern rackets and the prevailing power game, and that only elite players really know how to use the surface.

Traditionalists, and the All England Lawn Tennis and Croquet Club is certainly one, will have none of that talk.

Technology

The rules of tennis have remained much the same since the 19th century; the equipment, however, has not.

Balls

Tennis balls were originally hand-stitched, meaning no two were the same. Today uniformity is provided via a heat press that binds the nap (made of wool or nylon) to a rubber core. Each ball is filled with pressurized air and is tested by hand; International Tennis Federation rules state that a ball must bounce between 53 and 58 inches after being dropped onto concrete from a height of 100 inches, and each must be two-and-a-half inches (6.35 centimeters) in diameter and weigh two ounces (56.7 grams). Players request new balls because they lose bounce and when the nap gets raised they slow down. Spares are kept courtside, refrigerated at 68 degrees Fahrenheit.

There are four kinds of balls, from Type 1 (fastest) to Type 3 (slowest), as well as a ball used specifically at high altitudes. If a tournament is played at more than 4,000 feet, pressureless balls must be acclimatized locally for at least 60 days.

Rackets

The increased speed of the game is a result of fitter, stronger players, but also because of the massive leap in racket technology. Until the 1970s the rackets underwent little change. They were made of wood and had to be kept in a press to keep them from warping between matches. Bjorn Borg won 11 majors in the 1970s and 1980s using a wooden racket, and he held on to it when he made his comeback in 1991. He was blown off the court by players using graphite.

An early prototype of the modern racket was the Wilson T2000, created by French legend Rene Lacoste and introduced in 1968. It was made of lightweight tubular steel that had less wind resistance, and Jimmy Connors used one until the mid-1980s. The small head and long, split neck became one of Connors' signatures during his heyday, leading to a boom in sales of the racket, even though the design didn't suit the weekend hacker.

The first oversized rackets were introduced in the 1980s. The oversized heads have larger sweet spots but offer less control, and many top players choose smaller rackets. There is little head size difference between men's and women's rackets, but women tend to use rackets with smaller handles, and no frame can exceed 29 inches in total length.

Rackets are now made of graphite and fiberglass or a composite of several man-made materials, which makes them extremely light and virtually indestructible. The materials provide stiffness, which is essential for top players to control the ball, while getting lighter and lighter, providing less resistance and generating increased racket speed. The next wave is piezoelectric technology, with a circuit board in the handle converting energy from the impact of a ball and sending it back to the frame, dampening the vibration and further stiffening the racket.

Strings

Strings have been most resistant to change. The most expensive ones are still made of animal gut, often from cows. Professionals like their elasticity, liveliness and tension stability, but some synthetic materials, such as nylon, polyester and Kevlar, have started to make inroads. The tension of the strings is very personal, with high tension leading to more spin and control and lower tension creating power. Gauge, or thickness of the string, is another factor; thinner strings have more power, control and spin, but they break easily. Most professionals have their rackets restrung after every match.

Players have attempted to gain an advantage with clever stringing techniques, staying ahead of the curve and ITF regulations. Australian Barry Phillips-Moore used a double-strung racket, a creation of German Werner Fischer that resembled a poorly woven basket and was called a "spaghetti racket," which created massive topspin and unfamiliar bounces. American Michael Fishbach saw Phillips-Moore on the European circuit and brought the idea to the United States, using the racket to gain entry into the 1977 U.S. Open and upsetting former number one Stan Smith once he got there. Weeks later Ilie Nastase used a spaghetti racket to end Guillermo Vilas' then-record 53-match winning streak on clay,

with Vilas quitting after two sets to protest. The stringing technique was promptly banned.

The Digital Age

While the most expensive rackets and constant restringing are the domain of the professional, even the weekend hacker can access the latest technology. New smart courts, with high-definition cameras and sensors on players, are starting to become commonplace, and anyone with a smartphone can access the data.

Tiny microchips are also being used in smart rackets and balls, and the ITF instituted a rule beginning in 2014 that bans any piece of equipment that "collects, stores, transmits, analyzes or communicates information on player performance" in real time during matches. There are no such rules for training, however, or for gathering the data and analyzing it when a match is over.

A ball-tracking technology called Hawk-Eye has been used at more than 60 tournaments on tour since 2006, when the ITF gave it official accreditation. It determines where the ball lands and displays it on screens around the stadium and on TV. It's hard to argue with a camera that sees 1,000 frames per second, but removing some of the human element from the umpire (and the errors inherent in that role) also deprives fans of the tantrums that made players such as John McEnroe and Connors so (in)famous.

The inexorable march of technology will continue to improve the equipment. But, tennis is still a one-on-one battle, waged physically and psychologically. The mental aspect of the game is the hardest to control and quantify, and the mind is one mystery that technology is just beginning to understand.

International Play

The International Lawn Tennis Challenge Trophy is the granddaddy of all international tennis prizes, a bowl donated by 20-year-old Harvard student Dwight Davis, who wanted to foster friendship through the game and whose name the Cup would soon bear.

Davis enlisted Dr. James Dwight, a Harvard grad and president of the United States Tennis Association, to get the tournament started. Dwight used his connections in England to recruit the opponents, and he drew up the rules and officiated the first matches.

The Davis Cup has always been a men's tournament, and it was first contested at the Longwood Cricket Club in Boston in

Serena Williams (left) and Venus Williams smile together on the podium after receiving their gold medals in women's doubles at the 2012 Summer Olympics. The gold was the third for the sisters in Olympic doubles tennis.

1900 — the home court of both Davis and Dwight — between the United States and the British Isles. The Americans won the first challenge and remain the most successful country in tournament history with 32 titles. They are followed by Australia, which boasts 28 championships, and Great Britain and France, who are tied at 9. A total of 13 countries have lifted the Cup, and 130 nations battled for the trophy in 2013, making it the world's largest annual international team competition.

It was a tournament for amateur players until 1969, when professionals in good standing with their national federations were permitted to join. In 1973, five years after the dawn of the open era, it welcomed all players. Australia won that year with arguably the greatest team in tournament history — Mal Anderson, Rod Laver, John Newcombe and Ken Rosewall.

The current format is a best-of-five series, with no more than four players on each team playing four singles and one doubles match over three days. Countries take turns hosting; when two nations are drawn, the nation that previously hosted the competition becomes the visitor. If the countries haven't played each other since 1970, however, the host is chosen by the flip of a coin. The home team chooses the location and surface.

The most successful player in tournament history is Italy's Nicola Pietrangeli. Over a Davis Cup career that ran from 1954 through 1972, but didn't include any titles, the two-time French champion holds the records for most wins in singles (78), doubles (42) and overall (120).

Bjorn Borg of Sweden holds the record for most consecutive tournament wins. After losing to Manuel Orantes in the opening match of the 1973 European quarterfinal against Spain, he won all 33 singles matches he played until his last appearance in the competition in June 1980.

The first international women's competition was the Wightman Cup, an annual best-of-seven match series between the United States and Great Britain, starting in 1923. American Hazel Hotchkiss Wightman donated the trophy. The competition was contested until 1989, when it was mutually agreed that the series should be discontinued because it was no longer competitive (the Americans held a 51-10 record overall).

Because the Wightman Cup was confined to just two countries, Australian Nell Hopman and England's Mary Hardwick

Hare successfully petitioned the International Tennis Federation to create a world tournament for women.

The ITF named the new competition after itself: the Federation Cup was born in 1963 and became the Fed Cup in 1995. As with the Davis Cup, the United States won the first tournament and is the leader in all-time victories, with 17 titles. Eleven countries have won it, with Australia and the Czech Republic tied for second with seven apiece.

Arantxa Sanchez Vicario leads the way with most match victories in singles (50) and overall (72), and she won five titles with Spain. American Chris Evert has the longest winning streak in tournament history at 29, between 1977 and 1986.

Australian Margaret Court was 20-0 in singles in her Federation Cup career, a record matched by Martina Navratilova, who is the only woman to win the title playing for two different countries — Czechoslovakia in 1975 and the United States, after her defection, in 1982, 1986 and 1989.

Men and women both compete internationally at the Olympics; tennis was played from the first modern Games in Athens in 1896 until it was dropped after the 1924 Paris Games because of a dispute and mutual distrust between the ITF and the International Olympic Committee.

In the 1980s ITF president Philippe Chatrier approached IOC president Juan Antonio Samaranch about having the sport return to the Games. Samaranch agreed, reinstating it for the 1988 Seoul Olympics. He believed the best tennis players in the world should appear, and so the IOC decided to allow professionals to play, paving the way for professional athletes in other sports to take part in future Olympics.

Steffi Graf started the new era of Olympic tennis with a bang; she won the first and only "Golden Slam" in 1988 by winning all four majors and the singles gold medal. Four years later she was upset by 15-year-old American Jennifer Capriati in the gold-medal match in Barcelona.

The Americans dominated at home at the Atlanta Games in 1996; Andre Agassi and Lindsay Davenport both won singles gold, and Mary Joe Fernandez and Gigi Fernandez won the women's doubles. Only the Woodies — Mark Woodforde and Todd Woodbridge — kept it from being a clean sweep by winning gold in men's doubles for Australia.

The Williams sisters both added a golden shine to their legacy by winning singles titles — Venus in Sydney in 2000 and Serena in London in 2012. They also teamed up to win doubles gold in Sydney, at the 2008 Games in Beijing and in London.

Sanchez Vicario is also a legendary Olympian, leading all women with five tournaments played, and her four medals — two silver and two bronze — are tied with the Williams

sisters and second to the five won by Kitty McKane of Great Britain (three in 1920 and two in 1924).

The current men's elite have also burnished their reputations with Olympic success. Roger Federer won the doubles gold for Switzerland with Stanislas Wawrinka in 2008 and took home silver in London after losing to Brit Andy Murray in the gold-medal match at Wimbledon. Rafael Nadal was the gold medalist in singles in 2008, adding to his career Grand Slam.

Doubles

There are twice as many people on the court but only nine more feet of width to play with, so doubles tennis requires strategy and teamwork as well as quick reflexes and thinking.

"I know that it helped me play better singles working on my doubles game," says John McEnroe, who won nine major titles in men's doubles and one in mixed, to go with his seven singles majors.

But McEnroe is now calling for the abolition of doubles at the Grand Slam tournaments. He believes the game would be better served by using the money from doubles to promote the singles game, which would create the opportunity for lower-ranked players to develop and rise through the ranks. He also thinks it has become boring.

Doubles tennis doesn't get the same exposure or respect as the singles game; that doesn't really affect players like Martina Navratilova and the Williams sisters — legends of the game for which doubles titles add a lucrative cherry on top of their careers.

But for people like Bob and Mike Bryan, the Woodies and Daniel Nestor, it matters. While not exactly the poor cousins of tennis — prize money is still substantial for the top doubles players — they don't have the same level of fame or endorsement potential, and they're rarely mentioned in a discussion of the world's best players.

What the Bryans have accomplished is nothing short of extraordinary, however. They've won a male-record 92 titles and counting, shattering the previous record of 61 held by the Australians Todd Woodbridge and Mark Woodforde. Mike Bryan won two doubles titles without his brother, giving him the male record of 94 total titles.

The Bryans were the top-ranked team nine of 11 years through 2013, and after the duo won gold at the London Olympics they took four straight major titles, bridging the 2012 and 2013 seasons (much like Serena Williams did in women's

Doubles partners and siblings Bob and Mike Bryan celebrate after winning the doubles championship at Wimbledon in 2013. The win was the pair's third at Wimbledon.

singles in 2002–03, which the tennis press dubbed "the Serena Slam"). The Bryans have the U.S. Davis Cup doubles team record at 21-3, and the pair helped win the 2007 title.

Had the brothers won the 2013 U.S. Open they would have become the first men's team to win a doubles Grand Slam since Australians Ken McGregor and Frank Sedgman did it in 1951. The Bryans' 15 major doubles titles are one short of the male record held by Woodbridge.

Befitting his personality, Serbian-born Canadian Nestor has also quietly carved a niche for himself in the pantheon of all-time doubles greats. Still active, he has 83 career doubles titles, tied with Woodbridge and behind only the Bryans on the all-time men's list.

A three-time Olympian, Nestor won gold in Sydney in 2000 with Sebastien Lareau, and he was half of the ATP Doubles Team of the Year in 2002 and 2004 with Mark Knowles and in 2008 with Nenad Zimonjic. After taking the 2014 Australian Open mixed doubles crown with French partner Kristina Mladenovic, he also has 12 major doubles titles — eight in men's and four mixed.

Nestor and the Bryans are the only doubles players in history to have won all four majors, all of the Masters Series events, the year-end championships and Olympic gold at least once.

On the women's side, Martina Navratilova, who won her final major mixed doubles title at the 2006 U.S. Open with Bob Bryan, sits atop the women's doubles mountain, as she does in singles. She's won 41 major doubles titles — 31 women's and 10 mixed. Overall, Navratilova has collected a record 177 doubles titles and set the women's team mark of 79 with Pam Shriver.

Margaret Court holds the record among all players, male or female, with 62 major titles overall, 38 of which are in doubles — 19 each in women's and mixed. Billie Jean King earned 27 doubles majors — 16 in women's and 11 mixed — and Shriver won 21 women's doubles and one mixed doubles title at the majors.

Like the Bryan brothers, the Williams sisters have a DNA advantage over other teams and have used it to rule the doubles world in the 21st century. Venus and Serena play doubles only at the majors, where they've won 13 together (and two each in mixed), and at the Olympics, where they have collected three doubles gold medals (2000, 2008 and 2012).

The last two men to win a major title in both singles and doubles are Lleyton Hewitt and Pat Rafter. The two Australians decided to play doubles together in their native country at the 2014 Australian Open.

Hewitt, 31, and the 41-year-old Rafter lost in the first round, but they carried the grand tradition of great Australian champions Roy Emerson, who won 12 singles and 16 doubles titles at the majors, John Newcombe (seven singles, 18 doubles), Sedgman (five singles, 17 doubles) and Rod Laver (11 singles, nine doubles).

Those titles were compiled in the mid-20th century; current players are skipping doubles tournaments to avoid injury and save energy so they can focus on singles — the glamour game. Roger Federer, Rafael Nadal, Novak Djokovic, and Andy Murray have collectively won 38 singles majors and exactly zero in doubles.

"Most doubles players, I hate to say, are the slow guys who were not quick enough to play singles," according to McEnroe's view of the modern game.

The Bryan brothers, the top-ranked team for 344 consecutive weeks at the end of 2013, a record for any duo in history, are an exception.

"They're electrifying. They're probably the best doubles team that ever played," says 1972 U.S. Open doubles winner Cliff Drysdale.

But he understands that the competition in doubles isn't what it used to be. "That said, the singles players are not playing doubles anymore. So there's always an asterisk."

It's a sentiment shared by Chris Evert, a three-time doubles winner at the majors.

"The years that Navratilova and Shriver dominated, McEnroe and Peter Fleming dominated, they were having really easy singles matches until the quarters or semis," she says. "They used that as practice. But it's just really tough for the big names, the top players, to play doubles or mixed. It's a shame because doubles is very, very entertaining."

Fashion

Fashion has taken a turn toward casual over the last several decades, yet the outerwear of most athletic pursuits remains too technical, too specific and often too gaudy to be worn by any self-respecting fashionista. The jersey, specifically of the soccer/ football variety, is ubiquitous, but it doesn't belong outside the stadium or a gathering of like-minded fans. Golf shirts are seen away from the links but mainly in retirement communities, traditional polo and cricket wear is too uppity for the mainstream, and cycling attire is a little too…tight.

But tennis is the rare sport with apparel that's crossed over into the wardrobes of the world. The odd fashion fault aside, the sport has been on the leading edge of worldwide trends and has created several enduring styles and brands that are as at home on the court as they are on the street.

In the early days women wore corsets, full-length skirts, wide-brimmed hats and fur. France's Suzanne Lenglen was one of the first women to be an international sports star, and her higher hemlines, shorter hair and headbands were all a strong influence on French and European fashion. Her tour of the United States also spread her style among the carefree of the roaring '20s, helping usher in the era of the flapper.

On the court, long skirts gave way to cocktail-style dresses and drop waists, and the bandeau or visor became the headwear of choice. In the '30s and '40s the sleeves came off and silhouettes were more feminine and tailored, while skirts slowly crept up. Trailblazer Katharine Hepburn played tennis in high-waisted, form-fitting shorts in the 1952 movie *Pat and Mike*, and that decade brought the cinched-waist tennis dress and popularized the cardigan.

The 1960s was a time of social upheaval, and the Mod movement influenced tennis wear, especially in the miniskirts being worn. Tight shorts of the 1970s were coupled with the wide collars and loud patterns of the disco age, and the 1980s was a decade of color, especially pastels.

In the 1990s the pastels became fluorescents and spandex became popular, and in the 21st century the players became models and designers. Anna Kournikova, in her midriff-baring outfits, became more famous for being winsome than for winning, and fellow Russian Maria Sharapova is just as comfortable on the runway as she is under stadium lights.

Sharapova is a career Grand Slam winner and a dedicated follower of fashion. She's a fixture at couture shows and designs her own clothing for the court and the red carpet.

Venus and Serena Williams also have a hand in the creation of their clothing, and they favor the loud and elaborate. Even at Wimbledon, where rules dictate that all players wear predominantly white, they tend to find ways around the rules with accents and revealing cuts.

The Williams sisters followed in the footsteps of Anne White, a marginal player who made a name for herself at Wimbledon in 1985 with an all-white spandex catsuit.

Opponent and future Hall of Famer Pam Shriver called it the "most bizarre, stupid-looking thing I've ever seen on a tennis court," and officials asked White to wear something else when their match resumed after being suspended for darkness.

"I had no idea it would be so controversial," said White. "It wasn't my intention, as I took my tracksuit off, for anyone to spill their strawberries and cream."

There has not been as much flux in male tennis fashion; pants gave way to shorts and sweaters to short sleeves, but few players could be considered trendsetters.

There were hair idols in the 1970s — players such as John McEnroe and Bjorn Borg sported unruly and flowing locks — and in the 1990s Andre Agassi's denim, spandex and garish color schemes were briefly popular. Rafael Nadal burst onto the scene in the early part of the 21st century with long shorts and sleeveless shirts, but like Agassi, he became more traditional in his attire as he matured.

Men's tennis brought several enduring brands and styles, however. Rene Lacoste was an innovator in tennis and golf technology and was the first to wear the lightweight knit polo-style shirt that became a staple. The crocodile logo, which was created for him after he bet a crocodile-skin suitcase on a match in Boston, remains on the chests of the young and fashionable worldwide. Founded in 1933, the Lacoste brand has extended to footwear, fragrances, watches, eyewear, sheets and towels.

Fred Perry and Stan Smith would have made a tremendous doubles team, having both won Wimbledon singles titles three decades apart, and in today's business casual world the combination would be at home in the boardroom.

Both wore simple, classic designs that have withstood decades of change and trends. Stan Smith's simple white Adidas tennis shoe has battled the Converse Chuck Taylor as the footwear of choice for the classic and comfortable American since the early 1970s.

Fred Perry proposed a pipe for his logo when he launched his brand in 1952, but the crest of the British Davis Cup uniform was chosen instead, because partner Tibby Wegner thought women wouldn't want a pipe on their clothing.

So the laurel wreath became a subculture badge, and the cotton pique shirt became popular with the top players and the mods. It's been adopted by generations of British youth in the decades since, from Rude Boys to Britpop fans, and remained in the game with Murray wearing Fred Perry early in his career. (Murray had switched to Adidas by the time he became the first British man to win Wimbledon in the 77 years since Perry's three-peat from 1934 to 1936.)

Stella McCartney — daughter of another iconic Brit, Beatle

Caroline Wozniacki celebrates a point won against Garbine Muguruza during their third-round match at the 2014 Australian Open. Wozniacki wore this Stella McCartney number to rave reviews.

Paul — has one of the most recognizable names in 21st-century fashion. She's designed haute couture for fashion house Chloe and under her own label, as well as for numerous music and movie stars.

McCartney has also designed for Adidas since 2005; she created the British team's fashion and performance apparel for the 2012 London Olympics, and her ability to marry style and function has made her popular with tennis players. She cracked the code for fashionable and active women, with clothing that can be worn by a yoga mom or Caroline Wozniacki at Rod Laver Arena.

Bleacher Report had this to say about Wozniacki's attire at the 2014 Australian Open: "Elegant and feminine, the dress featured a two-tiered pleated skirt and adjustable elastic tank straps." The Danish star was high on the list of Bleacher Report's best- and worst-dressed players at the year's first major. "Except for the sporty straps trimmed in blue, this number might be mistaken for a cocktail dress."

Former world number one Wozniacki lost in the third round, but she looked damn good doing it.

THE 21ST CENTURY

Modern-era champions

The 21st century's two biggest stars and rivals, Roger Federer (left) and Rafael Nadal, congratulate each other on a well-played match: a 6–1, 6–3 victory for Nadal at the 2013 Italian Open.

Novak Djokovic

CHALLENGER TO THE THRONE

Novak Djokovic holds up the 2013 ATP World Tour Finals trophy after defeating Rafael Nadal in the best-of-three final, 6–3, 6–4.

A court jester, for several years Novak Djokovic was known more for his spot-on impressions of rivals Roger Federer and Rafael Nadal than for his success against them. He was an occasional burr under their saddles as the two rode toward immortality, but it didn't really look as if he was any threat to their duopoly.

His comedy act arose from the darkness that had enveloped his native Yugoslavia and later from the insecurity he felt around the top players.

"Nole," as his family knows him, was born in 1987 to parents Srdjan and Dijana, who owned a pizza and snack bar in the mountain resort of Kopaonik. He called his a "beautiful" childhood.

His dad was a skier and the family was athletic, but they didn't play tennis until the government decided to build a tennis centre in Kopaonik in the late 1980s. The pro there was Jelena Gencic, who had coached Monica Seles. She became a lifelong mentor to the young Nole, encouraging him to expand his horizons by reading poetry and listening to classical music.

But the idyllic life was torn apart when NATO planes started bombing Belgrade in 1999. Djokovic and his family would spend their nights in a bomb shelter, and during the day he played on pockmarked courts without nets.

The war crippled the country and the family's finances, so they sold their gold and borrowed money from a loan shark to send 13-year-old Nole to Munich to train under Nikola Pilic.

In 2002 Djokovic was the under-16 European champion, and he turned pro in 2003 at 16. A year later he played in the Davis Cup for the first time, and in 2005 he qualified for the Australian Open and Wimbledon, where he reached the third round. In 2006 he won his first professional tournament and became the youngest player in the top 20.

The first hint of greatness was at the Rogers Cup in Montreal in 2007, when Djokovic beat numbers three to one in order — Andy Roddick, Nadal and Federer — to win the title. He also reached the final of the U.S. Open and the semifinals of the French Open and Wimbledon.

Novak Djokovic reacts after winning his quarterfinal match against Jo-Wilfried Tsonga at the 2012 French Open. Djokovic would make it to the finals before losing to Rafael Nadal.

Novak Djokovic stretches out for the backhand return to Roger Federer in their semifinal match at the 2012 French Open. Djokovic prevailed, 6–4, 7–5, 6–3.

Having gained the requisite experience, Djokovic took his first major Down Under, beating Jo-Wilfried Tsonga for the 2008 Australian Open after beating Federer in the semifinals.

A year later Djokovic won the first ATP tournament held in his home country, one of his most cherished victories, and he finished the 2009 season ranked third in the world. But even as he scaled the tennis mountain he suffered from what he called "the Curse," a psychological affliction that kept him from reaching the summit. When the stakes were highest, his body would shut down and he would give up.

Djokovic held number three for most of 2008 through 2010, and it appeared he was stuck there. His conditioning was suspect, which led people to question the legitimacy of the many injuries he seemed to have.

Playing in the intense heat of the 2010 Australian Open, Djokovic started to hyperventilate and then vomited in the fourth set of a match against Tsonga. He lost in five sets and called it the lowest point in his career.

To rid himself of the Curse and his litany of injuries, Djokovic tried changing his training regimen and location, had nasal passage surgery to improve his breathing and brought in former world number four Todd Martin as a second coach, both for a calming influence and to get in better shape.

Around this time Djokovic was contacted by Dr. Igor Cetojevic, a physician and acupuncturist, who said he believed Djokovic had an imbalance in his digestive system that was causing his breathing problems. Cetojevic suggested he eliminate gluten and dairy from his diet and cut down on tomatoes. The man whose parents owned a pizza parlor could no longer touch the stuff, and the difference was night and day.

Down 11 pounds, Djokovic exploded in 2011. He won 43 straight matches, the longest streak of any active player, and went 70-6 for the year. He beat Andy Murray to win his second Australian Open and Nadal for his first Wimbledon title. Calling it his favorite tournament, after the match he ate a few blades of the hallowed Centre Court grass, and in Belgrade

100,000 fans celebrated the return of the conquering hero in front of the parliament building.

Djokovic capped the year with his first U.S. Open title, beating Nadal once again. A semifinal loss to Federer at the French Open earlier in the year kept him from being the third man in history to win a Grand Slam, but no one could stop his rise to the top, and Djokovic took over the number one ranking for the first time.

After the historic season, Djokovic won the international Laureus World Sportsman of the Year award and was given the Karadjordjeva Star Medal, for "special merits and success in representing Serbia." He was also named one of *Time*'s 100 most influential people in the world.

The newfound commitment to fitness and diet paid off in 2012. Djokovic downed Murray in the semifinals of the Australian Open, a match that took nearly five hours to play, and then beat Nadal in five hours and 53 minutes, the longest major final in history, to win his third Australian title.

Djokovic won his fourth Australian Open in 2013, becoming the first man in the open era to win three straight Down Under, and at Wimbledon that year he beat Juan Martin del Potro 7–5, 4–6, 7–6 (7–2), 6–7 (6–8), 6–3 in the longest semifinal in tourna-

Novak Djokovic serves to Leonardo Mayer during their second-round match at the 2014 Australian Open. Djokovic defeated Mayer but fell to eventual champion Stanislas Wawrinka in the quarterfinal.

as the most famous Serb in the world, he's also a political lightning rod. Most athletes avoid politics like the plague, but he doesn't back down and will expound on the breakdown of the former Yugoslavia when asked.

Dr. Igor Cetojevic suggested he eliminate gluten and dairy from his diet and cut down on tomatoes. The man whose parents owned a pizza parlor could no longer touch the stuff.

---

ment history. The days of languishing in long matches were forever behind the Serb star.

However, in the Wimbledon final he lost to Murray, the first British man to win at the All England Club in 77 years. After dealing with a hyperpartisan home crowd, Djokovic congratulated Murray on Centre Court and was lauded for his grace in defeat. It earned him some of the respect that's been slow to follow his triumphs on the court.

Not everyone loves the "Djoker;" he's been accused of immodesty, and his entourage rankles some of his fellow players and the media with their brash behavior and T-shirts sporting a giant picture of Djokovic's face.

He also spends time in a hyperbaric chamber, which isn't illegal but is another thing that rubs players and the tennis establishment the wrong way. Even the World Anti-Doping Agency weighed in, saying it violates "the spirit of sport."

Continually seeking self-improvement, mentally as well as physically, Djokovic is fascinated by the human mind and incorporates philosophy and spirituality into his routine. And

For some his success has been an unwelcome intrusion on the Federer–Nadal rivalry — one of the greatest in the history of tennis. But, given that by the end of the 2013 season Djokovic had won 543 matches and 41 singles titles, including six majors, he is, as tennis guru Nick Bollettieri states, "perhaps the best put-together player that [tennis has seen] in over sixty years."

With Federer on the downside of his career and Nadal's wonky knees an ongoing concern, history may prove that the clown prince was the real king of the court all along.

Career Highlights

Australian Open
Singles champion 2008, 2011–13

Wimbledon
Singles champion 2011

U.S. Open
Singles champion 2011

Olympics
Bronze medalist in men's singles 2008

Davis Cup Team Member
2004–11, 2013

Roger Federer

A LEGEND IN OUR MIDST

Rafael Nadal (left) returns a Roger Federer offering during the 2006 Wimbledon final. Federer won 6–0, 7–6 (7–5), 6–7 (2–7), 6–3 for his fourth consecutive title. It was the first of three straight years the two would meet at the Wimbledon final.

The discussion of the tennis GOAT — greatest of all time — may or may not end with Roger Federer, but there's certainly no better place to start.

Born in 1981 to Swiss father Robert and South African mother Lynette, the man who was raised in Basel plays with Swiss precision. It's a fluid, cerebral game; he makes difficult shots look effortless, and his footwork and intelligence always have him in the right spot.

And like his native country, he has few enemies. Even Rafael Nadal, the man who has foiled and frustrated Federer on many occasions, has nothing but respect and admiration for the man. The feeling is mutual.

Federer is an artist among athletes, playing a complete, aesthetically pleasing game. But it took him a while to learn to fight, not just to make the court his canvas.

By the time he was 13, Federer was spending his weekdays at the Swiss national training center and his weekends at home. In 1998, at 17, he was the number one junior player in the world. And in 2001, now a pro, 19-year-old Federer snapped Pete

Sampras' 31-match winning streak at Wimbledon. He lost in the next round, however, and was still searching for focus and mental strength.

The death of close friend and coach Peter Carter in a car accident in 2002 forced it upon him. Devastated, Federer realized that nothing is guaranteed in life, saying the tragedy gave him perspective and made him a fighter.

And while he started the 2003 season strongly, it wasn't until a first-round loss at the French Open that Federer realized the commitment and hard work needed to reach the top. He earned his first major title with a win over Mark Philippoussis at Wimbledon a month later. In 2004 he went on to win his first Australian Open and his second Wimbledon title.

The fortitude had arrived. Lleyton Hewitt, known as the scrappiest player on tour, had outworked Federer as their careers rose together, but in 2004 Federer beat him six times and on every surface, culminating in a 6–0, 7–6 (7–3), 6–0 beatdown at the U.S. Open final, the first time anyone had been "double-bageled" in the final.

Roger Federer serves to Teymuraz Gabashvili of Russia during their third-round match at the 2014 Australian Open. Federer defeated Gabashvili but fell to Rafael Nadal in the semifinal.

Roger Federer, in his tennis whites, serves to Philipp Kohlschreiber during their third-round match at Wimbledon in 2009. Federer made it to the final for the seventh consecutive year, taking his sixth Wimbledon crown.

Federer took the number one ranking from Andy Roddick in 2004 and held it for a record 237 weeks. Between 2004 and 2006 he set records with winning streaks in tournament finals (24) and against players in the top 10 (26). He won 10 or more titles for three straight years and 34 over that span. He also posted the highest winning percentage (94.3) and the highest percentage of tournaments won (69.4) over the three seasons. In 2006 he reached 16 finals in 17 tournaments entered and won a record 12.

Federer is elegant, and he seems born to play in the traditional all white of Wimbledon. He collected his third straight championship at the All England Club by besting Roddick in the 2005 final, and his fourth victory was over Nadal in 2006. It was the first of three years they'd face each other on Centre Court, cementing the legend of their rivalry.

Federer won again in 2007, but in 2008, playing for a record sixth straight Wimbledon title, it was Nadal's turn. Many con-

sider it the best match ever played, "a battle of such enthralling beauty and unimaginable majesty that it could not have been scripted," according to author Steve Flink. Federer was two sets down and fought back to tie it, but he ultimately succumbed 6–4, 6–4, 6–7 (5–7), 6–7 (8–10), 9–7. The loss ended his 40-match winning run at the All England Club.

The 2009 final against Andy Roddick could only be a letdown after that, except it wasn't. It was Federer's 20th major-final appearance, breaking Ivan Lendl's record, and he prevailed 5–7, 7–6 (8–6), 7–6 (7–5), 3–6, 16–14. It was the longest Wimbledon final in total games and the longest final set ever played in a major title match. Federer also set a major-final record with 50 aces.

With the victory Federer had his 15th major title, passing Sampras to become the all-time men's leader. He had tied the record a month prior by winning the 2009 French Open, which also completed his career Grand Slam. He was the sixth man to achieve the feat and one of three to do so on three different surfaces.

The best players thrive when the spotlight is brightest and the pressure most intense, and Federer is unmatched in Grand Slam tournament history. He won his first seven major finals in his first seven major-final appearances, a streak that ended with a loss to Nadal at the 2006 French Open. He has also been champion at least four times at three different majors and has reached the final of every major at least five times. On top of that he set Grand Slam tournament records with 23 straight semifinal appearances, from Wimbledon 2004 to the Australian Open in 2010, as well as the most total semifinals (33) and the most quarterfinals in a row (26).

Starting with his 2006 Wimbledon title, Federer played in 10 consecutive major finals, winning eight of them, and was in every major final in 2006, 2007 and 2009. The lack of a French title kept him from winning a Grand Slam in three separate years—2004, 2006 and 2007—when he won the three other majors. Only eight men have won three in a year, and only Federer has done it on three occasions.

Federer's last major title was Wimbledon in 2012. His final opponent was Andy Murray, who was vying to be the first British man to win Wimbledon in 76 years. Federer put the party on hold for another year, extending his record with his 17th major. Murray avenged his loss a month later as

Roger Federer waves to the crowd after defeating Andy Roddick in the 2009 final to win his sixth Wimbledon title. The match had the most games played of any Grand Slam final, 5–7, 7–6 (8–6), 7–6 (7–5), 3–6, 16–14.

time following the exploits of his beloved FC Basel and with his wife Mirka, a former pro, and twin daughters, Charlene Riva and Myla Rose. That may have to wait until after the 2016 Rio Olympics, however, where he's pledged to compete for the one singles bauble missing from his trophy case.

In 2006 David Foster Wallace wrote the essay "Federer as Religious Experience," and the true believers know he is capable of the miracle.

"The metaphysical explanation is that Roger Federer is one of those rare, preternatural athletes who appear to be exempt, at

---

Federer is an artist among athletes, playing a complete, aesthetically pleasing game. But it took him a while to learn to fight, not just to make the court his canvas.

---

he beat Federer on the same court with gold on the line at the London Olympics.

At the end of the 2013 season, even with his loss to 116th-ranked Sergiy Stakhovsky at Wimbledon and a drop to world number six, Federer was named ATPWorldTour.com Fans' Favourite for an 11th straight year. He was also selected by his peers as winner of the Stefan Edberg Sportsmanship Award for a ninth time and won the Arthur Ashe Humanitarian of the Year for a second time, in recognition of the work of the Roger Federer Foundation.

Since 2003, Federer has earned a record 27 ATP World Tour Awards and was named Laureus World Sportsman of the Year four times. His 302 weeks at number one are the most in history, and he's won 932 matches, 77 tournaments and nearly $80 million in career prize money.

When the 32-year-old does call it a day, he can spend more

least in part, from certain physical laws," says Wallace. "And Federer is of this type—a type that one could call genius, or mutant, or avatar...Particularly in the all-white that Wimbledon enjoys getting away with still requiring, he looks like what he may well (I think) be: a creature whose body is both flesh and, somehow, light."

Career Highlights	
Australian Open	**U.S. Open**
Singles champion 2004, 2006–07, 2010	Singles champion 2004–08
French Open	**Olympics**
Singles champion 2009	Silver medalist in men's singles 2012
Wimbledon	Gold medalist in men's doubles 2008
Singles champion 2003–07, 2009, 2012	**Davis Cup Team Member** 1999–2009, 2011–12

Lleyton Hewitt strikes a return to Marin Cilic during the semifinal of the 2013 Queen's Club Championships. Hewitt fell 4–6, 6–4, 2–6.

Lleyton Hewitt

TOOTH AND NAIL

For much of the 20th century, Australia was a tennis power, with successive generations of players winning majors and the country dominating the Davis Cup. But with the popularity of swimming, cricket, soccer, golf and rugby, the best athletes Down Under seem to have migrated to other sports.

The 21st-century heir to the tennis legacy was born in 1981, the son of an Australian rules football player. After nearly following father Glynn into the country's most popular sport, Lleyton Hewitt plays tennis like he's smashing heads on the field.

Glynn and Cherilyn, a former professional netball player, took their son Lleyton to his first Australian Open when he was 5. Ten years later, in 1997, he qualified for the tournament a month before he turned 16, the youngest player in its 108-year history.

In 1998 Hewitt won an ATP tour stop in Adelaide, his hometown, at the age of 16, beating Andre Agassi in the semifinals on his way to making headlines as the lowest-ranked winner in tour history, at 550th.

Hewitt made his Davis Cup debut the following year, beating American Todd Martin in five sets in his first match. Before the semifinals, Russia's Yevgeny Kafelnikov promised to teach the upstart a tennis lesson. Hewitt beat him in straight sets, and Australia went on to win the 1999 title.

In 2000 Hewitt won four tournaments, the first teenager to win that many since Pete Sampras 10 years earlier, and he earned his first major title, a doubles win with Max Mirnyi at the U.S. Open. He was the youngest man in the open era to win a major doubles crown.

Hewitt took his first singles major at the 2001 U.S. Open, beating Kafelnikov 6–1, 6–2, 6–1 in the semifinal and Sampras 7–6 (7–4), 6–1, 6–1 in the final. Proving that was no fluke, he won the year-end Masters tournament in Sydney, dismissing Pat Rafter and Andre Agassi in straight sets on the way to the final, a victory over Sebastien Grosjean, also in straight sets.

The strong finish vaulted Hewitt to the number one ranking at the age of 20 years, 10 months, the youngest man to be ranked number one in the world, bettering 21-year-old

Lleyton Hewitt powers a return shot to Marcos Baghdatis at the 2014 U.S. National Indoor Tennis Championships. Hewitt bested Baghdatis before losing to Michael Russell in the quarterfinal.

Lleyton Hewitt throws himself across the court to return a shot from Britain's Tim Henman during the 2002 Wimbledon semifinal. Hewitt hung on for the win and then defeated David Nalbandian for his second major victory.

Ellsworth Vines in 1932, and the first Australian to be on top since John Newcombe in 1971.

Hewitt held his top ranking and won his second major at Wimbledon in 2002, dropping only two sets in the entire tournament and dominating David Nalbandian in the final, 6–1, 6–3, 6–2. In the victory Hewitt didn't approach the net even once. He then capped the year with a Masters win in Shanghai, where he beat Roger Federer 7–5, 5–7, 7–5 in the semifinal and Juan Carlos Ferrero 7–5, 7–5, 2–6, 2–6, 6–4 in the final after being down 1–3 in the fifth set.

Called "Bart Simpson with a Yonex," Hewitt is a demonstrative and combative player, a dude with spiky blond hair under a backwards baseball cap who screams at himself and tries to intimidate opponents. Tellingly, his favorite movie is *Rocky*. Hewitt relishes the underdog role, and his wins are gutted out, not based on sublime talent. His passing shots, service returns and topspin lobs are strengths, but he lacks the big serves and

powerful groundstrokes of many of his contemporaries.

Hall of Famer and Australian Davis Cup captain Rafter calls Hewitt a "little mongrel," a compliment based on his scrappiness. And he's grateful that Hewitt has been a loyal Australian, playing for his country whenever he's been called upon.

But sometimes Hewitt's fire has burned the wrong people. He's made derogatory remarks about Australian fans, umpires and line judges. He changes coaches like underwear, has a frosty relationship with the media and had a long-running fight with the Association of Tennis Professionals after he was fined for not doing an interview.

Like Jimmy Connors, Hewitt may be successful only when he's angry, fighting enemies real and imagined, and also like Connors, another Hewitt quality is persistence. He refuses to surrender to the ravages of time.

In 2010 he took three months off after the Australian Open to rest his ailing left hip, which he had surgery on in 2009, and came back to beat Federer at the Halle tournament in Germany later that year. His multitude of maladies include a broken rib in 2005, a right knee injury in 2006, a back injury in 2007 and a right hand injury in 2010. He also missed three months in 2011 following surgery on his left foot to insert a metal plate in his toe.

In 2013, at 32 years old and ranked 66th in the world, Hewitt beat sixth-ranked Juan Martin del Potro in the second round of the U.S. Open. The four-hour, five-set victory over the 2009 U.S. champion was his first win over a top-10 player at the U.S. Open since beating Sampras in the 2001 final.

But he earned something he didn't have before — appreciation and perspective. Hewitt could almost be called mature.

"It's an amazing feeling," said Hewitt after the match. "A year-and-a-half ago I got told I probably wouldn't play again with the surgery I had. For me, I love being out in that atmosphere, sucking up every second of it."

The crowd was on his side, an appreciation of his career and his determination and resolve. Hewitt already had the respect of his opponents.

"I was happy for Lleyton," said Rafael Nadal. "He's a great fighter after a long time with a lot of injuries to have the chance to be back. To be still on the tour with motivation to keep play-

Lleyton Hewitt holds the Wimbledon championship trophy after defeating David Nalbandian in the 2002 final. Hewitt won the match 6–1, 6–3, 6–2 for his second major championship.

Called "Bart Simpson with a Yonex," Hewitt is a demonstrative and combative player, a dude with spiky blond hair under a backwards baseball cap who screams at himself and tries to intimidate opponents.

---

ing, keep fighting is something that I admire a lot in him. "

Todd Martin, who played against John McEnroe, Ivan Lendl, Andre Agassi and Pete Sampras, said the best shot he ever faced was Hewitt's backhand passing shot, and Marat Safin called him the game's biggest fighter.

Hewitt credited his run at the U.S. Open to a marathon training session he had with Federer on the first day of the tournament. And Federer says that early in his career Hewitt was a role model, and he still respects him.

"I am one of the guys who has always believed in Lleyton, even though people were writing him off and being negative," said Federer. "The guy has given everything and more to Australia, to tennis. He's done a lot. So I admire that he's still playing, that he loves it."

Hewitt, who was also part of the Davis Cup–winning team in 2003 and represented Australia at the 2008 Beijing and 2012 London Olympics, has won nearly 600 matches and $20 million in prize money, and in 2014 he played in his 18th consecutive Australian Open.

"I still get really motivated for the majors, and that's the main part that still drives me; why I'm still playing the game are Davis Cup and the majors," says Hewitt. "I still enjoy training and doing all the hard work, and if I didn't enjoy that, or found it too hard or whatever, then I wouldn't still be playing."

Hewitt finished the 2013 season ranked 62nd in the world, 10 spots lower than Australian number one Bernard Tomic. After a rocky early relationship, Hewitt has made nice and is mentoring Australia's most promising player. They play alongside each other on the Davis Cup team, and Hewitt knows that if the glory days are going to return to Australia, he has to inspire the next generation.

Career Highlights

Wimbledon	**Davis Cup Team Member**
Singles champion 2002	1999–2013
U.S. Open	
Singles champion 2001	
Doubles champion 2000	

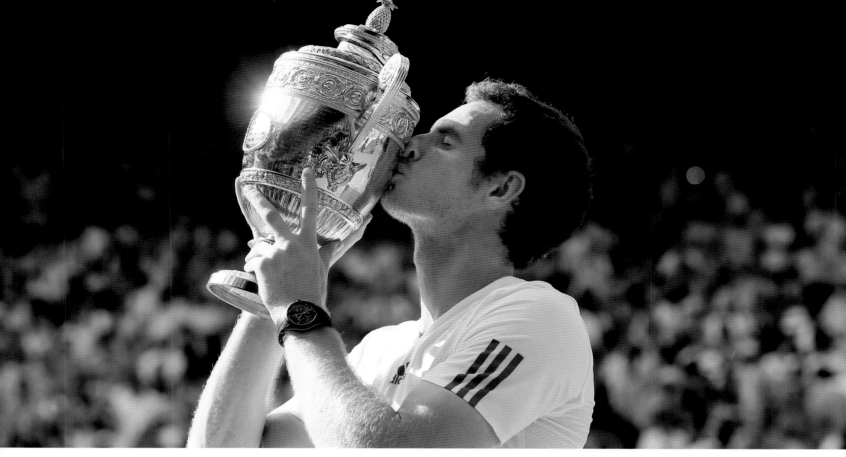

Andy Murray of Britain kisses the Wimbledon championship trophy after defeating Novak Djokovic at the All England Club in 2013. Murray's victory marked the first time a British man had won Wimbledon in 77 years.

Andy Murray

BREAKTHROUGH BRIT

It had been 77 long years. Not since a Briton had won a Wimbledon singles title, that was Virginia Wade in 1977, but since a British man had won "the Championships," the jewel in the nation's sporting crown.

Tim Henman knocked on the door in the late 1990s and early 2000s, but a Wimbledon title was always going to be an overachievement for him. Andy Murray had the talent, but he also had the misfortune of playing in the same era as three of the greatest of all time — Roger Federer, Rafael Nadal and Novak Djokovic. It seemed as though the British would be thwarted for another generation, that the statue and specter of Fred Perry, winner from 1934 to 1936, would haunt the grounds of the All England Club for the foreseeable future.

For a fortnight every summer since 2005, the nation's hopes had been foisted on Murray, and if that wasn't enough pressure, a member of his own family already had a Wimbledon championship: older brother Jamie won the mixed doubles title with Jelena Jankovic in 2007.

It was Jamie whom Andy looked up to and chased when the two were growing up. After a tryout with the youth team of the iconic Glasgow Rangers, Andy decided to focus on tennis, and it soon became clear that he was the better of the Murray brothers.

In 1999, at the age of 12, Andy entered the prestigious Orange Bowl tournament in Florida and won. He relocated to Barcelona to train when he was 15 and took home the 2004 U.S. Open junior title when he was 17, leading the BBC to name him the Young Sports Personality of the Year. In 2005 he became the youngest British player to compete in the Davis Cup and entered his first Wimbledon as a wild card a month after turning 18.

By 2007 Murray had won three Association of Tennis Professionals titles and had entered the top 10, but he soon hit the Big Three wall. He lost the 2008 U.S. Open and 2010 Australian Open finals to Federer and the 2011 Australian Open to Djokovic, during a stretch when Federer, Nadal and Djokovic won 29 of 30 Grand Slam tournaments.

Andy Murray returns to Fernando Verdasco during their quarterfinal match at Wimbledon in 2013. Murray survived a five-set scare, 6–4, 6–3, 1–6, 4–6, 5–7, to advance. He later won the championship over Novak Djokovic.

CHALLENGES REMAINING

ERDASCO 3

URRAY 3

Andy Murray eyes the ball as Fernando Verdasco delivers a return shot during their quarterfinal Wimbledon match in 2013.

His most crushing loss, however, came in his fourth major final, at Wimbledon in 2012. Murray was the first British man to make the final since Bunny Austin in 1938, but once again he fell to Federer, who won his seventh Wimbledon and 17th major career title. Murray didn't know if he'd ever come that close again, and he admitted that at that point in his career he simply felt like "a loser: nothing more, nothing less."

The joke in the United Kingdom was that when Murray won he was British, and when he lost he was Scottish. It is a barb not uncommon to Scots, but with political rumblings of a Scottish secession from the United Kingdom, the jab carried weight, and Murray steadfastly maintained his allegiance to Scotland.

"We Scots have a fierce pride in the things we do that others can never appreciate," says Murray. "I am the British number one, but I would prefer to be the British number one from Scotland every time."

Andrew Barron Murray was born in Glasgow in 1987, and he witnessed one of Britain's darkest chapters when he was grow-ing up in Dunblane. A local shopkeeper, who was known to the Murray family, killed 16 students and one teacher before turning the gun on himself at Dunblane Primary School on March 13, 1996. Eight-year-old Andy was in school when it happened.

Murray has a reputation for being dour, but after he opened up and broke down about the tragedy in a BBC documentary on the eve of Wimbledon in 2013, he earned a new level of respect and sympathy from the British public.

The 2013 tournament was different in several ways. Murray had hired Ivan Lendl as his coach in 2012, and the two men had something in common: they're the only two players to lose their first four major finals. Lendl went on to win eight majors, but never a Wimbledon crown.

"I don't know how many people at the time thought that Ivan was the right person for me, but I felt that there was some-thing intriguing about his career and how it had played out. I liked the fact that people had found him difficult to appreciate and he wasn't at all about the fame: it was about the winning for him."

The partnership worked. A month after the 2012 loss to Federer in the Wimbledon final, the Olympic tennis tournament was played at the All England Club. Murray and Laura Robson earned the silver in mixed doubles, but once again the main cause for fans was singles, and Murray beat Federer to win gold for the host nation.

Getting the better of the Swiss legend in such an important match was a huge boost to Murray's confidence, and it showed in the U.S. Open at Flushing Meadows later that summer when he beat Djokovic 7–6 (12–10), 7–5, 2–6, 3–6, 6–2 to win the title. It was his first major championship and the first won by a Briton since Wade in 1977.

So in 2013 there was reason to believe the Wimbledon drought would finally end. Murray reached the final for the second year in a row, this time meeting world number one Djokovic. The two had been born a week apart and had played each other since they were 11. It was their 19th professional encounter, with Djokovic holding an 11-7 lead.

After winning the first set, Murray trailed 4-1 in the second but rallied to take it, then he fell behind 4-2 in the third. He

Andy Murray serves to Novak Djokovic during the men's championship match at the 2012 U.S. Open. Murray won the five-set final to claim his first major title.

celebration began, one of the biggest street parties in Britain since World War II ended.

Sir Andy was awarded the Order of the British Empire by Prince William in October 2013, a ceremony he nearly missed because the ATP had scheduled a random drug test that day (he passed).

"We Scots have a fierce pride in the things we do that others can never appreciate, I am the British number one, but I would prefer to be the British number one from Scotland every time." –Andy Murray

---

fought back and reached match point, and with Britain holding its breath he dropped it. Djokovic then fought off the second and the third championship points. The 15,000 fans at Centre Court, thousands watching a giant screen on the grounds at "Murray Mount" and millions more around the country started to sweat. Ten minutes and eight points after the first match point, Djokovic hit the ball into the net and Murray won, 6–4, 7–5, 6–4.

When it was over Murray let out a primal scream, years of personal frustration and decades of national angst released into the clear blue London sky.

"That last game will be the toughest game I'll play in my career. Ever," said Murray to the fans after the match. "Winning Wimbledon — I still can't believe it. Can't get my head around that. I can't believe it.

"I obviously wanted to try and win this for myself, but also I understand how much everyone else wanted to see a British winner at Wimbledon, so I hope you guys enjoyed it."

They did; the nation let out a collective sigh of relief and the

With the weight of the OBE medal on his chest replacing that of 60 million people on his shoulders, Murray can breathe a little easier. And, by having reached the final of four of the last five Grand Slam tournaments he entered in 2012 and 2013, along with his 28 ATP titles, Murray's name can now be added to the pantheon of the generation's biggest stars.

And finally, when Fred Perry is spoken in the same breath as Andy Murray it will be to celebrate the last two British men to win at the All England Club, not to invoke national insecurity.

Career Highlights

Wimbledon
Singles champion 2013

U.S. Open
Singles champion 2012

Davis Cup Team Member
2005–09, 2011, 2013

Olympics
Gold medalist in men's singles 2012
Silver medalist in mixed doubles 2012

Rafael Nadal

Spain's Rafael Nadal returns a shot to compatriot David Ferrer in the men's final of the 2013 French Open. Nadal won the match to claim his record-setting eighth French Open title.

VAMOS!

Like a warm breeze from the Balearic Islands, Rafael "Rafa" Nadal Parera brought a refreshing style and sex appeal to tennis when he blew in with his long hair, sleeveless shirts and shorts below the knees. His arms have their own fan club, and changing shirts during a match leads to wolf-whistles from the normally staid tennis crowd.

A 6-foot-1, 188-pound ball of energy, "El Nino" is in constant motion, adjusting his clothes and his hair in what are now famous tics known as "manias" to the Spanish, meaning madness or frenzy. His heavy left-handed forehands are laden with topspin, and he outruns every ball and opponent with unbridled enthusiasm. His savagery on the court belies his good nature off it, and he plays with a fury that can't be explained by a difficult childhood or Svengali coach or any of the other dark motivations that have driven the most competitive players. There isn't a nicer, more ferocious guy on tour.

"I don't think anybody's played the game with the same kind of positive energy and emotion," says Hall of Famer Mats Wilander. "No one. Not even Lleyton Hewitt and not Jimmy Connors. Even though they are the great fighters, apart from Nadal, they're not as positive as Nadal. He is always positive. He's just a new breed. We've never seen anything like him."

Born in 1986 in Manacor, Spain, on the island of Mallorca, Rafa grew up across the street from the local tennis club where his uncle and lifelong coach, Toni Nadal, was the resident pro.

Passionate about soccer, Rafa learned sportsmanship on the pitch when his father, Sebastian, encouraged him to congratulate his opponents no matter the result. As he approached the age of 13 he still took soccer very seriously, and with another uncle, Miguel Angel, having played in three World Cups, it was a viable career option. But he chose tennis, and in 1997 he was the national 12-and-under champion.

Nadal turned pro in 2001 at the tender age of 15, winning his first ATP match in his hometown. In 2003 he reached the top 50, and in 2004 he and 1998 French Open champ Carlos Moya helped Spain beat the United States for the Davis Cup title. At 18 years old, Nadal beat Andy Roddick to become the youngest player to win a singles match in a Davis Cup victory.

Rafael Nadal serves against Richard Gasquet during the semifinal of the 2013 U.S. Open. Nadal went on to win the championship, defeating Novak Djokovic 6–2, 3–6, 6–4, 6–1.

Rafael Nadal returns a Roger Federer offering during their singles final on Centre Court at the 2008 edition of Wimbledon. Nadal prevailed against Federer, ending the legend's bid for a sixth straight championship.

After growing up on the clay courts of Mallorca, Nadal took the two most prominent clay competitions on tour, the Italian and French Opens, in 2005, beating world number one Roger Federer in the French semifinals. He defended both titles in 2006 and 2007, beating Federer in the final of the 2006 Italian Open and in the French Open final both years.

Guillermo Vilas held the clay record with 53 consecutive wins, but Nadal decimated it, reaching 81 straight before Federer ended it in Hamburg in 2007.

But Federer never did beat him at the one major contested on clay, and the 2008 French Open was a master class by Nadal; he didn't lose a set the entire tournament and dismissed Federer once again in the final, for his fourth straight French crown.

If Federer's legacy is best embodied by the all white of the All England Club, Nadal's is personified by the deep red clay of Roland Garros — which often covers the star from his headband to his toes.

While Nadal was dominating in Paris, Federer was making London his second home, winning the Wimbledon title from 2003 to 2005. When Nadal reached his first Wimbledon final in 2006 his opponent was Federer, with the man from Switzerland winning his fourth straight title on his favorite surface.

The rematch in the 2007 final was a Centre Court classic, and once again Federer prevailed, 7–6 (9–7), 4–6, 7–6 (7–3), 2–6, 6–2.

A year later, after beating Federer in the 2008 French Open final, Nadal finally overcame the lord of the manor, winning 6–4, 6–4, 6–7 (5–7), 6–7 (8–10), 9–7 for his first Wimbledon title. That 2008 final has been called the best match ever played, and tennis fans were getting spoiled with two of the greatest players in history meeting regularly on the game's biggest stages.

After conquering grass, hard court was the final frontier for Nadal, and he won his only Australian Open title in 2009 with a five-set final victory over Federer, naturally. Nadal had beaten him in three major finals on three different surfaces over the course of eight months.

The rest of the year was a difficult one for Nadal, however. He had recurring tendinitis and excruciating pain in his knees, and his parents were going through a divorce. His loss to 25th-ranked Robin Soderling in the fourth round of the 2009 French Open was a monumental upset, his first at Roland Garros after 31 straight wins and four titles.

Nadal rebounded in 2010, coming an Australian Open title short of a Grand Slam. He avenged his loss to Soderling in the 2010 French final, winning in straight sets for his fifth French title in six years, and beat Tomas Berdych for his second Wimbledon crown. He also won his first U.S. Open over Novak Djokovic to complete the career Slam and become the seventh man to win all four majors.

As the reigning champion from the 2008 Beijing Olympics, Nadal was forced to withdraw from the 2012 London Games with another knee injury. He ended up missing seven months with a partially torn patellar tendon; he returned after the 2013 Australian Open to stage one of the greatest and most unlikely comebacks in tennis history.

A triumphant Rafael Nadal reacts after defeating Novak Djokovic during their semifinal match at the 2013 French Open. Nadal later claimed the championship, his fourth straight and eighth overall.

slim 23–19 edge over the Serb. The 42 head-to-head matches are the most in the open era, and in 2012 Djokovic beat Nadal in six finals, including Wimbledon and the U.S. Open.

"I don't think anybody's played the game with the same kind of positive energy and emotion ... he is always positive. He's just a new breed. We've never seen anything like him." – Mats Wilander

---

After questioning early in the year whether he'd be able to return at all, Nadal went 75-7 in 2013 and won 10 tournaments, including a victory over fellow Spaniard David Ferrer for his eighth French Open, a record for any man at one Grand Slam event.

By season's end Nadal had 658 career match wins and 60 tournament victories: the only active player ahead of him is Federer. Despite the razor-thin margins of victory in many of their matches, the overall record skews heavily in Nadal's favor: 22-10 at the end of the 2013 season.

One of the reasons the rivalry has been so fascinating to watch as the pair scratch and claw for their respective places in tennis history is that their styles contrast in every way, yet they share a mutual respect, admiration and even friendship.

But just as Nadal has stymied Federer's march to an untouchable number of Grand Slam tournament victories, Djokovic could be a roadblock to Nadal's becoming the greatest of all time.

If the matches haven't been quite as memorable as Nadal–Federer, there have been more of them, with Nadal owning a

But at the 2014 French Open, Nadal beat Djokovic 3–6, 7–5, 6–2, 6–4 for his Ninth French Open title and 14th major. That win tied the Spaniard with legend Pete Sampras and put him three wins behind Federer's all-time record of 17. He's still just 28 and has won eight majors since 2010, so if his knees cooperate and the French Open remains on the calendar every summer, Federer's record appears vulnerable.

"Every tennis lover would like, someday, to play like Federer," says French tennis writer Philippe Bouin. "But every man wants to be Rafael Nadal. Which is different."

Career Highlights

Australian Open
Singles champion 2009

French Open
Singles champion 2005–08, 2010–14

Wimbledon
Singles champion 2008, 2010

U.S. Open
Singles champion 2010, 2013

Olympics
Gold medalist in men's singles 2008

Davis Cup Team Member
2004–06, 2008–09, 2011, 2013

Andy Roddick celebrates a point against Fabio Fognini in third-round action at the 2012 U.S. Open. Roddick's eventual victory over Fognini marked his last professional win.

Andy Roddick

AMERICAN ICON

Andrew Stephen Roddick was born in Omaha, Nebraska, in 1982 and grew up in Austin, Texas, where he played tennis with future New Orleans Saints quarterback Drew Brees. By the time he was 11 his family realized they had a prodigy on their hands and moved to Florida to further his young career.

But Andy didn't go to Nick Bollettieri's academy or any other Floridian tennis hothouse. His parents sent him to a normal high school, where he played varsity basketball and was a regular kid — as much as you can be when you're the number one junior tennis player in the world.

In 2000 Roddick was the first American since Butch Buchholz in 1959 to win the Australian Open boys' title, and he added the U.S. Open and four other singles titles and seven doubles titles on the junior circuit that year.

The first noteworthy victory of Roddick's professional career was over Pete Sampras in the third round of the Key Biscayne tournament in 2001, 11 years after 8-year-old Andy snuck into the players' lounge at the U.S. Open and beat Sampras at a video game.

Sampras won the 14th and final major title of his career at the 2002 U.S. Open, beating Roddick's hero, Andre Agassi, in the final. The next year the mantle was passed.

In the semifinals of the 2003 U.S. Open, Roddick saved match point against David Nalbandian with a service winner and went on to win the match to face Juan Carlos Ferrero in the final. Putting an exclamation on his first and only major title, Roddick hit three straight aces to finish his 6–3, 7–6 (7–2), 6–3 victory.

Roddick won five other singles titles in 2003 and had a 19-match winning streak. At the end of the season he was the number one player in the world, the first American since Agassi in 1999 and still the last to hold it. He was also the youngest player in history to win the ATP Player of the Year award.

Roddick was dating singer/actress Mandy Moore at the time, and he hosted *Saturday Night Live*, just the second tennis player to be asked, after Chris Evert. He was named Sexiest Athlete in 2003 by *People* magazine, and in 2004 he won ESPN's ESPY Award for Best Male Tennis Player.

Andy Roddick makes a backhand stab to return David Ferrer's shot in their third-round match at Wimbledon in 2012. Ferrer bested Roddick in four sets.

Andy Roddick eyes a forehand return to David Ferrer at Wimbledon in 2012. In his career, Roddick thrice made the Wimbledon final but was never able to secure victory.

He had officially crossed over into pop culture territory, but that kind of (over)exposure tends to breed resentment among peers. And even when Roddick strived to be one of the guys, he gave the impression that he was cocky and just a little too sure of himself.

Publicity also leads to expectations. Roddick was following in the long line of American greats and was the next great American hope immediately after the generation of Sampras, Agassi, Courier and Chang. But he had the misfortune of his prime years coinciding with those of Roger Federer, arguably the best player in history and the man who took Roddick's number one ranking just 13 weeks after he earned it.

Federer bested Roddick in the 2004 and 2005 Wimbledon finals and the 2006 U.S. Open final, but the closest and most painful loss for the American came at the 2009 Wimbledon final.

The match set records for the most games played in a Wimbledon final and longest fifth set in major-final history.

Roddick didn't drop serve until the final game of the last set, but Federer won 5–7, 7–6 (8–6), 7–6 (7–5), 3–6, 16–14.

It was a heroic effort, and rarely had a loss engendered so much respect and sympathy for a player. The crowd chanted Roddick's name afterward, even as the player on the other side of the net made history; with the win Federer surpassed Sampras, who was watching from the royal box, to become the man with the most major titles in the history of the game with his 15th.

"He's an artist," conceded Roddick, who had lost 19 of his 21 matches against Federer. "I basically hit the crap out of the ball."

A right-hander with a two-fisted backhand, Roddick whipped his wicked forehand from the baseline and had one of the most potent serves ever. He hit the fastest in history up to that point in 2004 at a Davis Cup semifinal match against Vladimir Voltchkov of Belarus in Charleston, South Carolina. It was recorded at 155 mph.

Roddick played in the Davis Cup on 10 occasions, winning memorably in 2007 with a 6-0 record in singles as the United States beat Russia in the final in Portland, Oregon. It was the Americans' first Cup since 1995 and the last the country has won.

In 2012, on his 30th birthday, Roddick announced that, like many American greats before him, the U.S. Open would be his last tournament. After more than 800 matches and injuries to his knees, ankles, shoulder and back, his body had told him it was time.

As they had done with Jimmy Connors in 1991 and Agassi in 2006, the U.S. Open crowd showered their native son with affection, and Roddick basked in it.

"When I was with Andy, I said, 'If you let 'em, those 25,000 people will help you win,'" said Connors, who coached Roddick briefly. "And it takes him to say that he's retiring to see it and to feel it. I guess, better late than never."

The energy and adrenaline pushed Roddick to the fourth round, but Juan Martin del Potro ended his tournament and career with a 6–7 (1–7), 7–6 (7–4), 6–2, 6–4 win.

Roddick's career winning percentage was .742, including .744 at the majors. He won 32 tournaments and more than $20 mil-

Andy Roddick makes a return to Fabio Fognini in the third round of the 2012 U.S. Open. Roddick retired after his fourth-round loss to Juan Martin del Potro.

"[Federer is] an artist. I basically hit the crap out of the ball." – Andy Roddick

---

lion in prize money, and he was in the world top five for 124 weeks between 2003 and 2006 and the top 10 every year from 2002 to 2010.

An avid golfer, Roddick played in the 2013 AT&T Pebble Beach Pro Am, and he plays World Team Tennis, which he has an equity stake in. He also spends time running the Andy Roddick Foundation, which he started in 2000 on the advice of Agassi, who said his one regret was not starting his charitable foundation sooner. It has raised $11 million to give kids in low-income communities the opportunity to play sports and get an education, and he's opening the Andy Roddick Foundation Sports & Learning Center in Austin, where he lives with his wife.

The all-American boy is now married to the head cheerleader, or in this case the *Sports Illustrated* swimsuit cover model, Brooklyn Decker, and they "are proud parents of two English bulldogs, Billie Jean and Bob Costas." The first to honor Billie Jean King — player, activist and namesake of the U.S. Open tennis center, and the second an inspiration for his new career in broadcasting. With his experience, good looks and charisma it was no surprise when Fox Sports 1 hired Roddick as a cohost of their nightly highlight show.

"He's a proud man, and has reason: He without question maximized his talent," says friend and Davis Cup teammate Jim Courier. "He's unlucky to have faced Roger, because he'd have had four, five, six [majors] — who knows? But Andy will tell you how lucky he is because he got one."

Roddick agrees.

"I got to play in a crowd, play in Wimbledon finals, be the guy on a Davis Cup team for a while. Those are opportunities not a lot of people get."

Career Highlights

U.S. Open	Davis Cup Team Member
Singles champion 2003	2001–2009, 2011

played on Centre Court. Davenport was serving for the Wimbledon title at 6–5 in the second set and was 2 points away from victory four times, but she couldn't close it out and Venus won 4–6, 7–6 (7–4), 9–7. The match set a Wimbledon women's final record at two hours and 45 minutes.

The physical toll of her long career caught up to Davenport in 2006. After finishing the 2004 and 2005 seasons ranked number one in the world, back and shoulder problems sidelined her, keeping her out of the French Open and Wimbledon. She also announced late in 2006 that she was pregnant.

Married in 2003 to husband Jonathan, Davenport gave birth to son Jagger in 2007. She returned to the game later that year and won four more tournaments, the last tying Virginia Wade for seventh place on the list of female singles winners in the open era at 55.

However, only three of her career tournament wins were Grand Slams, the same number Jennifer Capriati won while accumulating only 14 career tournament victories. Davenport also finished the year ranked number one four times — in 1998, 2001, 2004 and 2005 — which was an especially rare feat for her having claimed only three major titles.

Lindsay Davenport holds her baby, Jagger Jonathan Leach, after her victory over Daniela Hantuchova in the final of the 2007 WTA Bali Open. Davenport is one of only a handful of players to win a tournament after having a child.

"I never was about playing in front of people or getting attention. That actually freaked me out when I was playing pro tennis, and it caused me a lot of anxiety." – Lindsay Davenport

---

"It seemed to me that when she got a little hungrier — 'maybe I should set the bar higher' — things got more complicated," said tennis writer Jon Wertheim. "The first three times she appeared in a Grand Slam final, she won the prize. After winning the 2000 Australian, she came up empty, sometimes under devastating circumstances. Her body language and tendency toward self-flagellation suggested that maybe she was better off when she set lower standards for herself. Still, she ought to walk off the stage proud, having achieved more than anyone would have predicted when she first turned pro."

In 2008 Davenport surpassed Graf in career prize money at nearly $22 million and made her third Olympics, playing doubles in Beijing, before leaving the tour because she was pregnant with daughter Lauren, who was born in 2009. In 2012 she gave birth to her third child, daughter Kaya.

Always a popular player and an engaging personality, Davenport made a successful transition to tennis commentary and had a cameo appearance on the TV show *CSI*. A busy schedule and three kids keep her from playing a lot these days,

but her well-rounded childhood and life away from the game kept her from burning out.

"I always loved the sport," says Davenport. "It's amazing — you get some former players that don't ever want to play again. I have a lot of friends that were on the tour that are like that. But I'm not there. I like to play. I like to watch it. I like to study it still. I don't have the time right now, but hopefully in 10 years when my kids are older, I'll have the time. I look forward to that."

Career Highlights

Australian Open
Singles champion 2000

French Open
Doubles champion 1996

Wimbledon
Singles champion 1999
Doubles champion 1999

Federation Cup Team Member
1993–94

U.S. Open
Singles champion 1998
Doubles champion 1997

Olympics
Gold medalist in women's singles 1996

Fed Cup Team Member
1995–2000, 2002, 2005, 2008

Martina Hingis serves against Amelie Mauresmo during the round-robin portion of the 2006 WTA Tour Championships. Hingis was unable to win against the eventual runner-up, Mauresmo.

Martina Hingis

THE SWISS MISS

There have been a lot of precocious tennis talents over the years, but Martina Hingis really put the child in child prodigy. She played in her first tournament at the age of 4 and won the junior title at the 1993 French Open at just 12 years old, the youngest junior champion in the history of the majors.

Ironically, the French Open is the only singles major Hingis didn't win as an adult, but there was little else she didn't accomplish. She was world number one for a total of 209 weeks — from 1997 to 2000, the fourth-longest tenure in Women's Tennis Association history — and she also spent 35 weeks as the top-ranked doubles player. That rare combination made her one of only five women in history to hold both rankings simultaneously.

It almost seemed predestined. Hingis was born in Kosice, Czechoslovakia, now Slovakia, in 1980, an only child to parents who were both nationally ranked players. Her mother, Melanie, a disciplinarian and perfectionist, named her in honor of legend Martina Navratilova and coached her from birth.

After her parents divorced, Melanie believed Martina's

career would flourish away from the communist regime of their native country, and the two defected to Switzerland.

"I was almost eight years old," recounts Hingis. "It was a big thing because at the time I didn't want to move. I was very happy with life in Czechoslovakia. I had all my friends there, and I didn't know what was happening. Of course I was very upset, crying. I couldn't speak the language. I couldn't understand anything."

Hingis says the move brought her and her mother closer together. The defection also allowed her to travel freely to international tournaments, something she couldn't do while living in Czechoslovakia under communist rule. Melanie, meanwhile, married a Swiss businessman and became Martina's constant companion on tour; her father, Karol, remained in Slovakia and on the periphery of Martina's life and career.

On the court, "the Swiss Miss" found yet another home in the Australian Open. There she made the singles final six straight years, winning both the singles and doubles titles for three consecutive years from 1997 to 1999. The first made her

Martina Hingis celebrates after winning the final of the 1997 Australian Open. Hingis defeated Mary Pierce 6–2, 6–2 to win her first Grand Slam title.

Martina Hingis serves to Victoria Azarenka during their third-round match at the 2007 U.S. Open. Hingis, the 1997 champion, failed to advance.

the youngest major winner in senior history, at 16 years, three months old, and she became the youngest to be ranked number one.

1997 was a banner year for Hingis. On top of her Aussie finish she became the second-youngest Wimbledon singles champion by beating Jana Novotna in the final. Only Lottie Dod had won the title at a younger age, prevailing as a 15-year-old in 1887. Hingis, however, already had a Wimbledon doubles title under her belt, winning with Helena Sukova in 1996 when she was 15.

Hingis also won the U.S. Open in 1997, but her loss to the ninth-seeded Iva Majoli in the final of the French Open (a tournament in which she played through injury after falling from her horse earlier in the year) precluded her from her Grand Slam aspirations. Two years later Hingis was back in the French final. She took the first set 6–4 against Steffi Graf and led the second set at 3–1 and 5–4 but couldn't close it out. Argued line calls led to a hostile Parisian crowd and Hingis melted down,

losing 4–6, 7–5, 6–2 and leaving the court in tears.

Hingis returned strongly in 1998, winning her second straight Australian Open singles title in straight sets over Conchita Martinez and the doubles crown with 15-year-old Mirjana Lucic. At a combined age of 32, they were the youngest team to win a major doubles title. Paired with Novotna the rest of the season, Hingis won the next three majors to secure a doubles Grand Slam, the third woman in history to accomplish the feat.

At 5 foot 7 and 130 pounds, Hingis was slight by modern tennis standards, but she beat bigger, stronger opponents by outwitting them. Her mother taught her to play tennis like a game of chess, and she accurately placed balls where it was most difficult for her opponents to reach and return them.

"I can't overpower them, so why should I try? I just use their force to make them less powerful. Tennis is not only a physical game. It's mental and finesse. So I try and avoid their efforts."

On facing the power of Venus and Serena Williams, Hingis says: "There's always someone out there. But most of the time I still manage to get out of it, and win, because I use other methods. I have my speed, I have my hand and my brains — and I have my mum."

But she didn't always have her mum; in 2001 Hingis decided to find a new coach, citing the need for some autonomy and independence at the age of 20. Melanie wasn't happy with Martina's interest in fashion, the opposite sex and having a social life, while Martina didn't get along with her mother's new boyfriend. When questioned about the split, both insisted that they remained close and were just taking a professional break.

It didn't last long; the two were reunited for the 2002 season after Hingis recovered from surgery on her right ankle. She began the year with her fourth Australian Open doubles title, but she also suffered a taxing loss in the singles final against Jennifer Capriati. In a match that took more than two hours and was played in heat that reached 125 degrees Fahrenheit on the court, Hingis was up 6–4, 4–0 and had four match points in the second set, but Capriati set a major-final record by saving each one, and she eventually prevailed 4–6, 7–6 (9–7), 6–2.

Martina Hingis raises the Venus Rosewater Dish on Wimbledon's Centre Court in 1997. Her defeat of Jana Novotna in the final made Hingis the second-youngest Wimbledon champion.

winning league most valuable player in 2012 and 2013, as well as coaching Russian Anastasia Pavlyuchenkova.

After being inducted into the Hall of Fame in 2013, Hingis announced she was making a comeback in doubles, partnering with Slovakia's Daniela Hantuchova.

"I can't overpower them, so why should I try? I just use their force to make them less powerful. Tennis is not only a physical game. It's mental and finesse. So I try and avoid their efforts." – Martina Hingis

---

A few months later Hingis went under the knife to repair ligaments in her left ankle, but chronic problems with her ankles, knee and hip forced her to retire in 2003 at only 22. She came back three years later and won her only mixed doubles major at the 2006 Australian Open with Mahesh Bhupathi. She also made it to the singles quarterfinals as a wild-card entry and beat Venus Williams on her way to the 2006 Italian Open title. She had risen to the number seven ranking, but her return was short lived.

After testing positive for cocaine at Wimbledon, Hingis retired again in 2007. She denied ever taking drugs but chose to accept her two-year suspension and leave the game instead of fighting to prove her innocence.

Hingis' career total was as balanced as her game, with 43 singles titles and 37 in doubles, including 10 Grand Slam tournament victories — nine doubles and one mixed doubles — to bring her career total to 15 major championships.

In "retirement" Hingis didn't stray far from the court, playing for the Washington Kastles in World Team Tennis and

"I always had it in the back of my head in the last six years," said Hingis. "Now, being so much closer to it, being closer to the game, closer to the matches, I was like let's try it again and see if I can have a great time."

There was speculation it was the start of a singles comeback as well, something Hingis threw cold water on.

"At 17, everything seemed to be so easy. Now, I'm almost twice the age."

Career Highlights

Australian Open	U.S. Open
Singles champion 1997–99	Singles champion 1997
Doubles champion 1997–99, 2002	Doubles champion 1998
Mixed doubles champion 2006	**Wimbledon**
French Open	Singles champion 1997
Doubles champion 1998, 2000	Doubles champion 1996, 1998
Fed Cup Team Member	**International Tennis Hall of Fame**
1995–98	2013

Maria Sharapova serves during the 2014 Australian Open. Sharapova's best finish at the tournament was as champion in 2008.

Maria Sharapova

STYLE AND SUBSTANCE

Maria Sharapova is a child of the 21st century. Born in the former Soviet Union with no memory of the Iron Curtain, she went from near poverty in Siberia to an elite tennis academy in Florida to become a capitalist's dream and social media darling.

With more than 11 million followers on Facebook, Sharapova is one of the most popular athletes in the world of any sport or gender. Her personal website is heavy with tweets, pictures and sponsors—but light on tennis.

Like Russian predecessor and starlet Anna Kournikova, Sharapova's looks feed her popularity with tennis fans and advertisers. The difference is Sharapova has game and hasn't lost sight of what put her in the spotlight.

Born to Yelena and Yuri in 1987 in Nyagan, a town of about 50,000 in Western Siberia, Sharapova played in an exhibition with Martina Navratilova in Moscow when she was 6. At 9, Maria and Yuri set off for the United States with almost no money in their pockets and without Yelena, who couldn't join them for two years because of visa difficulties.

Even among the very best young players in the world at

Nick Bollettieri's tennis school in Bradenton, Florida, Sharapova stood out because of her height and devastating groundstrokes. Budding agent Max Eisenbud was struck by the 12-year-old's preternatural talent and took her under his wing. He helped handle the family's immigration problems, guided her financially and set up lucrative sponsorships. He remains her agent, manager and friend to this day.

Success came early for Sharapova. She won her first Grand Slam title at Wimbledon in 2004 when she was 17. As the 13th seed she dismissed two-time defending champion Serena Williams in the final with relative ease, 6–1, 6–4, after being down 1–4 in the second set.

Sharapova was the third-youngest woman to win Wimbledon, after 16-year-old Martina Hingis in 1997 and Lottie Dod, who was 15, in 1887. She was also the first player since Evonne Goolagong in 1971 to win on just her second try.

After beating Williams again to win the 2004 WTA Tour Championships, "the Siberian Siren" was suddenly one of the most famous athletes in the world.

Maria Sharapova, defending Wimbledon champion, serves to Nuria Llagostera Vives during their first-round match at the 2005 edition of Wimbledon. Sharapova succumbed to eventual champion Venus Williams in the semifinal match.

Maria Sharapova lets out a guttural scream as she returns Alize Cornet's shot during their third-round match at the 2014 Australian Open. Sharapova has thrice been to the finals of the Australian Open, winning once.

Sharapova first reached the number one ranking in August 2005, and in 2006 she won the U.S. Open in particularly dominant fashion. She dispatched that year's Australian Open and Wimbledon champion and top seed Amelie Mauresmo 6–0, 4–6, 6–0 in the semifinal and ran over French Open winner and second seed Justine Henin 6–4, 6–4 in the final.

A third major title came two years later at the 2008 Australian Open, where Sharapova beat Ana Ivanovic 7–5, 6–3 in the final after dominating top-ranked Henin 6–4, 6–0 in the quarterfinals.

Later that year Sharapova ran into misfortune, as she suffered a right shoulder injury that required surgery and kept her off the tour for 10 months. She endured an arduous rehabilitation regimen and finally saw the light when she beat Italian clay-court specialist Sara Errani 6–3, 6–2 in the 2012 French Open final. The clay courts at Roland Garros had always given Sharapova trouble — she had once compared her movement on clay to that of a "cow on ice" — and with the win she became only the 10th woman in history to complete the career Grand Slam.

She also regained the number one ranking for the first time in four years. Back in top form, Sharapova proudly referred to herself as a "warrior" for the determination and resiliency she exhibited in her comeback.

Those warrior-like qualities were the same traits that Marat Safin once suggested made Sharapova more American than Russian. It was praise, according to the men's former number one, as he believed her toughness was forged in the United States and something the Russian women on tour were lacking. But Sharapova is proud of her roots and dismisses those who say she's more American than Russian.

"I love where I'm from," she said after her French Open win. "I don't live there because of the circumstances, but all my family is there. The culture and the feeling, it's what's inside, not what's outside that determines that."

Representing her country, Sharapova had the chance to add a golden hue to her career Slam at the 2012 London Olympics. On the same Wimbledon court where she won her first major eight years earlier over Serena Williams, the two battled again. This time Williams came out on top, winning the gold-medal.

In 2013 Sharapova recruited Hall of Famer Jimmy Connors to be her coach, but that lasted just one match. She fired him after a loss to American teenager Sloane Stephens, saying it wasn't "the right fit for this time in my career."

With no coach and bursitis in her damaged shoulder, Sharapova withdrew from the 2013 U.S. Open, capping a frustrating season that dropped her to number three in the world after a resurgent 2012.

Off the court, rumors swirled. The first was about her legally changing her surname to "Sugarpova" for two weeks to advertise her new candy line; the second involved her relationship with Bulgarian tennis player Grigor Dimitrov, who had been linked to Williams in the past. That sparked a war of words through the media between Sharapova and Williams on the eve of Wimbledon in 2013. And while such rivalries are good for ratings, this one is becoming a little lopsided on the court. Williams is leading Sharapova 14-2 after beating her in

Maria Sharapova reflects on her victory over Justine Henin at the 2006 U.S. Open. The championship marked her second major title.

With sublime talent and a mass international appeal come heightened expectations, and in some ways it seems as if Sharapova hasn't quite lived up to her early promise and success, despite the career Slam. But she remains an elite player, a

---

Harvard Business School uses her as a case study of brand success, and she's been the world's highest-paid female athlete for nine years in a row.

---

the 2013 French Open final for her 13th straight win against the Russian.

Where Sharapova comes out on top is the world stage; Harvard Business School uses her as a case study of brand success, and she's been the world's highest-paid female athlete for nine years in a row, making about $29 million between June 2012 and June 2013, according to *Forbes*. Williams is second on the list, at $20.5 million.

Fashion is Sharapova's favorite pastime and another source of income. At 6 foot 2 and 130 pounds, she fits right in with the runway models, and she's created a line of Nike tennis apparel and Cole Haan shoes.

Philanthropy is another passion; the Maria Sharapova Foundation is "committed to helping children around the world achieve their dreams," and in 2007 she became Goodwill Ambassador for the United Nations Development Programme. She's donated over $100,000 to the area of Belarus affected by the 1986 Chernobyl nuclear disaster and recently launched a scholarship program for students there.

favorite in any tournament she enters and one of the biggest draws on earth.

After this long in the spotlight it's easy to forget that she's still well shy of 30, and she doesn't plan to fade away.

"There's nothing that I've done in my life that has given me the same experience as being on the court…you can be the greatest model in the world but if somebody doesn't put you on the cover of a magazine, you're never going to be famous. This sport, it's all in your own hands and that's what I love about it, you control your own wins and losses."

Career Highlights	
Australian Open Singles champion 2008	**U.S. Open** Singles champion 2006
French Open Singles champion 2012, 2014	**Olympics** Silver medalist in women's singles 2012
Wimbledon Singles champion 2004	**Fed Cup Team Member** 2008, 2011–12

Serena Williams

Serena Williams returns the offering of Maria Sharapova during the final of the 2013 French Open. Williams beat the defending champion to earn her first of two majors in 2013.

THE POWER PLAY

Equal parts aloof and engaging, flighty and focused, Serena Jameka Williams has a personality as strong as her game, and both have dominated women's tennis for a decade and a half.

Williams plays with a chip on her shoulder that was nurtured by her father, Richard, a Svengali figure who created a Williams-against-the-world attitude using slights against the family, whether they were real or perceived. He took over press conferences to accuse fans of racial slurs and officials of unfair treatment, motivating his daughters and thrusting himself into the spotlight. Whether he did this to take the pressure off his children or because he was a narcissist is open to debate.

Born in Saginaw, Michigan, in 1981, Serena moved with her family to Compton, California, the infamously gang-infested part of Los Angeles, when she was a toddler. She picked up a racket at the age of four, and playing against Richard, mother Oracene and sister Venus on the public courts, her immense talent was obvious very early, but she was largely sheltered from the junior circuit growing up.

Williams turned pro the month she turned 14 in 1995 but played only one match that year and none in 1996. Her first real taste of success was at a tournament in Chicago in 1997, beating seventh-ranked Mary Pierce and number four Monica Seles on her way to the semifinal.

Physically mature and committed to the tour in 1998, Serena was a rising star with musculature, athleticism and overwhelming power never before seen in women's tennis. Her closest contemporary is her sister, who is 15 months older, slighter and taller than 5-foot-9 Serena. Serena, however, beat her to the family's first Grand Slam tournament victory as she captured the 1999 U.S. Open on her second trip to Flushing Meadows. She was the first black woman to win a major since Althea Gibson was U.S. champion in 1958.

The sisters have met in eight Grand Slam tournament finals. Venus won the first at the 2001 U.S. Open, when they became the first siblings to meet in a major final in more than a century, but Serena won six of the next seven over her big sister, including four major finals in a row — the French Open, Wimbledon and the U.S. Open in 2002 and the Australian Open in 2003.

Serena Williams celebrates beating Maria Sharapova 6–2, 7–6 in their semifinal match at the 2014 Brisbane International. Williams won the championship, defeating Victoria Azarenka in the final.

Serena Williams stretches to make a backhand return to Maria Sharapova at the 2013 French Open final. Williams' victory marked just her second French Open title.

With that she became the fifth woman in history to hold all four major titles at once, but because it didn't happen in one calendar year, it was dubbed "the Serena Slam."

Life on the top proved difficult for Williams, however. She had major victories at the 2003 and 2005 Australian Opens, but slowly her desire to play waned as she dealt with injuries, depression and off-court interests.

Tennis icon and commentator Chris Evert penned an open letter to her, offering "advice, not criticism," suggesting that the life span of an elite athlete is short and should be seized with both hands. She also believed Williams had the chance to be the greatest of all time.

To deal with the pressure, Williams, who came back to the tour after a brief hiatus to win the 2007 Australian Open, developed multiple personalities. Psycho Serena plays tennis, Summer "helps me out a lot, does my fashion things," Megan is "mean and mischievous" and Takwanda is "rough, not a Christian. She was at the U.S. Open in 2009."

That particular U.S. Open was a low point in Williams' career; she was the defending champion but on the verge of losing to Kim Clijsters in the semifinal. On match point Williams was called for a foot fault, after which she lashed out at the line judge, brandishing her racket and unleashing a stream of profanities. The outburst cost her a point and the match, and she was fined a record $82,500.

Commentator and tennis Hall of Famer John McEnroe, a fiery and temperamental competitor himself, encouraged her to apologize. But a stubborn Williams refused, saying she felt like she was unfairly picked on.

Williams never truly expressed contrition, but a life-threatening pulmonary embolism two years later gave her some perspective and maturity. She was rushed to the hospital in 2011 with a blockage in an artery in her lung; she had cut her foot on some glass in 2010, an injury that required two surgeries, kept her in a cast for 20 weeks and may have been a contributing factor.

"I remember I asked, 'Will I be able to play tennis again?' I never thought I would ever have to ask that question. I never really liked practicing, but now every time I go on court I'm, like, 'This is fun.' I enjoy every moment more now."

The health scare made Williams' 2012 season all the more remarkable. She won the gold medal at the London Olympics at Wimbledon — where she'd taken her fifth singles title a month prior — dismissing Maria Sharapova in the gold-medal match as if it were a walk along the Thames. The 6–0, 6–1 final took just over an hour; she lost only 17 total games in her six Olympic matches.

The medal made Williams the first person in history to win each major and Olympic gold in both singles and doubles. It also matched Venus, who won singles gold in Sydney in 2000. (Together the pair were golden for the United States as a doubles team at the 2000, 2008 and 2012 Olympics.)

Williams finished the 2012 season with a 6–2, 2–6, 7–5 win in the U.S. Open final against Victoria Azarenka, and there was no letup in 2013. She frustrated Maria Sharapova in the French Open final, winning 6–4, 6–4 for her second championship at Roland Garros 11 years after winning her first, and repeated as U.S. Open champion, again over Azarenka.

Serena Williams hugs the U.S. Open championship trophy after dispatching Victoria Azarenka 7–5, 6–7 (6–8), 6–1 in 2013. It was the second straight U.S. championship for Williams, both times over Azarenka.

While there are no guarantees in life and even fewer in sports, it seems likely that Williams will match the 18 major singles titles won by Evert and Martina Navratilova, and with continued health it's not out of the realm of possibility that she

---

"I'm playing more. I'm practicing more. I'm on the court more; I'm doing more than I've ever done. I'm taking tennis more serious and I appreciate the moments more." – Serena Williams

---

Asked how to beat Williams before the match, Azarenka replied: "You've got to fight, you've got to run, you've got to grind and you've got to bite with your teeth for whatever opportunity you have."

Azarenka fought gamely on a windswept court, breaking Williams twice when she was serving for the championship in the second set, but lost 7–5, 6–7 (6–8), 6–1, the seventh time she'd fallen to Williams at a Grand Slam event.

It was Williams' fifth U.S. Open and 17th major title. At the age of 31 she showed she's still as dominant as ever when she's healthy and ready to play. After her near-death experience she came back with renewed focus and fitness, her 67-4 record in 2013 a tribute to her hunger and the work she put in.

"I still do so much fashion; I have a new Web series coming out," said Williams, who has her own Nike tennis apparel and a line of handbags and jewelry, after the 2013 U.S. Open win. "But the difference is I'm playing more. I'm practicing more. I'm on the court more; I'm doing more than I've ever done. I'm taking tennis more serious and I appreciate the moments more."

could reach or exceed Steffi Graf's 22 or even Margaret Court's all-time record of 24.

"The greatest tennis player we've ever seen," said Evert after Williams beat Carla Suarez Navarro 6–0, 6–0 in the 2013 U.S. Open quarterfinals. "She doesn't have the best record, but nobody's had a game like her."

Career Highlights

Australian Open
Singles champion 2003, 2005, 2007, 2009–10
Doubles champion 2001, 2003, 2009, 2010

French Open
Singles champion 2002, 2013
Doubles champion 1999, 2010

Wimbledon
Singles champion 2002–03, 2009–10, 2012
Doubles champion 2000, 2002, 2008–09, 2012
Mixed doubles champion 1998

U.S. Open
Singles champion 1999, 2002, 2008, 2012–13
Doubles champion 1999, 2009
Mixed doubles champion 1998

Olympics
Gold medalist in women's singles 2012
Gold medalist in women's doubles 2000, 2008, 2012

Fed Cup Team Member
1999, 2003, 2007, 2012–13

Venus Williams is all smiles as she hoists the Venus Rosewater Dish as the champion of the 2000 edition of Wimbledon. It was her first major victory and first of five career singles titles at the All England Club.

Venus Williams

SHE'S GOT GAME

"Venus Williams Is Straight Outta Compton!"

So read the posters Richard Williams plastered on telephone poles in the notoriously rough neighborhood when his daughter was young, echoing the famous lyric from rap group N.W.A.

Far from the country clubs and elite tennis academies, Venus and sister Serena honed their games together on the hardscrabble courts of south central Los Angeles.

To Venus it was simple: she succeeded because of "belief and training," which included throwing footballs and baseballs to improve her serve, skipping for footwork and taking dance and taekwondo classes for movement.

Rumor has it that the sisters learned to drop to the court when they heard gunshots, and Richard spoke of returning to help out the gang members who guarded their practices. Much of their childhood became the stuff of legend, fed by their father, who became one of the more enigmatic and polarizing figures in tennis. It's a childhood that informed their attitude and shaped their image in the game.

Born in 1980, Venus Ebony Starr Williams is the older, taller

and more lithe of the two pro-tennis-playing Williams sisters; the pair have three older sisters from their mother Oracene's first marriage.

With Venus posting a 63-0 record on the United States Tennis Association junior tour by the time she was 12, Richard and Oracene started to worry about the notoriety they had in Compton and decided to move the family to Florida for a tennis education. After a few years under the tutelage of Rick Macci, who'd coached Jennifer Capriati and Mary Pierce, Richard took over the guidance of their careers once again.

Venus would become one of the most accomplished female tennis players in history but only the second best in her household. As sibling rivalries go, however, this one is lacking. The two are best friends and a formidable doubles team, with a bond that can be forged only through sharing DNA. Together they've won three doubles gold medals at the Olympics, in Sydney, Beijing and London, and seven doubles titles at the majors.

Venus joined the professional tour in 1994 when she was 14 at a tournament in Oakland, pushing future Hall of Fame

Fifteen-year-old Venus Williams returns a shot to Asa Carlsson at the 1995 Acura Classic. Carlsson won the match, but the youngster turned heads in her first full year on the professional circuit.

Venus Williams shows off one of her elaborate outfits — a trademark of the star — during her fourth-round match against Tsvetana Pironkova at the 2011 Wimbledon Championships.

player and U.S. Open champion Arantxa Sanchez Vicario to three sets before losing.

Focusing on school, Venus didn't enter a major until 1997, losing in the first round at Wimbledon before making a thrilling debut at the U.S. Open. Ranked 66th, she survived two match points in the third-set tiebreaker to win the semifinal 7–6 (7–5), 4–6, 7–6 (9–7) over Irina Spirlea in a match that took almost three hours. Williams fell 6–0, 6–4 to top-seeded Martina Hingis in the final, but she put the world on notice.

"I'm tall. I'm black. Everything's different about me," said the 6-foot-1 Williams at the tournament. "Just face the facts."

Williams won her first major title at the All England Club in 2000, a place that couldn't be further removed from the courts of her youth but would become her second home. After beating number one Hingis in the quarterfinals and Serena in the semis, she downed second-ranked Lindsay Davenport 6–3, 7–6 in the final to lift the fittingly titled Venus Rosewater Dish.

Proving that was no fluke, Williams beat the top two players again to win the 2000 U.S. Open, defeating Hingis in the semifinal, after being down 3–5 in the third set, and Davenport in the final. It also earned her a $40 million contract with Reebok.

Capping a breakthrough year, Venus won two Olympic gold medals in Sydney, taking the singles with a win over Russia's Elena Dementieva and the doubles with her sister. She was the first woman to win both golds since Helen Wills Moody in 1924.

A year later Williams defended her Wimbledon title, and then, at the 2001 U.S. Open, the sisters became the first set of siblings to face each other in a major final in more than a century. Venus won that match 6–2, 6–4 for her second straight American championship.

Serena then beat Venus in three straight major finals in 2002 — the French Open, Wimbledon and the U.S. Open — and by 2005 it looked as if Venus' best years were behind her. That season, however, she once again knocked off the top two seeds to win a major. Seeded 14th, she beat number two Maria Sharapova in the semifinal and top seed Davenport in the final for her third Wimbledon title. Williams saved match point at 4–5 in the third before rallying to win 4–6, 7–6 (7–4), 9–7 in two hours and 45 minutes, which set a record for the longest women's final at the tournament.

A series of injuries meant Williams played only a few tournaments in 2006, but confounding people as always, Venus earned her fourth Wimbledon crown in 2007. Ranked 31st, she was the lowest-ranked woman to ever win the tournament.

In 2008 she defended her Wimbledon crown by beating Serena in the final; in doing so she became just the third woman with at least five Wimbledon titles to her name, joining Martina Navratilova and Steffi Graf.

Back at the All England Club for the 2012 Olympics, she and Serena steamrolled their way to the doubles gold medal. It was a welcome result after being diagnosed with Sjögren's syndrome, a disorder of the immune system that can induce severe joint pain, in 2011.

Off the court the sisters share a home in Palm Beach, Florida. As in their childhood, living together drives the sisters to want to be better — even if that sometimes causes moments of sib-

Venus Williams returns to Maria Jose Martinez Sanchez during their third-round match at the 2011 Wimbledon Championships. Williams defeated Martinez Sanchez 6–0, 6–2.

a shock to the very white world of tennis, and neither sister has returned to Indian Wells since.

The specter of racism has stayed with Williams. In 2009 she won a tournament in the United Arab Emirates that Israeli player Shahar Peer had been denied a visa to play in; at the tro-

---

"Not to win the first major was tough for me. I thought as older sister I should step up. I didn't know how to fight, it didn't come naturally to me." – Venus Williams

---

ling strife, which the pair spoke about in a 2013 documentary called *Venus and Serena.*

"Not to win the first major was tough for me," admits Venus of Serena's 1999 U.S. Open win. "I thought as older sister I should step up. I didn't know how to fight, it didn't come naturally to me. It came naturally to Serena. I had to learn from her example."

But at the very start it was Serena who was jealous.

"It was very difficult being in shadow of Venus," says Serena. "Venus was always in the newspapers and media. I was never supposed to be good…I was a copycat. That's the reason I played tennis."

Early in their careers some accused the family of fixing their head-to-head matches, with Richard deciding ahead of time who would win. At a tournament in Indian Wells in 2001, Venus withdrew from her semifinal match against Serena, and at the final two days later the crowd booed her and Richard as they took their seats to watch. There were claims of racist taunts from the fans, with Richard turning to respond to those assembled with a raised left fist in a black power salute. It was

phy ceremony Williams called out the hosts and the Arab royalty in attendance, saying it was "a shame that one of our players couldn't be here."

At the press conference afterward Williams explained that it "made me think of all the people who gave something for me to be here. I am not here to rock the boat or upset anyone — I'm just here to try to do what's right."

Career Highlights	
Australian Open Doubles champion 2001, 2003, 2009–10 Mixed doubles champion 1998	**U.S. Open** Singles champion 2000–01 Doubles champion 1999, 2009
French Open Doubles champion 1999, 2010 Mixed doubles champion 1998	**Olympics** Gold medalist in women's singles 2000 Gold medalist in women's doubles 2000, 2008, 2012
Wimbledon Singles champion 2000–01, 2005, 2007–08 Doubles champion 2000, 2002, 2008–09, 2012	**Fed Cup Team Member** 1999, 2003–05, 2007, 2012–13

INDEX